City of Clerks

City of Clerks

Office and Sales Workers in Philadelphia,

1870–1920

JEROME P. BJELOPERA

University of Illinois Press

URBANA AND CHICAGO

© 2005 by the Board of Trustees
of the University of Illinois
All rights reserved
Manufactured in the United States of America

∞ This book is printed on acid-free paper.

1 2 3 4 5 C P 5 4 3 2 1
Library of Congress Cataloging-in-Publication Data
Bjelopera, Jerome P.
City of clerks : office and sales workers in Philadelphia, 1870-1920 /
Jerome P. Bjelopera.
p.   cm. — (The working class in American history)
Includes bibliographical references and index.
ISBN 0-252-02977-1 (cloth : alk. paper)
ISBN 0-252-07227-8 (pbk. : alk. paper)
1. Clerks—Pennsylvania—Philadelphia—History.
2. Clerks (Retail trade)—Pennsylvania—Philadelphia—History.
I. Title. II. Series.
HD8039.M4U5325   2005
331.7'6165137'097481109034—dc22   2004023675

Contents

Acknowledgments

I began examining the lives of industrial-era clerical workers in Philadelphia while I was a graduate student at Temple University in the mid-1990s. My first intense study of the selling floor and office, however, occurred when I was a teenager working in the stockrooms of a suburban department store outside Cleveland, Ohio. Although I cannot say that I made any erudite observations of in-store class structure or gender politics as a pimply, gangly teen, some amazing salespeople and managers befriended me and guided me through an initially bewildering world. As I organized the shelves behind the scenes and hauled out goods to be sold in the store's housewares and china departments, Bonnie, Flo, Charlie, Julie, Columbia, and Mary Anne made my brief stint in retail rewarding and always interesting.

I have benefited from the understanding and wisdom of family and friends who endured countless conversations about office and sales work and witnessed many of my meltdowns. I cannot sufficiently thank my mother, Mila, and my sister, Mary Ann Stropkay, as well as her husband, Eric. My mother has been a particular inspiration. I cannot begin to catalog the innumerable sacrifices she has made for her children, and she has always encouraged me. The kind words, unflagging support, and good humor of my wife's immediate family—notably Ronald, Bernardine, Nicole, and Ryan Smallcomb, as well as Vincent and Dorothy Magarosky and Dorothy Omashel—have buoyed me throughout this project. Jeff Pratt and Brian Victor have listened intently and commented on many versions of the arguments laid out in the manuscript. During one pivotal conversation, Alexandria Solt helped me work through some fundamental concepts regarding the then in-flux study.

Like most other scholarly authors, I owe a mountain of gratitude to archivists, librarians, colleagues, editors, and teachers. Debra Schrammel and Gary Schecter made me feel at home and gave me brilliant research leads at the Peirce College Archives. Marjorie McNinch, from the Hagley Museum and Library, carefully guided my exploration of the Strawbridge and Clothier collection. Margaret J. Jerrido, Brenda L. Galloway-Wright, George D. Brightbill, and Cheryl Johnson, all at the Temple University Urban Archives, offered incisive direction to my investigations into their collections. John Kennedy, from Temple University's Paley Library, advised me at two critical junctures in my research. Tom Bile and Salvatore Saporito helped with the three maps that appear in chapter 6. Kenneth L. Kusmer, my academic adviser, led me to this topic for my first seminar paper in graduate school. He surely did not know what he was in for. Regardless, he patiently read and extensively commented on numerous versions of the manuscript. I greatly appreciate his guidance and scholarly example. In the early stages of writing, I could always rely on Wilbert L. Jenkins's keen eye and indefatigable optimism. Bettye Collier-Thomas, Judith G. Goode, and James W. Hilty shepherded this manuscript through the dissertation process. The thorough comments of Ileen A. DeVault, Alice Kessler-Harris, and an anonymous reader for the University of Illinois Press helped me to rethink and rework some important sections of the book and only strengthened my work. The press's editors Richard Wentworth, Laurie Matheson, and Bruce Bethell have been a tremendous help. Benjamin Rader, Maureen Smith, Duncan R. Jamieson, Randolph Roth, and Janet Irons read parts of the manuscript or material related to it and lent important recommendations. At the *Pennsylvania Magazine of History and Biography,* Ian M. G. Quimby and Sharon Holt pored over an essay that forms part of chapter 5. It originally appeared as "White Collars and Blackface: Race and Leisure among Clerical and Sales Workers in Early Twentieth-Century Philadelphia" (*PMHB* 126 [July 2002]: 471–90). A handful of influential teachers have made quite a difference in my life. Without them, this book would not have been possible. James Pilewski, Francesco Cesareo, Marian Morton, James Krukones, and David Robson inspired me to become a teacher and a historian. I learned much in their classrooms.

While I taught at Bradley University in Peoria, Illinois, between 2000 and 2003, I counted on the support and encouragement of Andrew Kelley, Jennifer Brady, Kerry Ferris, Brad Brown, and Stacey Robertson. For a period Andrew and I met weekly to work on our own projects and bounce ideas off of one another. These vital sessions kept me plowing along, and Andrew's deft wit kept me sane. Long ago I lost count of how many times Andrew and Jennifer invited me to their house for dinner and abided endless talk about academia. Kerry shone as an example of professionalism and strength. She reminded me that fighting for justice is the right thing to do, regardless of the odds or the opposition. Brad and Stacey lavished me with good counsel. I was truly lucky in my colleagues at Bradley.

I owe the most to Danielle Smallcomb. Without her this book never would have been completed. Danielle read, listened, debated, edited, endured, comforted, and celebrated all along the way. She walked with me when I was in stride. When I stumbled, she picked me up and put me on the right course. Her brilliant observations, down-to-earth suggestions, boundless confidence, and, above all else, love have meant the world to me. Danielle, a simple dedication can neither explain nor pay back my vast debt to you. But at least it's a start.

Introduction

Upon graduating from a Philadelphia business college in 1876, sixteen-year-old T. James Fernley was offered a position as an office boy in a local wholesale hardware firm. He viewed this job as an "apprenticeship." After spending a year learning the business from the inside, doing basic clerical work, and mastering skills such as salesmanship and bookkeeping, the young man boldly left his employer and founded his own wholesale hardware business, which grew and prospered over the next two decades. Fernley's speedy rise from office boy to successful entrepreneur differed greatly from the experiences of others toiling behind the desks and on the selling floors of Philadelphia businesses during the industrial era. Charles D. Kirby spent most of his career at Strawbridge and Clothier, a Philadelphia department store. Following several years in a smaller firm, he joined the store in 1885 as a salesman in the umbrella department, where he stayed for the next quarter-century, eventually becoming the head of the umbrella counter. Between 1888 and 1894 Clara May Leidy labored as a bookkeeper in two businesses. She left the workforce in order to marry.[1] This study is about thousands of people like Fernley, Kirby, and Leidy who worked in the stores and offices of Philadelphia between 1870 and 1920. It is a history of the rise of the clerical workforce, an indispensable group in America's industrial economy, recounted from the context of one of the nation's major cities.

Historians have written voluminously about those above and below office workers and salespeople in the industrial social order,[2] with numerous scholarly studies exploring the work lives, communities, institutions, family and kinship patterns, and leisure pursuits of blue-collar workers. The history of clerical employees during the age of smokestacks—the late nineteenth and early twentieth centuries—has received far less attention. Besides being important in its own right, the experience of these nonmanual workers also has obvious relevance to our understanding of the postindustrial period. Since World War II the prominence of white-collar jobs in the American economy has vastly expanded. The roots of the postmodern information and service-based sector can be found within the industrial era. Although considerably smaller than the blue-collar working class, the office and sales workforce grew more quickly than the manual workforce during 1870–1920. This book explores the early history of this neglected occupational group.

Office and sales employees formed a key component of the industrial workforce. Clerks, bookkeepers, secretaries, and stenographers processed the paperwork that businesses needed to prosper, and salespeople connected millions of customers with the products of the industrial age. These lower-level white-collar workers occupied an emerging middle ground in industrial America's social structure. Immediately above them on the occupational ladder stood proprietors and professionals; below were skilled blue-collar workers. A number of fundamental factors underscored this intermediate status. Unlike many professionals, clerks and salespeople seldom attended four-year colleges, but they had significantly higher levels of formal education than did blue-collar workers. Most either received training in two-year business colleges or attended specialized commercial high-school programs that prepared students for clerical work. Like professionals and small-business owners, clerks and salespeople worked with their minds as well as their hands, but like most factory operatives, clerical employees were continuously supervised by management. Men and women toiling in offices and stores complained about their low salaries, but they secured additional forms of compensation. They labored in clean, relatively safe work environments and earned regular vacations, things of which few blue-collar workers could boast. Most important, lower-level white-collar workers did not experience the periodic unemployment that plagued many blue-collar Americans. As a consequence, prior to the 1930s few of them became homeless during economic downturns.[3]

Scholars typically trisect the white-collar workforce into professional, proprietary, and clerical categories. The growth of the third category in the age of smokestacks represented an important shift away from the preindustrial white-collar world, in which proprietary jobs outnumbered all other occupational groups. In 1870 proprietors formed the largest sector of the white-collar workforce in Philadelphia, accounting for 45 percent of all nonmanual jobs, while clerks and salespeople constituted 41 percent. By 1900 this relationship had been reversed. Office and sales employees made up 53 percent of all nonmanual workers in the city, while proprietors accounted for only 31 percent of the white-collar workforce. By 1920 the gap between the two groups had grown wider, with office and sales workers holding 58 percent of white-collar jobs and business owners, 21 percent.[4] The pronounced growth of the clerical realm in the late nineteenth and early twentieth centuries is thus central to any study of nonmanual employment—indeed, central to understanding the impact of industrialization on urban economies.

Studies examining industrial-era clerical employees have taken several approaches. A handful of books have cogently addressed specific types of workers, such as telephone operators, traveling salesmen, and department-store saleswomen.[5] For the most part, however, labor historians pursuing the goal of history "from the bottom up" have directed their efforts toward blue-collar workers. An exception is Ileen A. DeVault's work. DeVault's study of clerical employees in Pittsburgh focuses on the importance of white-collar jobs to the children of skilled blue-collar workers.[6] At the turn of the twentieth century, however, women constituted a rapidly growing segment of the clerical realm. Perhaps not surprisingly, then, historians of women and gender have made the most significant contributions to our understanding of clerical workers. They have especially explained the on-the-job experiences of women and the construction of gender in the workplace.[7] These studies have shown how the introduction of new office machinery, including the typewriter, spurred this growth. Simultaneously, business owners and managers began to view some types of employment as ideally suited for women—namely, stenography, secretarial work, and department-store selling. Further, recent scholars examining women in the office and on the selling floor have emphasized the proletarianization of clerical work in the industrial period, for the office or sales jobs that women took offered little chance for promotion and paid less than similar jobs held by men.

Unlike previous studies, this book pushes well beyond the threshold of the workplace in tracing the lives of clerical employees. As its title implies, *City of Clerks* anchors clerks and salespeople firmly within the context of the industrial metropolis by examining their leisure pursuits, residential patterns, educational backgrounds, and the place of clerical workers in the urban economy—all of which have received little scholarly discussion. The issues central to this narrative, then, include not only gender but also race and ethnicity, which have been largely neglected in the historiography of this group.[8] Moreover, I focus on both male and female workers, for we need a fuller understanding of the lives as well as the work patterns of this group in the context of the rapidly industrializing American city. To get at these issues, this study draws on resources such as the records of the Peirce

School, the most prominent business college in industrial Philadelphia, and of Strawbridge and Clothier, a major department store and landmark in the city. The voice of the clerical workforce emerges from this material.

While forming an important occupational group in the industrial order, the clerical workforce consisted of an ever-changing mix of typically young, unmarried individuals. In fact, for much of the period between 1870 and 1920, most people struggling to eke out a living in the office world or on the selling floor saw their jobs as temporary or transitional. Working behind a sales counter or cluttered desk provided numerous men and women the opportunity to avoid their parents' fates, struggling for years in blue-collar jobs. Many viewed office and sales work as a way station in their lives as they pursued other goals. Countless men who labored behind desks or counters sought upward occupational mobility. Some, like T. James Fernley, experienced significant success. Others, like Charles D. Kirby, remained mired in clerical careers as the industrial order matured. Nevertheless, throughout these decades visions of career advancement continually inspired men to try their hands at office or sales work, to plan for brief stints as bookkeepers and clerks until they learned the secrets of running a business or were promoted into management. As the case of Clara May Leidy suggests, unlike their male counterparts, most women typically expected to marry their way out of the office or selling floor. It would be the rare female clerical worker who would rise to any significant position in management.

Between 1870 and 1920 developments in the clerical realm fueled the rise of a large lower middle class in the industrial economy. The sheer expansion of the ranks of office and sales employees in this period was coupled with declining chances at career advancement available from these jobs. By the turn of the twentieth century, businesses created legions of dead-end office and sales positions and increasingly staffed sales counters and offices with women. These changes helped solidify the place of these workers in the occupational hierarchy of the industrial city, firmly sandwiching them between middle-class and blue-collar occupational categories. By the early twentieth century the possibility that men could use such work as a springboard into more firmly middle-class occupations had shrunken significantly. Clerical work began to take on appearances that it maintains today.

C. Wright Mills's classic study *White Collar: The American Middle Classes* has enormously influenced scholarly views of the history of nonmanual workers.[9] Mills broadly argued that the growth of corporate America transformed the largely proprietary preindustrial middle class into an expanding, propertyless group trapped in the industrial era's bureaucratic ranks. For Mills, the industrial-era middle class represented a degraded version of its preindustrial precursor. While imaginatively laying out broad changes in middle-class occupations, his study depicts industrial-era middle-class Americans as shallow, soulless people who found little pleasure and less release in their lives. Mills described a middle class full of harried workers with no authentic culture. These workers were "estranged from community and society in a context of distrust and manipulation; alienated from work and, on the personality market, from self; expropriated of individual rationality and politically apathetic—these are the new little people, the unwilling vanguard of modern society."[10] At the bottom of the middle-class social order that Mills delineated resided the most "estranged" workers, the office and sales employees who made up the clerical workforce. There is a core element of truth in Mills's depiction. As I will explain, some workers felt alienated, quit their jobs, or stole from their employers. Mills's overall view, however, is too bleak. One aim of this book is to provide a corrective to such dismal depictions of passive white-collar Americans, a view that over the decades has become an all-too-common stereotype of this group. This study will lend agency to the lives of clerical workers. It will show that typical male office and sales employees viewed their work as an opportunity to improve their lives. Thousands of people chose lower-level white-collar employment as much more palatable than manual labor. Working behind a desk was certainly safer than toiling in a textile mill or cannery. Although clerical employees suffered from a variety of indignities on the job, including low pay and sexism, their careers were not especially degrading or alienating. Similarly, much like their blue-collar counterparts, industrial-era clerks and salespeople developed a rich leisure life beyond the workplace.

The first three chapters of this study are devoted to issues of employment and class. Chapter 1 offers a general discussion of Philadelphia's office and sales workforce and its changing relationship to the city's overall white-collar workforce between 1870 and 1920. Placing clerks and salespeople within the context of middle-class economic opportunity allows us to assess the changing importance of clerical work to the city's economy as a whole. Chapter 2 focuses on the workplace experiences of low-level white-collar workers. It surveys how office employees and salespeople looked for work and the variegated aspects of the clerical work world. Chapter 3 further explores work-related themes. It investigates the class backgrounds of people seeking business-college educations in preparation for office or sales employment. The city's clerical ranks at the turn of the century were filled primarily by people whose parents had toiled in nonclerical jobs. Office and sales employees came from a variety of class backgrounds. Many children of skilled laborers moved into white-collar occupations, as did the progeny of small-business owners and professionals. This chapter analyzes intergenerational mobility across the collar line using the extensive records of the Peirce School, Philadelphia's premier business college of the time. I use federal manuscript censuses to trace students from the 1880, 1900, and 1910 schoolyears and uncover the class backgrounds of their families. Finally, I discuss the ethnicity of students preparing for clerical occupations and examine Peirce's role as an institution mediating entrance into the office and sales workforce.

The next three chapters move beyond the realm of work. Chapter 4 assesses the leisure activities of Philadelphia's clerks, examining this group's involvement in the new consumer economy that began to emerge in the 1890s.[11] The city's clerical workers engaged in mixed-gender as well as same-sex leisure pursuits. Office workers and salespeople formed their own social and athletic clubs. At the same time, as consumers they became heavily involved in the emerging youth-oriented leisure economy of the industrial era. Chapter 5 connects leisure experiences with the realm of work. It begins by discussing the image of the ideal worker that the majority of Philadelphia's clerks strove to emulate. Some workers rebelled against this paragon by engaging in on-the-job theft and embezzlement and by flouting workplace norms. Additionally, the clerical workforce shaped its own racial identity in relation to the vision of the model worker. This process occurred at the intersection of work and play in the lives of the city's office and store employees. While at play, many of Philadelphia's office and sales workers indulged in the racist masquerade of blackface minstrelsy, either as amateur actors or as spectators. The racial content of minstrelsy represented an inversion of the workplace virtues that clerks absorbed. Through the pastime of minstrelsy, these Philadelphians came to see workplace ideals as "white" ideals. This popular leisure activity helped shape a common sense of whiteness for an occupation group that was increasingly drawn from a variety of ethnic backgrounds. Chapter 6 further elucidates this group's relationship to the industrial city by exploring the evolving residential and family patterns of Philadelphia's clerical workers. I examine where clerks lived in the city and analyze the composition of clerical households according to race, ethnicity, and marital status. Federal manuscript census schedules yield invaluable information about the ethnic, racial, gender, and class composition of clerical residential zones. Particularly important to an understanding of this occupational group are the workers who, in increasing numbers, lived in lodging houses in Philadelphia's furnished-room district. In this part of the city many clerical workers challenged Victorian mores regarding sexuality and temperance.

* * *

The social and economic contours of an era often have their origins in the broad and gradual changes that shaped its predecessor. The office and sales workforce, no less than the working class, was central to urban industrial society in the United States. Understanding the work lives, residential patterns, and leisure experiences of the clerical workers between 1870 and 1920 helps us to more clearly conceptualize the maturation of the industrial order and provides insight into the initial stage of postindustrial society. In many ways this study approaches the age of smokestacks "from the middle out" rather than from "the bottom up." The rise of the clerical workforce forms an important element in the multilayered histories of both industrial and postindustrial urban America. It is a story that, as yet, remains unfinished. This book brings the tale closer to completion.

1 Clerking and the Industrial-Era White-Collar Workforce

Industrialization profoundly influenced American society and culture,[1] with mechanization, incorporation, and immigration spurring the expansion of the blue-collar workforce. In the last three decades historians have focused much attention on the men and women who toiled in these jobs, but our understanding of the clerks, bookkeepers, stenographers, typists, and sales-people who worked in the stores and offices of industrial America remains partial at best.[2] Arno J. Mayer offers several reasons American and European scholars have paid less attention to lower-level white-collar workers. He argues that academicians have little sympathy for this social group. Mayer pointedly asks, "Could it be that social scientists are hesitant to expose the aspirations, life-style, and world view of the social class in which so many of them originate and from which they seek to escape?"[3] He contends that study of powerful elites or the working class and poor—the poles of Western social structure—has preoccupied scholars. They have neglected the middle. Most convincingly, Mayer describes the lower middle class's structure as complex, unstable, constantly changing, and thus difficult to study.[4] As Mayer's criticisms suggest, defining the position of office and sales workers in America's class structure poses problems. Their status in society shifted as the nation industrialized, and their location in the urban social order during the age of smokestacks must be described within the context of the entire nonmanual (white-collar) workforce. In the walking city full of artisans and small businesses of the early nineteenth century, clerical work served largely as training for men who were destined to become small-business owners in the preindustrial economic order. During the late nineteenth and early twentieth centuries, however, office and sales employment was transformed. This sector of the workforce grew tremendously, in sheer numbers surpassing both the professional and proprietary categories of white-collar work. In addition, women increasingly entered the previously male realms of the office and selling floor. The growth of clerical opportunity and the expansion of women's employment in office and sales jobs undermined the connections that this type of work had with apprenticeship for young men. The small, mostly male workforce that had worked behind the desks and sales counters of the walking city thus developed into a large and distinct occupational segment that included vast numbers of women in the industrial work world.

Two major factors make the Philadelphia of 1870 to 1920 an interesting city in which to view the early development of the industrial-era white-collar world. First, Philadelphia does not easily fit the typical urban, northern model of industrialization. In the later nineteenth and early twentieth centuries, northern industrial cities such as Detroit, Cleveland, Pittsburgh, and Chicago quickly developed economies based on heavy industry. In each of these cities several large-scale industries dominated development from the start.[5] At the same time, Philadelphia maintained a highly varied economy. The city's industrial firms came in all sizes. Product diversity, a wide variety of work settings, product and operation specialization, and family ownership colored Philadelphia's industrial complexion.[6] The city's blue-collar workforce was thus not concentrated in any one industry. In the early twentieth century this broad array of production encouraged the city's Chamber of Commerce to dub Philadelphia the "Workshop of the World."[7] Occupational variety also largely held true for Philadelphia's clerical workforce. The city's clerks and bookkeepers worked for a broad assortment of manufacturing and commercial interests ranging from huge department stores to small offices. The second factor making the city a fascinating backdrop for the study of lower-level white-collar workers concerns its ethnic makeup. The coal region of northeastern Pennsylvania siphoned off many of the unskilled immigrants who landed in Philadelphia. Millions of others favored the heavy industrial work to be found in the Midwest. This movement drastically affected the city's social structure.[8] Philadelphia did not experience the large waves of New Immigrants that washed over America's heavy industrial heartland. In the fifty years after the Civil War, Philadelphia's immigrant population never climbed higher than 27 percent of the total population, which especially featured Old Immigrant groups such as the Irish and Germans. Throughout the period about one-half of the city's denizens were native-born with native-born parents. During the same fifty-year period, at least three-fourths of those inhabiting New York and the metropolises ringing the Great Lakes were immigrants or their American-born children.[9]

In the preindustrial workplace, male office and sales workers had learned business skills in preparation for the day they would acquire their own small businesses. They were, as Stuart M. Blumin has dubbed them, "businessmen-in-training," apprentices.[10] The famous nineteenth-century Philadelphia financial magnate Jay Cooke worked a series of clerical jobs before striking into banking. Cooke gained his first exposure to business during his childhood in northern Ohio. He occasionally helped out at his uncle's dry goods store in the town of Sandusky. In 1835, at the age of fourteen, the young Cooke won his first full-time job at another dry goods business in town. During his year-long stint at this job, the adolescent learned the rudiments of office work. This training helped him land more lucrative positions. He spent a brief period in St. Louis clerking in one of the city's dry goods establishments. While in the "Gateway to the West," he took penmanship courses at a writing school, increasing his clerical proficiency. The Panic of 1837 devastated Cook's St. Louis employers, and the lad returned to Sandusky.[11]

Soon thereafter, William G. Moorehead, Cooke's brother-in-law and the owner of a packet-line company operating between Philadelphia and Pittsburgh, invited the young man to toil as a clerk in his firm. The sixteen-year-old Cooke seized the opportunity and moved to the "City of Brotherly Love." His daily routine at the company, the Washington Packet Line, mirrored the pace of work for preindustrial artisans.[12] Even though the teen complained that clerking in the city was all "business and bustle," frequent periods of relaxation and release punctuated his daily routine at work. The youthful clerk's typical day began at 5:00 A.M. In the early morning he wrestled with paperwork, such as manifests and waybills. Cooke also arranged for the day's passengers to be transported by omnibus to the rail depot. At 8:00 A.M. he ate breakfast and took time off to read the morning's newspapers. Cooke then turned to his daily business correspondence and typically made a trip to the bank. He spent part of the late morning and early afternoon strolling through local parks, because business usually slowed at that time. After this break the clerk picked up passengers arriving at a dock on the Schuylkill River, near the city's waterworks. On the dock he supervised his company's runners, or messenger boys, who waited to take care of arriving passengers and kept the firm apprised of the situation at the dock. The runners from competing establishments often tussled over perceived or real slights while waiting for arrivals, and Cooke had to pay fines whenever his workers brawled. Occasionally he was drawn into the melees. Cooke routinely ate dinner at 2:00 P.M. and supper at 8:00 P.M. He devoted the time in between to work and a variety of leisure activities, such as taking walks, seeing productions at local theaters, strolling through museums, or simply stretching out at his desk and gazing through the company's window at passers-by on Chestnut Street.[13] While the youthful clerk tired of the more tedious aspects of his job, such as soliciting passengers and sitting in a cramped office, he appreciated the trust his brother-in-law bestowed on him. The teen was allowed to manage Moorehead's private correspondence. His boss told Cooke intimate details about the business and, when away, even left him with the keys to his private treasury desk.[14] To the increasingly ambitious Cooke, the compensation for the tedium of clerical work was firsthand knowledge of the way a business operated. Of course, the clerk alleviated boredom by engaging in regular leisure throughout the day—reading the daily papers, rambling through the city, taking long meals, and even visiting a nearby hotel's bar for drinks.

Unfortunately, the business went under late in the summer of 1838. Cooke worked for several months as a bookkeeper in a hotel next door but returned to Sandusky in November. He was not away from Philadelphia for long, however. In April 1839 he returned to take a clerical position with E. W. Clark and Company, a banking firm. Cooke fell in love with banking, relishing the personal attention his bosses gave him. Indeed, the future financier watched them closely as well. He clerked there for just over three and a half years and never worried about becoming mired in a clerical career. Even salary increases were unimportant to him. Cooke was content to learn the banking business and earn the trust of the firm's proprietors. The young man saw this part of his life as an apprenticeship that prepared him to become a banker. In 1843 the bank made him a partner, and he subsequently rose to national prominence as a financier.[15]

The clerical work environment prior to industrialization, while dominated by men, was not exclusively masculine. Some dry goods stores, large and small, featured "shopwomen" who tended the counters and sold goods. George G. Foster, an observer of antebellum life in Philadelphia, noted that the shopwomen who worked in establishments throughout Center City were well-educated, performed as quickly and accurately as male clerks, and had the "ease and politeness of manners worthy of the drawing room." Typical shopwomen labored in establishments run by their husbands or fathers. These small stores were connected to the family residences, so female clerical employment often involved family ties and represented more an extension of the domestic sphere than a female invasion of the public arena.[16] Significantly, these jobs were not apprenticeships and did not offer women career advancement. Meanwhile, for male clerks and bookkeepers in the first half of the nineteenth century, upward occupational mobility existed as a very real possibility, something that most expected. Indeed, like Cooke, many other nineteenth-century industrial leaders began their careers as office workers.

In Pittsburgh a young Andrew Carnegie started his work life as a telegraph messenger boy in 1849, showed great promise, and advanced to telegraph clerk. John D. Rockefeller, who studied bookkeeping in a Cleveland high school, balanced the books of a produce retailer.[17] Although these rags-to-riches examples were extreme, they powerfully insinuated the possibilities of career advancement open to mid-nineteenth-century male white-collar workers.

Between 1870 and 1920 clerical work drastically changed. The modern clerical workforce arose in this era, and U.S. industry incorporated and bureaucratized to process the mountains of information necessary to efficiently and profitably run rapidly growing businesses. From 1890 to 1910, in what has been dubbed the "administrative revolution" or the "managerial revolution," U.S. businesses vastly expanded their office workforces.[18] In the fifty years following 1870, Philadelphia's office and sales sector rose from 7 percent to 19 percent of the entire workforce. It went from being a sliver of the working population to a sizable chunk. Larger bureaucracies and the advent of department stores demanded legions of clerks to count the debits and profits as well as to sell goods.[19] Additionally, office and sales work drew more women as the industrial order matured. This constituted their first opportunity to enter white-collar employment in large numbers, and their presence in the white-collar workplace helped transform the very meanings of clerical work. In 1870 about 80,000 clerical workers labored in the United States, but under 3 percent were women.[20] By 1920 America's clerical workforce numbered slightly over 3,000,000, and 45 percent were women. Women dominated certain newly created occupations at the turn of the century, such as typing and stenography. Other occupations, such as clerking, slowly transformed from male- to female-typed jobs. Employers tied the labor of women to the advent of new office technology, particularly the typewriter. Offices especially employed women in the most routinized forms of clerical work, which approximated light manufacturing.[21] Women dominated the industrial era's preeminent sales arena, the department-store selling floor, as well. Men occupied all levels of office and selling-floor hierarchies, while male-dominated management relegated women to the bottom tiers, kept them from ascending the corporate ladder, and expected them to leave the workforce once they married. Much like preindustrial shopwomen, these late nineteenth-century women could not harbor any realistic hopes of using their jobs to advance in the masculine business world.

Clerking grew in routinization and mechanization during the industrial period, and particularly in large establishments, its direct association with male apprenticeship diminished. In fact, male clerks and their superiors came to view the most routinized work, while necessary for the successful functioning of bureaucracy, as the purview of women and undesirable for young men. The preindustrial pace of work and office intimacy that Jay Cooke and his fellow clerks experienced faded away. Opportunities for upward occupational mobility declined.[22] Despite the changes in the clerical world, however, the shiny preindustrial vision of rapid advancement did not tarnish enough to dissuade men from entering lower-level white-collar employment. Many industrial-era male clerks still clung to dreams of business ownership. Unfortunately for them, the small counting-floor setting in which a shopkeeper passed on the secrets of his trade to his only clerk became harder to find. These more intimate settings had made it easier to learn the tricks of the trade, so to speak. The administrative revolution made it a growing rarity for clerks to work directly with business owners. Rather, they interacted with a wide variety of middle-level managers and received much of their training in specialized schools. Replacing apprenticeship, educational institutions such as clerical high-school programs and business colleges arose to instruct the emerging clerical workforce.[23]

Nevertheless, the antiquated, preindustrial dream of using clerical work as a route to small-business ownership tenaciously persisted for industrial-era male office and sales workers. Successful transition from clerical work into the proprietary world, however, required business acumen, monetary resources, and a bit of luck. The story of Joseph Blumenthal serialized by *System* magazine in 1916 served as an idealized example to industrial-era male clerks who dreamed of climbing into the proprietary ranks. Enough men shared Blumenthal's experiences to keep the dream of upward mobility alive for countless thousands of their counterparts. In 1898 the twenty-seven-year-old Blumenthal served as a salesman for D. Sulzberger, a Philadelphia extract manufacturer. Blumenthal's father had worked as a commission salesman, but Joseph wanted more. That year, with the help of his family, he started his own company, the Peerless Extract Works. He rented a fifteen-foot by thirty-foot room at 45 North Second Street for fifteen dollars per month. His five brothers joined him as partners. His sister, Edna, labored as the fledgling company's bookkeeper, receiving five dollars a week for her ledger work. In the first year the company drew modest profits, about $2,500. Sickness among family members and other family-related issues, however, such as siblings pursuing schooling rather than their jobs at the extract works, forced Blumenthal to shut down operations shortly after his first year of business. This failure did not discourage him. Rather, in 1900 Blumenthal doggedly created another extract business, Blumenthal Brothers, to help pay his extended family's bills. Unfortunately, profits barely covered the new expenses of three of his brother-partners. They had recently formed new families, and the brothers struggled to get by. They had children to care for, an expensive burden. In 1907, while walking home from work one evening, the six brothers gazed at a chocolate company's truck as it drove by. The sextet realized that transforming their business into a confectionery company might offer a way to increase profits. They began to lay plans for a much larger operation than the extract company. By 1910 they had secured thirty thousand feet of factory space, the proper equipment, and most important, a supervisor with specialized knowledge of chocolate production. A new company sprang to life. By the 1910s output and profits soared so high that the Blumenthal Chocolate Works outgrew its old digs. It relocated northeast of the city on 2.5 acres of open land near some Pennsylvania Railroad tracks. Through extraordinary effort and will, combined with the support of a talented family, Joseph Blumenthal rose out of the clerical workforce and into small-business ownership.

Thousands of other male office and sales workers attempted similar transitions with varying degrees of success. Blumenthal's experience highlights the allure that proprietary work maintained for late nineteenth-century male office and sales workers. Disregarding the reality of declining occupational mobility, many believed that the office or selling floor prepared them to seize the helms of future small businesses. Blumenthal had initially learned the nuances of the extract business as a clerk, but he was not satisfied merely to possess the knowledge. He took his understanding of the extract business with him when he decided to form his own company. In terms of upward mobility, Blumenthal's experience shared much in common with the lives of clerks from the preindustrial period, such as Jay Cooke.[24]

In larger business establishments ambitious male office workers increasingly focused on another route of upward mobility: climbing the corporate ladder. For example, in 1913 William Barton Johnson, a "clean-cut, aggressive" twenty-five year old, scrambled into the managerial echelons of the Pennsylvania Railroad as paymaster of the New York Division. He had begun his career with the railroad ten years earlier, as a clerk in Philadelphia.[25] Edgar T. Wismer experienced a similar climb up the class ladder. In 1886 he was hired as a cash boy for the Strawbridge and Clothier Department Store in Philadelphia. Soon thereafter he became a clerk in the auditing department, where he excelled. His superiors pushed him to become the head of the auditing department and then made him chief statistician for the store just after the turn of the century.[26] In this position Wismer gathered vital information about operations and helped formulate critical store policies. Even though work in offices and on selling floors lost its preindustrial aura of apprenticeship and high levels of upward occupational mobility, clerking still offered many of industrial America's white-collar men a springboard into much more remunerative and status-conferring positions.

Lumping industrial-era clerical workers with other white-collar workers in an undifferentiated middle class papers over important differences. Because of its growing size and importance in the industrial economy, this group must be studied as a discrete segment of the workforce.[27] Additionally, several other factors suggest classifying clerical workers as a distinct group within the industrial order. If I am to highlight the separateness of office and sales workers, however, I must justify excluding others—say, small-business owners and skilled blue-collar workers—from this group and define what qualities made clerical workers unique in industrial America's class structure.

First, industrial-era clerical workers did not control the means of production or own the businesses where they balanced ledgers or peddled wares. This distinguished them from small-business owners and professionals, such as lawyers and physicians, who had private practices. Second, unlike managers or foremen, they did not control the work of others. Clerical employees were paid workers subject to the searching gaze of management. This superficially seems to connect them with blue-collar laborers, but there was an important distinction: clerks and salespeople differed from the toiling masses of the industrial order in that their jobs did not require tremendous physical exertion. Clerks worked mostly with their minds, not their hands. A 1930 study aptly referred to office workers as "soft-handed" and blue-collar workers as "hard-handed" laborers.[28] Workers within the industrial-era office or in sales positions also had clean jobs. Literally, workplace grime did not stain white collars as much as it did blue collars. "Dig!" a poem that ran in 1913 in the alumni journal of Philadelphia's Peirce School, a business college, read:

> He wanted a job, and like everyone else,
> He wanted a good one, you know;
> Where his clothes would not soil and his
> hands would keep clean.[29]

The protagonist does not initially obtain what he desires. Rather, he receives a dirty job that requires him to dig with a spade. He accepts it, works hard, and is rewarded one victorious day when his employer replaces the spade with a pen. The poem glorifies the preeminence of clerical work and makes the case for clerks as hard workers. In the minds of the office workers whom the Peirce School trained, the pen was mightier than the spade.[30]

As simplistic as this may seem, office and sales employees cherished cleanliness as a status marker distancing themselves from skilled blue-collar operatives, because they could not rely on differences in pay. Indeed, some skilled blue-collar workers earned more weekly pay than did male clerks or salesmen. In the late nineteenth century the predominantly male clerical workforce earned salaries comparable to those among the upper echelons of the skilled workforce.[31] More broadly, in 1890 the average earnings of the city's office personnel hovered well above the composite wage levels for the entire workforce. Male office workers averaged $925.70 a year in pay; female clerical workers averaged $433.12. The average yearly wage for the city's entire male workforce leveled off at $609.97. For women, it was $301.48.[32] However, this significant gap in earnings shrank between 1890 and 1920. One specific, stark example suffices to give a sense of this decline. In 1890 the yearly earnings of railroad clerks across the nation hovered 13 percent above those of skilled blue-collar railroad employees. By the 1920s the gap had completely vanished, and clerical workers increasingly relied on different measures to differentiate themselves from those in the blue-collar realm.[33]

Despite this convergence, job security separated clerks and salespeople from skilled blue-collar workers, who suffered from periodic unemployment.[34] In the late nineteenth century, as Alexander Keyssar has noted, "working with a pencil rather than a wrench was an unmistakable emblem of job security."[35] Blue-collar workers, even skilled employees, regularly faced unemployment. At the turn of the century just over 28 percent of Philadelphia's carpenters and joiners went jobless for a month or more each year, as did 8 percent of the city's machinists. The situation was even worse for male unskilled laborers: one-third of them faced a month or more of unemployment every year. The figures for blue-collar women were staggering as well. Yearly, almost 20 percent of female textile mill operatives and 17 percent of women dressmakers suffered through more than thirty days of unemployment. At some point every year sizable segments of the manual workforce struggled to cope with joblessness. For clerical workers the picture proved much brighter. Only 4 percent of male clerks and salesmen experienced comparable unemployment, and female clerks averaged about the same.[36] Saleswomen fared the worst, with 6 percent finding themselves unemployed for at least one month annually.[37]

Industrial-era clerical workers were aware that they occupied a terrain above the labor aristocracy. The office and the selling floor were distinct from the shop floor. Most clerical workers worked in offices or stores in Philadelphia's central business district, and clerks and salespeople socialized with their white-collar coworkers both at and away from their places of employment. In addition, office and sales employees typically received more schooling than did the working class. In the 1909–10 schoolyear 234,000 students enrolled in commercial education programs nationally.[38] Emphasizing their position between the working class on the one hand and professionals and small-business owners on the other, clerical workers avoided connection with menial work and longed for full-fledged middle-class status. Many men ignored the shrinking opportunity for movement out of the lower reaches of the office and selling floor. No doubt as a result, little successful unionization occurred in the clerical realm prior to the 1920s. No major organized oppositional culture sprang up to tilt against employers for control of the workplace. Rather, lower-level white-collar workers tended to identify with those higher on the social and economic scale. In particular, men who aspired to rise into the professionalized managerial hierarchy or to become small-business owners eschewed collective antimanagement agitation. Poignantly, in 1905 the Retail Clerks' International Protective Association (RCIPA), one of the few clerical unions, lamented that one-half of America's male sales clerks dreamed of becoming small-business owners.[39]

Broad forces evident in the growth of the industrial-era office and sales workforce paralleled developments in the blue-collar realm. These forces distanced industrial-era clerks from their more solidly middle-class counterparts. The de-skilling that transformed the working class was mirrored in the clerical work world. During the second half of the nineteenth century, manual employment went from being the domain of skilled, native-born craftsmen to being dominated by unskilled or semiskilled immigrant-stock labor.[40] Mechanization, scientific management, and feminization likewise transformed the clerical workforce. These factors opened up more entry-level positions while constricting the responsibilities and potential upward mobility of many clerical laborers. Countless jobs went to the children of immigrants, who by century's end were entering the clerical workforce in substantial numbers, even in Philadelphia, a city with a relatively small immigrant population.

Industrial-era clerical work had a more complicated position in urban society than its preindustrial predecessor did. Between 1870 and 1920 office and sales employment came to rest between other, more firmly white-collar work opportunities above and skilled blue-collar jobs below it on the class ladder. In this period many denizens of the office and selling floor, particularly women, landed jobs without much potential for advancement. Clerical employment no longer simply served as direct apprenticeship into the small-business world for a small male workforce, as it had in the early nineteenth century. By the early twentieth century a vast army of clerks had arisen to serve big business. Many in this army did not learn their skills on the job but received specialized clerical training in high schools and private business colleges. In an interesting twist, however, employers and employees continued to view clerical work as temporary. Women rarely worked beyond marriage, and men still dreamed about upward mobility into the managerial world or their own businesses. Their bosses devised hiring systems that failed to promote women and advanced just enough men to fuel fantasies of upward climbing. This was a perfect scheme to maintain a fluid, tractable workforce. Both workers and management saw clerical employment as a way station on the path to other destinations in the lives of young clerks and salespeople.

More detailed discussion of the city's clerks must be contextualized by addressing their place in Philadelphia's overall white-collar workforce. The six U.S. censuses from 1870 to 1920 provide the best sources for describing the city's nonmanual workers. Unfortunately, different censuses used different ethnic, racial, or occupational designations. Employment figures in the 1870 and 1880 censuses rank immigrants by nations of origin but do not differentiate the ethnic or national backgrounds for native-born individuals. The 1890 and 1900 censuses list immigrants according to nativity as well as ethnicity. The 1910 and 1920 censuses focus once again on nativity. Nevertheless, these differences do not preclude discussion of the nonmanual workforce's changing composition for this period. In fact, the published censuses allow analysis of the white-collar workforce from two basic and necessary angles. First, they enable us to describe white-collar work by placing it in the context of Philadelphia's entire workforce. Second, they allow us to ascertain the relationships of nativity, gender, and race to white-collar work in general and to clerical work in particular.[41]

The manual and nonmanual labor pools both increased steadily in industrial-era Philadelphia. Simply examining expansion rates shows that the postmodern information and service-based workforce was conceived and quickened within the industrial order. Buildup in the white-collar realm outpaced that in the blue-collar sphere: the manual workforce increased half as quickly as the white-collar job world did, tripling between 1870 and 1920, while the white-collar workforce grew sevenfold. The proportion of the total workforce composed of white-collar workers doubled, from one in six to one in three workers.

It is more difficult to determine the extent to which individual workers could have noticed this difference in the expansion of the blue- and white-collar sectors. Over time, however, white-collar workers (the clerical ranks, proprietors, and professionals) likely noticed the amplification of opportunity within their own specific occupational segments of the nonmanual workforce simply through their interactions with others engaged in similar work. The clerical realm grew significantly. A bookkeeper or salesperson working in 1870 and still actively employed at century's end most likely noticed how quickly the clerking ranks had grown, swelling by a factor of five in the last three decades of the nineteenth century. By 1920 Philadelphia's clerical workforce was roughly ten times the size it had been in 1870. The professional workforce grew elevenfold in the same period. The augmentation of these two segments of the white-collar work world reflected the age's professionalization and bureaucratization as well as the late nineteenth century's organizational and managerial revolutions.[42] The proprietary workforce grew more slowly.[43] Nonmanual employment shifted away from being largely defined by entrepreneurial activity and toward a greater linkage with bureaucratic and professional employment.

At first glance these trends appear to indicate that professional and clerical work held equal significance in Philadelphia's industrial economy. A closer reading proves otherwise. In 1870 small-business owners constituted the largest white-collar occupational group and held 45 percent of all nonmanual positions (see table 1). By 1920 they had slipped to third place, holding just 21 percent of Philadelphia's white-collar jobs. By then office and sales workers accounted for 58 percent of the white-collar workforce and far outranked both small-business owners and professionals as a segment of the white-collar labor pool. Thus, the widening of the clerical sector significantly redefined the city's white-collar occupational structure. Indeed, one may describe this trend as a "clerical revolution."

The ascent of the clerical workforce and the decline of proprietors as parts of the white-collar world underscored a shift in the occupational trajectories

Table 1. Occupational Composition of the White-Collar World, 1870–1920

Occupational segment	1870		1900		1920	
	No.	% of white collar	No.	% of white collar	No.	% of white collar
Professional	5,203	14.2	24,788	16.9	57,862	21.3
Proprietary	16,460	44.9	44,742	30.5	56,032	20.7
Clerical[a]	14,970	40.9	77,141	53.6	157,313	58.0
Total white-collar	36,633	100.0	146,671	100.0	271,207	100.0

Sources: Secretary of the Interior, *The Statistics of the Population of the United States . . .* (Washington, D.C.: GPO, 1872), vol. 1, table 32, pp. 794–95; Department of Commerce and Labor, Bureau of the Census, *Occupations at the Twelfth Census,* special reports (Washington, D.C.: GPO, 1904), table 43, pp. 672–78; Department of Commerce, Bureau of the Census, *Population 1920, Occupations* (Washington, D.C.: GPO, 1923), vol. 4, table 2, pp. 1193–97.

[a]Includes office and sales workers. The "Clerical" category will comprise office and sales workers in all subsequent tables where the term appears.

of male clerical workers. In the 1870s pursuing white-collar employment was most often coupled with entrepreneurial motivation. At that time clerking still offered men rapid mobility into small-business ownership; office and sales work was directly linked to eventual self-employment and the capital and personal risks this involved. By 1900 the meanings of white-collar work had changed. The significance of small-business ownership in the nonmanual realm plummeted. The dominant sector of the white-collar workforce—clerical employment—became increasingly connected with specific bureaucratic skills imparted by business colleges and related educational institutions. Workers easily transferred this knowledge from job to job, and male clerks faced diminishing chances of ever owning their own enterprises. Essentially, proprietary opportunities shrank as the pool of office and sales workers grew. Subsequently, in the early 1900s, institutions such as business colleges, clerical high schools, and professional schools played a larger role as gatekeepers mediating the entrance of thousands into Philadelphia's offices and stores.

Thus, the growth of the office and sales workforce was tied to men's declining chances for entry to the proprietary sector, which grew the least among the three white-collar occupational segments between 1870 and 1920. As Ileen A. DeVault has noted, the shrinking overall potential for upward mobility in the office world resulted from the "increasingly pyramidic organizational structure of offices."[44] That is, the expanding pool of office and sales workers received direction from a relatively small group of managers. The clerical revolution in the white-collar realm highlighted a pyramidic reorientation not only of the office but of the entire nonmanual workforce.

Nativity and race provide other perspectives on industrial-era Philadelphia's economic opportunity structure (see table 2).[45] As mentioned previously, Philadelphia's population was predominantly native-born. Over time increasing proportions of the city's native-born white workers filled nonmanual jobs.[46] In 1870 one-fifth of Philadelphia's nonimmigrant white workers labored behind desks, at counters, or in storefronts tabulating figures, greeting customers, running a business, or practicing a profession. Fifty years later double that proportion did so. Being of native birth offered one a decent chance at landing white-collar work. Examining the situation from a different angle, the white-collar world was overwhelmingly native-born from 1870 to 1920. Native-born Philadelphians accounted for about 78 percent of the city's white-collar workers between 1870 and 1920.[47] Even more specifically, just under 90 percent of all office and sales employees from 1870–1920 were native-born (see table 2). Nevertheless, clerical employment provided an often-traversed bridge between an immigrant world dominated by manual work and a world of less physical labor. The 1900 and 1920 censuses more pre-

Table 2. Philadelphia's Clerical Workforce Analyzed by Nativity and Race, 1870–1920

	Percentage of workforce		
Nativity/race	1870	1900	1920
Native-born white	88.1	87.8	86.9
Second-generation	—	32.8	35.7
Immigrants	11.9	11.1	11.6
African-American	—	1.0	1.5

Sources: Secretary of the Interior, *The Statistics of the Population of the United States*... (Washington, D.C.: GPO, 1872), vol. 1, table 32, pp. 794–95; Department of Commerce and Labor, Bureau of the Census, *Occupations at the Twelfth Census,* special reports (Washington, D.C.: GPO, 1904), table 43, pp. 672–78; Department of Commerce, Bureau of the Census, *Population 1920, Occupations* (Washington, D.C.: GPO, 1923), vol. 4, table 2, pp. 1193–97.

cisely describe the native-born category, differentiating between individuals who had native-born parents and those who were born in the United States but had immigrant parents (hereinafter termed "second-generation"). In the first two decades of the twentieth century, about one-third of all native-born clerical employees were second-generation. The clerking work environment likely altered the second generation's ties to parents and past. Second-generation men and women in the office and sales workforce were encouraged to deemphasize their foreignness. For many, their work relied heavily on the use of English and regular interactions with native-born whites.[48] Also, few foreign-born men and women worked in the typical office or department store. In this context, an interesting juxtaposition of figures further highlights how clerical work served to mark success among immigrants in Philadelphia. Of all the immigrants in the city's workforce in 1900, only about 5 percent held office or sales jobs. Among the children of European immigrants in the same year, three times this proportion held jobs in the clerical realm; that is, they were three times as likely to land low-level white-collar work and climb up the economic ladder than were their parents.

From 1900 to 1920 the Great Migration swelled the number of African American workers in Philadelphia, but this period held little change for blacks in the white-collar realm. The 1870 and 1880 censuses did not distinguish African Americans from whites. The 1890 census combined African Americans, Chinese Americans, and Native Americans. In 1900, when the census did distinguish African Americans as a separate category, black workers made up about 7 percent of Philadelphia's overall workforce; in 1920, almost 10 percent. Throughout the period, however, African Americans accounted for only a tiny sliver of Philadelphia's white-collar sector—less than 2 percent.

White-collar workers also constituted a small and unchanging share of the city's total African American workforce—about 7 percent between 1900 and 1920. For black Philadelphians, job opportunities in the nonmanual sector were scarce, and their chances for such employment did not improve between 1870 and 1920. Thus, as a whole, the white-collar world's composition by nativity and race remained remarkably consistent from 1870 to 1920.

At the turn of the twentieth century, it was standard practice for Philadelphia's white business owners to reject African Americans seeking employment behind office desks or store counters. In his pathbreaking late nineteenth-century study of black Philadelphia, W. E. B. Du Bois found that "nearly all" black clerks and salespeople worked in establishments owned by African Americans. Du Bois highlighted the tale of an elegant stationery store owned by a black Philadelphian. Blatant racial discrimination had forced the proprietor out of a previous job as an assistant business manager at a white religious newspaper in Philadelphia. He turned to small-business ownership as the only way to control his career and remove the onus of racism from his job life—to run a business where he "'owned the stock, the store and the building'" and made all the decisions. One of the stationer's key decisions was to hire his sister as a clerk. She had received training as a typist and stenographer, but no white business owner would hire her.[49] The proprietor took responsibility for righting the wrongs his sister had experienced by allowing her to practice the skills she had learned.

Most white merchants believed that the mere presence of black clerks in their stores would turn away their white customers. When black candidates appeared on the thresholds of white businesses, their skin color determined their employability. Du Bois recounted the story of a white male lawyer's unsuccessful attempt to help a young black female business-college graduate find clerical work. White business owners who spoke with the lawyer agreed to employ the prospective clerk until they found out her race. In another incident, an African American man sent a letter of application to an employer for a sales position. His credentials landed him an interview. When he arrived for it, the firm informed him they had no positions. Prospective employers greeted African Americans with "very sorry" or perhaps simply ignored them. Occasionally the reception was even worse, as when one black clerk sought to fill a position in the suburbs and was greeted with racist derision: "What do you suppose we'd want with a nigger?" White employers refused one woman who tried to land a job at "almost every store" on the stretch of Market Street that divided Center City. Fully qualified black men and women who graduated from high school or college business programs simply could not find office work in white firms in the City of Brotherly Love.[50] The only way a black clerk could gain entry into a white business was through personal connections with the employer, and such friendships occasionally did open doors in the city. Du Bois found that only strong affiliations between African Americans and white business owners could possibly lead to employment: "A—— was intimately acquainted with a [white] merchant and secured his son a position as a typewriter in the merchant's office." The black Philadelphians who secured positions in white-owned department stores and offices as janitors or elevator operators could not expect to advance into clerical jobs. One ambitious black porter implored his white employers to give him a chance at promotion into clerical work. They refused and promoted whites instead.[51]

The few black Philadelphians who landed office or sales jobs in the white world did not enjoy the opportunity to use their employment as a springboard into more lucrative work. Of the 130 black office workers that Du Bois found in his extensive study, 30 worked in city or federal government offices that offered some security, if not mobility. A man in the city tax office enjoyed a particularly long and distinguished career as "perhaps the most efficient clerk in the office." Wanamaker's department store employed African Americans in its post office. A handful of black Philadelphians also toiled in white-owned railroad offices and banks. More often than not, however, African Americans in these positions faced hostility from white management and clientele. Promotion and upward mobility were out of the question for black clerks in the white world. Perhaps they dreamed of saving money and developing their own businesses, but their jobs offered less compensation than those of white clerks, which made saving money more difficult. An African American porter and shipping clerk earned six dollars a week while his white counterparts received eight dollars.[52]

A 1912 study of black workers in Pennsylvania by R. R. Wright found that little had changed since Du Bois had compiled the material for his book in the 1890s. Privately owned white firms in Philadelphia almost never employed black office or sales workers.[53] Wright examined 600 white-owned firms in the city. The only black clerical worker reported by the employers was a receiving clerk in a small department store. Most department stores hired African Americans but relegated them to semiskilled or unskilled jobs. They worked as waiters, porters, and elevator operators. Over a decade after Du Bois's study, blacks who sought clerical work in the white world still found their best opportunities in civil-service jobs. Philadelphia's post office served as both the city's and Pennsylvania's largest employer of black clerks. In 1912, 145 African American postal clerks worked in the city. Wright cautioned that the job responsibilities of lower-level postal clerks were nearer to unskilled work than to white-collar work. These positions had "much to do with hauling, picking up, and assorting mail." But he also hinted that some upward mobility from these jobs into "more responsible" positions occurred. Nor did black clerks working in African American businesses in 1912 enjoy much chance of upward occupational mobility. The city's black community supported few big businesses. Of 263 black businesses in turn-of-the-century Philadelphia, only 5 had more than 10 employees. In addition, most of the city's black businesses failed quickly. Thus, even if African American clerks or salespeople happened to earn enough to leave the office or store and establish their own businesses, the potential for success was minimal.[54]

In short, exclusion defined the work experiences of racial minorities, particularly black women, in the office and sales sector of Philadelphia's white-collar occupational structure. The limited job opportunities provided little upward mobility. The whiteness of the office and selling floor rendered African Americans barely visible to white clerical workers on the job. If white sales clerks encountered black employees in department stores, they usually labored in a lower-status service position, such as elevator operator, janitor, waiter (in store restaurants), maid, porter, or stockman. The previously mentioned white lawyer who had tried to find work for an African American woman eventually ended up temporarily hiring her himself. However, this well-intentioned individual cowered in front of his workers. The woman he hired was light skinned, and he forced her to "pass" as a white employee. Otherwise, he faced angering his white employees who equated black workers with menial labor. Even after the woman left to find work outside the city, the lawyer refused to tell his employees that they had worked beside an African American, likely because he feared their resentment.[55] The racist attitudes of employers, customers, and white clerical workers powerfully combined to marginalize black workers in most white-collar settings. Fear ruled the attitudes of whites who formed this triad of antipathy. White clerks shuddered at the idea that black employees might toil on equal footing with them and enjoy the potential for upward mobility that clerical jobs supposedly offered. As in the rest of urban America, white shoppers at department stores or the clients of Center City offices detested contact with African Americans.[56] Management worried about the impact that inserting black clerks into the workplace would have on their white employees and clientele.

Gender forms another important viewpoint from which the white-collar workforce can be analyzed (see table 3).[57] White-collar work defined the occupational lives of rapidly expanding portions of both the male and female workforces. In other words, the chance to attain nonmanual positions rose

Table 3. Women as a Percentage of the White-Collar Workforce, 1870–1920

Occupational	1870		1900		1920	
segment	Total	Percentage	Total	Percentage	Total	Percentage
Professional	1,594	30.6	5,979	24.1	15,197	26.3
Proprietary	1,714	10.4	3,908	8.7	6,973	12.4
Clerical	2,086	13.9	17,872	23.2	65,045	41.3
Total white- collar	5,394	14.7	27,759	18.9	87,215	32.2

Sources: Secretary of the Interior, *The Statistics of the Population of the United States . . .* (Washington, D.C.: GPO, 1872), vol. 1, table 32, pp. 794–95; Department of Commerce and Labor, Bureau of the Census, *Occupations at the Twelfth Census,* special reports (Washington, D.C.: GPO, 1904), table 43, pp. 672–78; Department of Commerce, Bureau of the Census, *Population 1920, Occupations* (Washington, D.C.: GPO, 1923), vol. 4, table 2, pp. 1193–97.

for both sexes. Nevertheless, men dominated the white-collar sector. Women held only about 15 percent of all middle-class jobs in 1870. This percentage more than doubled by 1920, and most of this growth came in the clerical workplace. In relation to professional and proprietary employment, the greatest gender-related changes in the clerical segment of the white-collar workforce transpired in the fifty years after the Civil War.[58] The shifts in the gender dimension of clerical employment occurred nationally and have particularly drawn the interest of women's historians because of their implications for the female workforce. Three major trends along gender lines shaped the surge of clerical employment between 1870 and 1920.

First, it is important to remember that although the participation of both men and women in office and sales work grew from 1870 to 1920, the clerical revolution occurred in two distinct, gendered phases. For women to a great degree and for men to a lesser degree, white-collar opportunity meant clerking between the Civil War and the Roaring Twenties. Women's overall participation in the clerical work world exploded in this era. In 1870 almost 39 percent of the female white-collar workers were employed in clerical jobs (see table 4). Although clerking women outnumbered those who ran businesses or plied professions in 1870, this difference was much more pronounced in 1920, by which time female office and sales workers composed an amazing three-quarters of the entire female white-collar workforce. Thus, just after World War I white-collar opportunity for women had become largely clerical. It is astounding that most of this transformation occurred in the first two decades of the twentieth century. About 75 percent of the climb in female office and sales employment opportunity happened after 1900.[59]

Although it did not match the rate at which women's participation in the clerical sector billowed, men's participation also intensified (see table 4). The male clerical workforce accounted for two-fifths of all white-collar

Table 4. Percentages of Philadelphia's Women and Men in White-Collar Occupations, 1870–1920

Segment	1870	1900	1920
Professional			
Women	29.6%	21.5%	17.4%
Men	11.6	15.8	23.2
Proprietary			
Women	31.8	14.1	8.0
Men	47.2	34.3	26.7
Clerical			
Women	38.7	64.4	74.6
Men	41.2	49.8	50.1

Sources: Secretary of the Interior, *The Statistics of the Population of the United States . . .* (Washington, D.C.: GPO, 1872), vol. 1, table 32, pp. 794–95; Department of Commerce and Labor, Bureau of the Census, *Occupations at the Twelfth Census,* special reports (Washington, D.C.: GPO, 1904), table 43, pp. 672–78; Department of Commerce, Bureau of the Census, *Population 1920, Occupations* (Washington, D.C.: GPO, 1923), vol. 4, table 2, pp. 1193–97.

men in 1870 Philadelphia, rising modestly to one-half in 1920. Employment in offices or stores was not the overwhelming occupational choice for men in the white-collar world as it was for women. Nevertheless, by 1920 male employment in the clerical workforce was double that in the proprietary or professional realms. Of equal importance, the augmentation of clerical opportunity happened earlier for men than for women. Most of the enlargement of the male clerical workforce occurred between 1870 and 1900. In fact, during the first decade of the twentieth century, the most significant growth occurred in the professions, resulting from the swelling of managerial jobs in the corporate world. Male office and sales employment expanded in the formative years of the new industrial order. As employers began to work out the changing meanings of clerical positions, the jobs were largely being filled by men. By the late 1910s cost-accounting techniques and Frederick W. Taylor's scientific management principles had swept the corporate office and retail sales floor. Taylorism's emphases on efficiency and accountability fit into the bureaucratic needs of rapidly expanding corporate America.[60] New jobs in emerging corporate bureaucracies often went to youthful, single women who were seen by employers as the cheapest, most tractable segment of the working population. Young women also had been connected with repetitive, de-skilled industrial work. To bosses, the employment of women behind office machines seemed logical. Many single women also jumped at the opportunity to obtain higher-status nonmanufacturing work. Male-dominated managers resisted Taylorism in their corners of the office and closed off potential upward mobility for new, often female, clerical workers.[61]

Importantly, the rise in female clerical opportunity did not diminish levels of male participation in the white-collar workforce as a whole. In the early twentieth century, office and sales workers still represented about half of all male white-collar jobs, which suggests that after the turn of the century, clerking was far from being something men simply avoided or from which they were excluded by employers' reconceptualizations of occupational terms. Two alternative interpretations seem plausible. On the one hand, definitions of work and perceptions of mobility remained sufficiently unclear and contested to entice large numbers of both men and women into the office or onto the selling floor. On the other hand, women flooded into new dead-end, sex-typed job opportunities in the clerical workforce. Meanwhile, men continued to fill positions that offered some mobility, but the creation of new, promising jobs slowed in the second decade of the twentieth century. These interpretations are not exclusive, however, and reality most likely lay in some combination of the two.

The second major trend that influenced the gender construction of the clerical sector was its growing but incomplete feminization. In 1870 men held 86 percent of office or sales jobs in Philadelphia. This dropped to around 59 percent in 1920. As with women's overall participation in the clerical workforce, much of this sector's feminization occurred in the first two decades of the twentieth century. Even by 1920, however, men still constituted a majority of these workers. Among the five largest clerical occupations, the proportion of women workers dwarfed that of men in only two, stenography and bookkeeping. The rest of the major clerical pursuits in 1920 were highly mixed by gender. For example, among the 52,712 clerks who did not work in stores, almost one-third were women. This indicates that men and women in similar occupational circumstances interacted on the selling floors and in the counting rooms of the early twentieth century. Men who worked in offices or at sales generally performed the same tasks as their female counterparts, whether they did so in separate settings or within the same environs. Instead of underlining a clear division between male management and female workforce, these figures accent some degree of role blurring and gender intermingling in the office and on selling floors.[62] Unlike the white clerical workforce, its African American counterpart did not show a high degree of feminization by 1920. Four-fifths of all black clerical employment went to men in 1920.

As a counterpoint to the rising presence of women in offices and stores, men dominated the professions and business ownership in the city between 1870 and 1920, and the ratio of women to men in these fields did not significantly change. Over this period men held between a three-to-one and a four-to-one numerical advantage over women in the professions. The difference was even more exaggerated among proprietors. Roughly nine of every ten Philadelphia businesses had men at their helms between 1870 and 1920.

Women business owners and professionals were concentrated in a handful of occupations in industrial-era Philadelphia. Women dominated boarding- and lodging-house ownership in the city, the sole proprietary category they controlled. Women accounted for 92 percent of the city's boardinghouse keepers in 1870 and 87 percent in 1900. Twenty years later the published federal census did not even enumerate male boardinghouse keepers, likely indicating their scarcity in the city. Women accounted for just under a third of all professionals in 1870, with almost nine-tenths teaching school. By 1920 educators still accounted for half of all professional women; nurses, another quarter. Male professionals controlled the clergy, journalism, law, and medicine throughout the late 1800s and early 1900s. Practicing law was particularly closed off to women. In 1883 Carrie Burnham Kilgore became Philadelphia's first female lawyer. Kilgore's admission to the bar followed nearly ten years of struggle. Becoming a lawyer embodied only the first step, however. She expected to encounter gender bias and outright belligerence from men in her profession. Some of the city's male lawyers exuded hostility toward women and were likely to "lie in wait to snub and insult and embarrass a woman, especially if she chances to be one of cultivation and refinement."[63]

The opportunities open to women in the professional and proprietary worlds focused on work that featured the rather Victorian feminine roles of child rearing and housekeeping. The expansion of employment prospects in the clerical realm offered a much more modern-minded vocational choice that moved away from domesticity and placed women firmly in the public worlds of the office and store. For many women, clerking presented a white-collar job option that got them out of the house both literally and figuratively.

The third gender-related trend was that distinctions of nativity remained a relatively constant factor for both men and women in the clerical workforce between 1900 and 1920. Women born of native parents provided slightly over 50 percent of female clerical workers during the period. Their male counterparts accounted for about half of the male clerical workforce. Female children of immigrants constituted around 40 percent of the workforce in the same period, and second-generation men held about one-third of male clerical positions in Philadelphia. Native-stock and second-generation clerical workers made occupational choices based on the internal dynamics of the socioeconomic groups from which they initially came. Class status, race, ethnicity, educational level, and gender played out in unique ways to encourage these individuals to seek jobs in the growing offices and emporia of Philadelphia. In turn-of-the-century Pittsburgh, the skilled blue-collar workforce—the labor aristocracy—encouraged its children to enroll in the Commercial Department of the steel town's public high school.[64] Labor aristocrats reasoned that the occupational status conferred by a child's employment in the clerical sector maintained the entire family's status at the top of the working-class hierarchy. For Philadelphia, these issues will be taken up in following chapters.

* * *

The development of a massive clerical workforce in industrial-era Philadelphia can be viewed from structural and social perspectives. Structurally, as part of the white-collar realm, clerical employment grew tremendously in the period. It expanded tenfold and in terms of total workers far outpaced the professional and proprietary sectors, so that by 1920 one can truly speak of the emergence of a prominent and distinct clerical segment in the economy. By 1920 this group was more than triple the size of either the proprietary or the professional portions of the white-collar world. Overall, the white-collar world tilted heavily toward office and sales work in the early twentieth century. By 1920, 58 percent of all nonmanual jobs in the city were clerical. This clerical revolution was the key component in the massive growth experienced by the white-collar sector.

The clerical workforce's development as a social group had its distinctive ethnic, racial, and gender contours. Throughout the period office and sales employees were overwhelmingly native-born. However, improved census recording techniques after 1900 highlight an additional insight about this statistic. In the first two decades of the twentieth century, one-third of clerks in Philadelphia had foreign-born parents. In other words, a substantial ethnic presence existed in the city's offices and on its selling floors. Not only did a sizable portion of the clerical workforce come from immigrant communities, but for second-generation men and women seeking employment in the city, office and sales work proved an oft-selected option in the early twentieth century. From 1900 to 1920 most children of immigrants who chose nonmanual employment clerked in stores or offices.[65] In even broader terms, in 1920 one of every four second-generation individuals in Philadelphia held an office or sales job. This constituted a significant leap from the situation only twenty years earlier.[66] In other words, the first two decades of the twentieth century saw a major opening of clerical opportunity to the native-born children of immigrants in the city.

Between 1870 and 1920 the level of female clerical employment grew faster than did the corresponding male figure, and regardless of gender, whites dominated Philadelphia's offices and selling floors. Much of this boon for women occurred between 1900 and 1920, while most of the acceleration in male clerical opportunity happened between 1870 and 1900. Nonetheless, even as late as 1920, the office and sales workforce was well mixed along gender lines. Between 1900 and 1920 second-generation women constituted around 39 percent of women working in the city's offices and stores. During the same period their male counterparts made up around one-third of the men employed in the offices and stores of the city. Thus, we can further flesh out the findings regarding nativity and the clerical workforce: the native-born sons and daughters of immigrants held large segments of clerical opportunity in early twentieth-century Philadelphia. Discrimination barred access to clerical jobs for African American citizens, however. Finally, one critical factor that combines both structural and social themes cannot be assessed from published census data. Studying the mobility of workers across the collar line demands a different approach and evidence. This critical question will be taken up in chapter 3.

2   In the Office and the Store

Two major fracture lines complicate the description of clerical work experiences. The first line of fracture is the diverse nature of white-collar work. Superficially, a department-store saleswoman seems to have had little in common with a male bank clerk. Nonetheless, significant connections united the work experiences of these and other clerical employees. From 1870 to 1920 thousands of workers in Philadelphia's offices and stores found jobs through similar mechanisms and toiled under similar conditions. Clerks, bookkeepers, and department-store saleswomen all worked with information in some way, well before the advent of the "information age." These employees did not produce goods or materials. They wrestled with statistics, facts, data, and documents, all the particulars involved in production and sales processes. The second fracture line is gender. It served to constantly distinguish male from female white-collar on-the-job experiences, shaping the ways in which men and women perceived their work. It influenced almost every aspect of the white-collar workplace. As in the blue-collar work world, gender divided workers in the office and on selling floors, and management shunted employees into certain jobs based on it. Focusing on themes shared by office and sales occupations overcomes the first fracture line and helps us view these workers as a relatively cohesive group in the industrial order. With clerking, however, one cannot easily smooth out dissimilarities grounded in gender, which profoundly differentiated the experiences of men and women.

Any discussion of the clerical work experience must start prior to the office door, for clerks and salespeople received their initiation into it with the hiring process. To illuminate the work lives of Philadelphia's industrial-era clerks, I begin with the formal institutional aid that thousands used to secure positions. Business colleges, such as the city's Peirce School, founded in 1865, had placement offices that matched their students and alumni with potential employers. The school's Employment Department found seemingly countless students their first jobs. Business colleges and public-school business-education programs offered effective, formal, institutionally mediated job placement services to clerical workers, a rarity for other occupations in the industrial city. As Walter Licht has found, most of Philadelphia's industrial-era businesses relied on informal hiring procedures, particularly for blue-collar jobs. Informal "family, ethnic, and neighborhood networks" dominated working-class Philadelphians' search for employment until the early twentieth century.[1]

With their advent in the mid-nineteenth century, business high schools and college programs cultivated job placement networks that connected prospective employees with employers. Peirce's first catalog recognized the school's intermediary role: "We cannot pledge ourselves to secure situations for all our graduates; the absurdity of doing so is manifest. But our best efforts are directed to secure positions for our pupils in accordance to their knowledge and ability."[2] The college's Employment Department, a formal institution designed to connect young men and women with their first jobs, emerged in the early 1890s. Peirce wove its pride for the department throughout its promotional publications.[3] In 1900 the school published a pamphlet that listed the 101 job offers that the department had recently received from the private sector.[4] In text alongside the list, the college emphasized that the placement program had more offers than it could fill and that a great variety of positions existed to entice students. In the early 1890s the Employment Department received over five hundred requests for workers annually. This grew to around two thousand every year in the first decade of the twentieth century, when, by its own measures, the school averaged six to ten applications for stenographers and bookkeepers for every day it was open.[5] In September 1909 Peirce received 159 requests for workers and filled 83. Their salaries ranged from six to twenty dollars per week.[6] Peirce placed one student, M. Luther Grimes, as an assistant bookkeeper with the Southwark Mills Company in the spring of 1893.[7] Peirce connected Ida B. Starck with a "Dr. White, the headmaster of the Phillips Brooks School," in 1905.[8] White hired Starck as his private secretary. In 1912 the Employment Department still had difficulty filling all requests with qualified male or female students. Simply too many openings existed.[9] In one of Peirce's promotional publications, a fictitious character named "Tom Brown" recalls his meeting with the school's Employment Department secretary in 1915: "'There are always several applicants [employers] for every man we graduate,' he [the secretary] said.

'In the last three months we have received 422 requests for our students to fill positions. At times these requests run as high as 250 a month. Now here is a request from a motor truck company, asking for an assistant to one of our graduates who has been there several years. I sent a boy out there this morning.'" Immediately thereafter the young man returns from the motor truck company and breathlessly intones that he won the job and thanks the secretary. The secretary goes on to inform Tom Brown that this student has not concluded his entire course of study.[10] After exhausting its pool of graduates, Peirce dipped into its reserve of qualified students who had not completed their degrees and placed them as well.[11]

By the turn of the century the Employment Department was receiving requests by phone, letter, and telegram. Some employers required fully prepared candidates. Others preferred new employees with little or no work experience so they could train them.[12] Students formally applied to the department for assistance, and it kept their applications on file. As employers' requests came in, the placement service carefully matched job descriptions to the talents and employment desires of the students on file. Depending on their relationships with the Employment Department, firms either immediately hired a recommended student or requested two or three applicants for interviews. The placement service strove to find work for all the students who requested its help, no matter how many interviews it took.[13]

The department was extremely helpful to students in periods of economic downturn. When the economy faltered, the number of employers asking Peirce to help them search for students naturally dropped. Nevertheless, the placement service maintained its contacts in the business community and continued to receive numerous applications for workers. From September to December of 1914, during a severe recession, the department accepted 315 requests from employers. Firms had made 542 inquiries during the corresponding period in 1913.[14] Although students and alumni did not have the same chances of getting work in periods of economic stagnation, they could still expect Peirce to receive numerous requests for good workers. This must have been more encouraging than seeking work without help in such periods.

Gender issues loomed large at both ends of the hiring and placement process. Employers submitted gendered requests for employees, and Peirce considered a student's sex as a major factor in its placement efforts. Applications for workers clearly exhibited the importance of gender in the hiring process. In 1906 the Allegheny Oil and Iron Company requested a youthful male stenographer. The Biddle Hardware Company desired an "experienced lady stenographer." The Victor Talking Machine Company wanted two young men for clerical work. Sometimes requests could be very detailed. In 1910 the J. L. N. Smythe Company submitted a letter stating that the firm was looking for "a good stenographer—a girl about 20 years of age, with at least one year's business experience": "At the present time, we can put our hands on at least a score of 'typewriters and stenographers,' who can take dictations and write letters, but we want a girl who will take an interest in her work, who can turn out a neat letter, properly punctuated, with all words spelled correctly—a girl to whom one can dictate a letter with the assurance that it will be right when finished."[15] This request reflected the construction of stenography as women's work. To drive home the connection, the letter incorporated the word *girl* three times in two sentences and failed to mention any possibility of upward mobility or promotion. The note firmly connected women with mechanized, routinized office work. The central traits of J. L. N. Smythe's desired "girl" included accuracy, interest in her work, and a solid understanding of punctuation. The letter failed to mention ambition or a general knowledge of business. The repeated allusion to youthfulness likely denotes that the company sought a tractable employee. Like this one, other requests were rarely gender-neutral.[16]

Even in cases where a prospective employer did not specify gender, the Employment Department utilized gender-specific standards to match men and women to jobs. It sent women applicants "only to institutions and business houses of which [it] had a personal knowledge."[17] Working conditions formed a central consideration in the placement of women. The prospective business's reputation had to meet minimum standards for the department to place a woman there. The school discovered whether Peirce alumni filled any managerial roles at the office or store in question and asked the former students to assess the job environment. This attitude revealed a Victorian sensibility about women among Peirce administrators. They believed that female students required the school's assistance in finding an employer who had a good reputation in hiring women and could offer them a safe location. School administrators thus balanced their modern-minded efforts to introduce women into masculine work settings with a paternalistic sense of women's needs. In the masculine work world, female students required extra intervention in their job search so that they would land in solid, safe, and respectable positions as defined by the school. Surely female students were occasionally the first women hired by particular firms, and the job candidates may have appreciated the reconnaissance done by the Employment Department on their behalf. This same vigilance did not apply to the assignment of men. Peirce assumed that men could fend for themselves in the public sphere and that male students either would not be duped into a bad or even dangerous work environment or, if duped, were assertive enough to extricate themselves easily.

As the school grew in local prominence, it developed an extensive web of contacts consisting of former students in the business world. Every year the institution sowed city firms with hundreds of workers. As Samuel H. Talman, secretary of the school's alumni association, boasted in 1905, "The old, reliable Philadelphia houses that secured their office help from Peirce School in the '70's continue to make it a custom to call on us whenever a vacancy occurs. In many cases those in charge of these firms are themselves Peirce graduates and have made themselves conspicuous in their respective lines of work."[18] As Talman suggests, the Employment Department often received repeat business from satisfied employers. Also, former students who climbed into managerial positions called on the school to find new hires to fill vacant sales counters and office positions under their direction. Harold Bryson, a former student who was in charge of the Cutter Electric Manufacturing Company's office, notified Peirce in 1906 that he needed an assistant bookkeeper. The school sent him three candidates. Bryson was very happy with the worker he finally chose, saying, "Before applying to Peirce School [the company] had advertised and received fifty answers, but not one desirable applicant." Bryson further declared that he would "hereafter" rely on Peirce's placement office for new hires.[19] Indeed, many businesses that tried the Employment Department ended up returning to it for future hires. W. Bruce Barrow, a "real estate man," telephoned the school in December 1905 seeking to replace a female stenographer he had hired from Peirce a year earlier. She had moved into a "more important position." Barrow received an immediate response from the school, which sent out a student the same day.[20]

In addition, former Peirce students who were dissatisfied with their current jobs turned to the department for help in securing new work,[21] and unemployed Peirce men and women applied for help in their job searches. In many cases the placement program met these requests rapidly. Thomas W. Stratton, who had graduated in 1904, telephoned the department in November 1905 because he had recently lost his job. The morning after Stratton called, the department steered him toward the Dixon Crucible Company for a bookkeeping position. When he visited their office, the manager, who was interviewing another candidate for the same position, dropped the candidate and, after briefly talking to Stratton, hired him at fifteen dollars per week.[22] On May 24, 1909, F. Hilda Mack, tired of working as a public stenographer, contacted the Employment Department for help. By June 3 she had landed a stenographic job with the DeLong Hook and Eye Company.[23]

Beyond relying on business colleges and clerical high-school placement programs, women seeking employment in Philadelphia's offices or stores found help from other formal institutions. One of these, the Bureau of Occupations for Trained Women, created in 1912 by the Philadelphia branch of the Association of Collegiate Alumnae, offered job-finding services for women willing to pay a one-dollar deposit. The bureau welcomed both individuals new to the workforce and those seeking occupational change. It aimed to provide nonteaching occupational options to women. With offices at 1302 Spruce Street, the bureau most often situated women in white-collar jobs but also offered positions in private households for individuals trained as nurses, dressmakers, seamstresses, and managing housekeepers.[24] Between 1912 and 1914, 967 women applied for work through the bureau, while another 840 simply visited the office to obtain "information about positions or for vocational advice."[25] Women did not have to have a four-year college background to use the service. Between 1912 and 1914, 75 percent of the women who applied for work through the bureau lacked any college training.[26] Applicants were either fairly young or older women; 48 percent were twenty-nine or younger. Women between thirty and thirty-five years of age accounted for only 15 percent of applicants, but those over thirty-five constituted a third of all job seekers. The organization provided a valuable service, particularly to older women, who may have encountered difficulty obtaining work from stubborn employers willing to hire only ostensibly acquiescent youths. In 1914 just over one-third of the positions filled by the bureau were from clerical categories.[27] Women in other cities also had access to similar institutions. In Chicago, for example, the YWCA was active in female vocational placement, including that for clerical work.[28]

Still, thousands of white-collar workers in Philadelphia could not or did not rely on formal placement services. Rather, they counted on informal connections in the work world or their friends and families. Many also scanned newspaper ads for openings. One such person, Alexander Knight, started in the carpet business in 1867 as a salesman with Phineas Hough, Jr., and Company on Second Street. He worked there for twenty years, until it closed. Knight was then unemployed for a few weeks. To find a new job, he relied on a personal connection with his acquaintance Andrew McKinstry, the founder of Strawbridge and Clothier's carpet department. McKinstry brought him into his department in the store.[29] Informal connections played a large role in Taylor Pilling's job search as well. Pilling was serving as a National Guardsman in the First Regiment Armory in October 1885 when one of his friends informed him that the cloth department at Strawbridge and Clothier required a salesperson. The day after hearing this, he landed the job.[30] Family connections, too, factored into the job hunt. For one thing, office and sales workers occasionally found employment with family members. In 1888 Clara May Leidy landed her first real office job as an assistant bookkeeper in the counting room of George S. Harris and Sons. She worked there for a year until her uncle, Jonas H. Huckel, drew her into his business office. R. Crosby Fairlamb found work in the offices of his father's building supplies company.[31] In addition, some workers depended on family more indirectly to secure work. For three years after he graduated public school at age sixteen, Robert T. Nowland labored in his uncle's general store in Middletown, Delaware. Nowland desired a change, traveled to Philadelphia, and secured a sales position at Strawbridge and Clothier's cotton goods counter. His uncle's letter of recommendation proved key to the young man's success in gaining the job.[32]

As Nowland's story suggests, the act of finding a job was more formalized for industrial-era clerks than it was for blue-collar workers. Employers often drew manual laborers from ranks loitering outside the factory door; alternatively, such laborers were sometimes brought into work through informal family or ethnic ties.[33] Indeed, although the ritual of résumés, recommendations, interviews, and offers seems ubiquitous today, this was not the case for the preindustrial white-collar work world. Employers in the preindustrial office often drew clerical workers from their personal contacts. Typically a new hire arrived on the recommendation of someone the employer trusted. When the Washington Packet Line closed its doors in Philadelphia during the late summer of 1838, the seventeen-year-old Jay Cooke lost his job as a clerk, but the proprietor of Congress Hall, a hotel next door to the packet line's office, hired Cooke to work as a bookkeeper immediately thereafter. The hotelkeeper, a Mr. Sturdivant, had likely heard of Cooke from his previous boss. The company that gave the young man his next job in Philadelphia, the banking firm of E. W. Clark, was located on the floor above Congress Hall. Clark and his partner, Edward Dodge, frequented Congress Hall, where they met and observed Cooke while he worked. He greatly impressed them. No doubt they also heard Sturdivant carry on about his bookkeeper's talents. Indeed, Sturdivant notified Cooke that the bankers had displayed interest in employing him.[34] If such personal contacts failed, however, and a business owner was forced to hire a stranger, the employer could rely on the intimacy of the preindustrial office, where he would have closely supervised new workers and might gradually give them more responsibilities as merited.

As the clerical workforce grew too large for employers to simply trust their personal connections and as notions of business apprenticeship broke down in the expanding industrial-era office, hiring procedures grew more rigorous. After all, workers in this new class performed some of the more important and sensitive work in the business world, from balancing accounts, taking dictation, and managing important files to handling cash and selling products to valued customers. To reassure bosses of their trustworthiness, office and sales workers increasingly had to undergo a ritualized hiring process that included one or more of the following: a written application for work, letters of recommendation, formal interviews, and as the office world mechanized, specific skill-based tests. This formal hiring process was in place by the 1870s. Male applicants experienced the most elaborate procedures, often because employers considered them for jobs that were more prestigious than those they assigned to women. In the late nineteenth century Peirce encouraged its students and alumni to apply for positions in writing, on good stationery, because before the typewriter became ubiquitous, firms sought office workers with excellent penmanship.[35] Beyond showing off candidates' handwriting, letters of application typically underscored their work experience and confidence in their own abilities. In an 1886 letter applying for a bookkeeping position in the newly formed Fourth Street National Bank, James Glentworth claimed much experience that he said had given him familiarity "with all the duties of that position as well as . . . a general knowledge of other departments."[36] William Houpt, in his letter of application for a teller position in the same bank, asserted that he had more than eleven years of business experience, seven in a bank setting. He added, "I understand general bookkeeping, and I believe of an average of figures [*sic*]." Houpt mailed a second letter reassuring the bank that he would accept any pay.[37] Some letters of application included references or short notes of recommendation. The reverse side of Glentworth's letter bore three brief endorsements from former superiors. Letters of recommendation accentuated the applicant's abilities and moral character, especially trustworthiness. In 1886 David Faust, president of Union National Bank, wrote to the president and board of directors of the Fourth Street National Bank regarding a candidate. Faust stressed that the candidate had worked at Union National since boyhood, eventually attaining the position of second teller's assistant before he moved on "to engage in other business." Faust added that the candidate was "intelligent, faithful, and attentive to his duties" and that the bank "had full confidence in his integrity."[38]

The job interview formed the next stage in the hiring process. As it still does today, advice abounded regarding the proper way to conduct oneself in an interview. For all applicants, appearance was the first step toward a successful interview. Commentators considered neat, conservative "good taste" appropriate. They suggested that one should not "wear gaudy apparel," because employers rejected people who attracted attention. A candidate's appearance was supposed to be subtle and reassuring to supervisors.[39] Proper dress and deportment held different meanings for male and female job seek-ers, however. For men, a well-kept appearance conveyed that they were hard working and ambitious. The successful male applicant made sure he had smartly polished shoes, a nice hat, neatly trimmed hair, a well-fitting shirt and tie, and clean fingernails.[40] Employers associated competence with ap-pearance. Looking "prosperous" helped men land work.[41] Advice columns directed toward men contended that an unkempt, "seedy" appearance ruined opportunities.[42] Looking clean and neat symbolized a well-ordered male mind. For women, cleanliness and modesty were at least partly related to sexuality. According to commentators, proper attire for a woman indicated that she had the ability to enchant her boss. In one advice column Peirce alumni read that "a young woman who ceases to care for her appearance will soon cease to please." She would "fall little by little until she degenerat[ed] into an ambitious slattern." The image of the fallen woman was echoed by another author, who suggested that the immodest office woman would find herself "on the downward chute to some man's low estimations."[43]

For both men and women, etiquette proved as important as dress in the interview, and advice columns spelled out acceptable deportment. One had to exhibit a fine balance of courteousness and self-assertion. Writers doled out stern warnings such as "don't fail to see the man to whom you are directed, but don't walk right into his private office uninvited. Don't fail to show that you have learned to be courteous, but don't act in a cringing manner or as if you considered yourself menial."[44] These directions inculcated aspiring office workers with the requisite attitude they needed to land a job and prosper in the hierarchical workplace. Managers expected women to be even more deferential than men at work, never to ask too many questions, not to show too much initiative, and never to be frivolous.[45]

Finally, the interviews often included an assessment of relevant skills. As scientific management took hold in the second decade of the twentieth cen-tury, large offices began rigorously testing applicants for specific positions. The federal government assessed potential stenographers for speed and abil-ity.[46] Other offices followed suit. By 1913 Philadelphia's Curtis Publishing Company had devised an elaborate system of testing the aptitude of potential office workers.[47] With luck, by following the proper rules and passing the proper tests, one landed a job.

In the late nineteenth and early twentieth centuries, the city's clerks were fairly youthful compared to the general workforce. In 1890, 39 percent of male clerical workers were between ten and twenty-four years old. The same age group provided 29 percent of the city's entire male workforce. It is probable that relatively few men spent their late forties in the same types of lower-level white-collar jobs that they held initially in their careers. Between 1820 and 1860 Philadelphia's male clerks had experienced high levels of upward occupational mobility.[48] This was clearly changing by the late nineteenth century, but as late as 1890 sizable numbers of men likely still spent only part of their lives clerking.[49] Even in the 1890s male business-school graduates had decent chances of moving into professional or proprietary jobs after starting their careers in subordinate positions.[50] Three decades later the male clerical workforce was growing older. Just above 32 percent of these men were below age twenty-five, which suggests that opportunity for climbing the corporate ladder was waning. More men had life-long clerical careers. Even in 1920, however, young men still entered the city's stores and offices hoping to advance rapidly in the business world. This may explain why, although declining, the proportion of men under the age of twenty-five in Philadelphia's clerical workplaces remained higher than that of such men in the general male workforce, which in 1920 stood at 21 percent.

The work experiences of Amos H. Hall and Charles H. Breerwood attest to men's movement out of clerking in the second half of the nineteenth century. Although they came from different generations, both men rose out of clerical positions in their early twenties. In 1866 Hall began work as a bookkeeper in a Philadelphia business office and remained there for two years. In 1868 he entered into partnership with H. W. Fisher and Charles F. Fisher and formed Fisher and Hall, a firm that made cedar vats and tanks. He spent the rest of his life in business for himself.[51] By the 1890s chances for men to venture into independent business ownership had shrunk, but new routes offered continued male mobility in the office world. As corporations emerged, one could climb the ladder of bureaucracy into the ranks of management and perhaps higher. In 1898 Charles H. Breerwood started out as a bookkeeper with C. B. Porter and Company, wholesale tinware merchants. After less than a year behind his desk, Breerwood changed jobs, hiring on with the Cheltenham Electric Light, Heat, and Power Company as a cashier. Climbing up the corporate ladder, he soon became an assistant secretary and in 1902 was elected secretary and treasurer, a management position.[52] He had moved out of the clerking ranks without moving out of his workplace. By the second decade of the twentieth century, however, an increasing segment of the male clerical workforce followed career trajectories that looked much like the previously mentioned Taylor Pilling's. Pilling worked as a salesman at Strawbridge and Clothier from 1885 to 1910, and he never left the selling floor.

Philadelphia's clerical women faced a different situation between 1890 and 1920. Most of the women who held lower-level white-collar jobs were younger than twenty-five in both years, 64 percent in 1890 and 59 percent in 1920. But women did not clamber up the occupational ladder and leave the desk or sales counter. Rather, they exited the workforce to marry. The female clerical world also grew older between 1890 and 1920, but it remained significantly younger than the entire female workforce. In 1890, 51 percent of the city's working women were younger than twenty-five; in 1920, 42 percent were. Typical of clerking women was Clara May Leidy, referred to previously. She worked as a bookkeeper and general office assistant in her uncle's business from 1888 to 1895. While in her midtwenties, she left to marry Dr. George H. Mayer, a dentist living in Mauch Chunk, Pennsylvania.[53]

Even if a woman toiled in an office or on a selling floor her entire life, she had only a slim chance of experiencing upward mobility. A tiny number of older women rose into the lowest ranks of management in the office and sales worlds. A few women became department-store buyers. Some older female clerical workers, however, simply moved from workplace to workplace, in and out of similar jobs with similar responsibilities. Others in big offices or department stores moved laterally from department to department, working similar types of jobs. Bosses celebrated the perseverance of those who persisted at the same job for most of their lives. Grace M. Hallam served as a stenographer in Strawbridge and Clothier's executive office for the greater part of her adult life. In 1909 the store's Quarter Century Club, which recognized employees who had survived twenty-five years in the store, inducted her. The club admired Hallam as "a good, steady, sincere worker, one who had 'trod the mill and not gone sour.'"[54] Hardly stunning praise, this statement reiterated the notion that, for women, personal ambition at work was out of the question.

Widowhood occasionally forced women who had been clerks or salespeople prior to marriage to return to the workforce. Elizabeth F. Scott graduated from Peirce in 1893, and soon thereafter the school placed her in her first job, in the offices of the Manufacturers Supplies Company of Philadelphia. She labored there for ten years until she left to get married to a Mr. Sontgen. Her marriage ended tragically when her husband died in a railroad accident in Camden in 1908. Mrs. Sontgen, having to support her mother and an invalid brother, asked Peirce's Employment Department for help in obtaining another job. They immediately placed her as a secretary to the Philadelphia lawyer Henry S. Cattell. She worked loyally and hard for Cattell until she died of appendicitis in 1915. Sontgen was an exception, however. She left her first job for marriage and probably never planned to reenter the workforce. Only extraordinary tragedy pushed her back into the work world. Female office and sales workers in their late thirties or forties labored because their lives departed from the general trends affecting white women in industrial American society.[55]

The clerical sector encompassed a great variety of jobs. Philadelphia's clerks toiled in places ranging from large department stores with thousands of workers to firms housed in modern steel-framed, curtain-walled, high-rise buildings to the offices of small businesses. Most labored in Philadelphia's central business district, which by the early twentieth century clustered around Market, Chestnut, and Broad streets at the very heart of the city. Thousands of clerical employees worked in impressive structures, such as Philadelphia's massive City Hall, the soaring Land Title and Trust Building, Wanamaker's Department Store, the Pennsylvania Railroad's Broad Street Station, and the terminal station and office edifice of the Philadelphia and Reading Railroad. For example, scores of office workers labored in the Reading terminal, which opened in 1893 at the corner of Market and Twelfth streets. They worked in the passenger rooms of the station itself and the adjoining baggage areas, as well as in the cab lobby and the express, treasurer's, ticket, and post offices. More clerks passed their days in the counting rooms and general offices of the railroad in the terminal complex.[56]

Wherever clerical workers were employed, job responsibilities differed widely from occupation to occupation—telegraphers had little directly in common with salespeople, for example. Despite this diversity of work settings and responsibilities, common themes emerged in the work lives of office and sales employees, themes that undergirded all clerical on-the-job experiences. Clerks and salespeople served as the foot soldiers in what Robert H. Weibe has called the "search for order" in industrial America.[57] Their jobs revolved around the maintenance of order in the industrial economy. They helped collect and process data that management interpreted to ensure an ideal flow of production and sales. Above all else, the clerical workforce organized, processed, and disseminated information. They acted as the sensory organs, the eyes and ears of, as Alfred D. Chandler termed it, the "visible hand" of management.[58] Without the material that the clerical workforce gathered and processed, management could not function effectively. Clerks collected and organized data regarding the nature of the business. They logged the hours that others worked, sorted important documents, indexed customer complaints, and kept track of supply levels. Bookkeepers and accountants monitored cash flow. Secretaries controlled the communication into and out of offices, typed memos, and organized schedules. Stenographers took ephemeral oral communication in the form of dictation from employers and converted it into clear, more permanent typewritten form. Even sales personnel brokered information. They informed customers about goods, and their managers showed great concern about the ways that sales personnel presented themselves to customers, how they talked about products, and how they represented the store to the public.

Industrial-era offices, one of the two broad environments within clerical experience (the selling floor being the other), came in all shapes and
sizes. This variation affected the allocation of work activities. Large offices
had entire bookkeeping, clerical, typewriting, stenographic, and secretarial
departments. Smaller offices relied on just a handful of workers who had
overlapping responsibilities. For instance, in a small office a secretary might
arrange schedules and type memos as well as take dictation, whereas this last
activity would have fallen under the purview of a stenographer in a larger
office. Still, there were many points of convergence. For one thing, clerical
workers utilized general skills that were easily transferable from job to job.
Bookkeepers, for instance, followed similar procedures and used similar
skills no matter where they worked. At a more general level, organization
and hierarchy dictated the nature of all office and sales work. Clear chains of
command and routes of upward occupational mobility existed. Likewise, all
these workplaces had clear sexual divisions of labor. Offices and sales floors
had male and female spaces as well as gendered jobs. More broadly, especially
by the early twentieth century, employers gender typed entire job categories,
regardless of work setting.

In Philadelphia during the fifty years following the Civil War, office workers
encountered differing career expectations, trajectories, and responsibilities
based on gender. Many men expected that the jobs they took would offer
upward mobility. Women understood that the positions they took would
neither pay as well as the posts men held nor offer advancement. Jobs such
as typewriting, stenography, and operating telephone switchboards crys-
tallized in the industrial period. These occupations had low prospects for
promotion, and employers, favoring a large, tractable, and cheap workforce,
tailored them to women. Remington first produced the typewriter in large
quantities in 1874, and women quickly became associated with the use of this
office machine.[59] By 1886 American companies produced 15,000 typewriters
annually.[60] When typewriting initially found its way into the published federal
census in 1890, the U.S. government ranked it under "female occupations."
Male typists did exist, but they were a rarity in the industrial office. In the
work world, the term *typewriter* soon stood for both the operator and the
machine she worked. Management measured a typewriter's quality in her
accuracy and speed, and a good one pounded out forty words per minute;
the best achieved sixty with unfamiliar copy.[61] Of course, we cannot know
the thoughts of long-dead typists, but "The Frantic Typist," a poem from the
Peirce School Alumni Journal, the organ of the school's alumni association,
conveys the work conditions of typists from a woman's perspective.[62] In large
firms typists often sat together pounding out memoranda and letters. In this

noisy and stressful atmosphere, women strained their eyes to read dictation and avoided distraction. Mistakes meant time-consuming editing or starting over. Typists had a love-hate relationship with their machines. The typist

> Abhors the type of the typewriter;
> The one would write what it is told,
>> The other what it wilt,
> There is a constant war—behold!
>> Much innocent ink is spilt.

The clatter of a woman's own machine as well as those surrounding her sparked headaches. Bosses constantly hovered over typists, and sometimes fierce competition emerged between operators sitting next to one another. The typist can only groan,

> Stare at the clock and long for home:
> Or clasp her head and moan "it aches"—
> Until her comrade hears her say
> And sweetly smiles—then makes mistakes—
> Crumples her sheet and glares her way. . . .

Large office bureaucracies frequently connected typists with stenographers. Typists transcribed the mountains of daily material stenographers took from dictation. To alleviate the tedium, many a typist no doubt fantasized while her fingers flew over the keyboard. Another poem from the *Peirce School Alumni Journal* described the daydreams of a typist recently returned from vacation:

THE TYPEWRITER'S FIRST DAY BACK

> I'm back from my vacation and the time was
>> short indeed;
> I wonder if I've lost my stroke, or got behind
>> in speed.
> Don't ask if I enjoyed myself, it makes me
>> smile to think;
> I'd rather guess my ribbon needs another soak
>> in ink.
> I had the very gayest time of any girl I know;
> And now I wonder what is up, this carriage
>> moves so slow.
> I got a ring or two of course, although my days
>> were brief;
> Oh! What a rattle-trap this is, and all this work—
>> great grief.

And Will is such a gallant chap, and Claude is
    just a dear;
I Wonder if the manager is hanging round me
    here.
And Alex Vanderbilt they say is coming into town;
This nickel frame will scarce reflect—my face
    is not so brown.
And I should have a grenadine; Oh! Yes, I
    really should;
The firm must buy a new machine, they say
    that times are good.
For now I know the latest step, the German and
    quadrille;
This type is so much out of line, it really makes me ill.
What! Twelve o'clock? How time does fly,
    and I am not half through;
Oh! Go to lunch with you? Well, yes; I don't
    care if I do.[63]

Although amateurish, the poem conveys the sense of a young woman's work-place daydream. She reflects on her vacation with every word she types. The choppy lines lend the feel of a carriage return. The poet's light tone conveys pleasant thoughts of men, dancing, and drinking interspersed with mundane concerns about her workplace and typewriter. While the verse of-fers a somewhat shallow depiction of the typist's thoughts (she emerges as flighty and obsessed with the opposite sex), it suggests her youth. One can only imagine what more realistic thoughts, worries, and dreams filled the aching minds of typists during their long hours in the office. In a more seri-ous vein, in 1896 the *Peirce School Alumni Journal* reprinted a brief series of suggestions about curing a headache that was geared toward office women. When an office woman returned home from work, she could apply various techniques to allay throbbing headaches incurred during the day's work. The advised "remedial agents" included walking in the fresh air, shampoo-ing one's hair in a weak solution of soda water, taking a nap, and running a hot sponge down one's neck.[64] Migraines, backaches, muscle strain, and general fatigue were of greater immediate concern for office women than tips for wooing a rich suitor.

    The radical transformations that influenced the industrial-era office most sharply etched their marks into the position of stenographer. This job, which emerged in the late nineteenth century, was initially performed by men and women. When, between 1890 and 1910, the specific duties attached to stenography were linked to machines, especially the typewriter and the graphophone, the job was largely feminized. A drawing of a female stenographer fashioned out of stenographic symbols in the *Peirce School Alumni Journal* embodied the notion that women and stenography were one in the same.[65] Stenographers, whether male or female, were more closely connected to their supervisors than were most other office employees. A stenographer knew the boss's correspondence and spent hours taking dictation, sometimes receiving sensitive, confidential material. Stenographers had to learn employers' "moods and eccentricities."[66] Commentators coached them to dissemble when they caught their boss's errors in dictation: "Don't say to your employer when a mistake does occur that 'he dictated it that way.' Even if he did he will not believe it. Say to him you misunderstood or did not catch his remark."[67] Stenography symbolically incorporated scientific management, or Taylorism. The shorthand that stenographers learned stressed efficiency and routinization—economizing the pen strokes and motion necessary to capture the relevant information. Stenographers understood the importance of punctuality at work and of being so smooth and efficient at taking dictation that they never interrupted a speaker. For most, daily work revolved around proficiently managing the mundane details in the office world, not learning grand business theory or lessons.[68] Stenographers were to be unfeeling. If an employer fired them, they were not supposed to whimper, cry, moan, or protest.[69] They toiled as intermediaries between their bosses and machines. Stenographers heard the dictation their bosses gave them, transcribed it into temporary stenographic symbols, and then either typed it into a letter or memorandum themselves or passed it on to typists to complete the task.

Only the rare male stenographer realistically expected significant upward mobility in the male-controlled business world. In the late nineteenth and early twentieth centuries, office managers defined a small minority of stenographic positions for men. Employers specifically looked out for these male hires and groomed them for better jobs.[70] The intimacy between stenographer and boss taught the male stenographer the nuances of enterprise and provided contacts in the business world. Thus, the male stenographer interested in advancement could, through good manners and politeness, ingratiate himself with the boss and move up in the office world. Abram D. Hallman answered a request for a male stenographer that the Philadelphia Traction Company (PTC) placed with the Peirce Employment Department in 1895. He won the job, proved to be a hard worker, and earned his employer's trust. Hallman's bosses raised his responsibilities and gave him work of "increased importance." The PTC promoted Hallman to transfer agent and in 1904 elected him assistant secretary and treasurer. By 1909 he had risen to the elected executive position of secretary.[71] In a development much like that in the realm of stenography, telephone companies employed women as operators nearly from the start, because these positions involved a high level of routinization. Telephony required specialized skills for operating machines, and telephone companies considered women perfectly suited for this type of work. They also believed that women possessed a gentler, more patient demeanor and better customer service skills than men. By 1900, 80 percent of operators nationwide were women.[72]

After 1900 the business world redefined other lower-level white-collar occupations, such as secretarial work and telegraphy, from masculine jobs offering high potential for career advancement to low-mobility, female positions. After 1910 secretarial work feminized because large firms required vast numbers of inexpensive assistants. Between 1910 and 1920 it became the highest-status female clerical job while it declined as a route into managerial positions for ambitious men. Secretarial posts entailed greater responsibilities and required greater initiative and creativity than did other female office jobs. Secretaries controlled their boss's correspondence and fixed their errors. They oversaw schedules and performed a myriad of other office duties. As Margery W. Davies has pointed out, they simultaneously acted as "buffers" between the outside world and supervisors and as their bosses' "servants."[73]

Rosabeth Moss Kanter has noted that as secretarial work feminized, businesses divided it into occupations that exhibited "marriage-like" characteristics and those that were "factory-like."[74] Marriage-like positions directly descended from the secretarial jobs that men held in the preindustrial and early industrial period. Many of these "private" secretaries served individual proprietors exclusively. For men in much of the nineteenth century, these positions had offered sure routes to individual business ownership. Where better to learn the business than constantly at the business owner's side? Essentially, in many offices, industrialization created a ponderous bureaucracy with too many bosses for this route of male mobility to remain open. Not everybody could serve the head of the company and learn all there was to know about the business's operations. Regardless, as late as the second decade of the twentieth century, a few men could still be found as secretaries serving the highest corporate levels. For example, Stanley Zimmerman, a graduate of Peirce and Princeton University, worked as the secretary to the vice president of the Pennsylvania Steel Company in Steelton, Pennsylvania.[75] Despite this tradition, however, women flooded into private secretarial jobs. The same article in the *Peirce School Alumni Journal* that mentioned Zimmerman also mentioned five women and only one other man who worked as secretaries. Differing from the marriage-like slots, factory-like secretarial positions met the general needs of a business. The workers who filled these jobs toiled in general office pools, often combining clerical, bookkeeping, and stenographic tasks in their daily routines. Employers defined these situations even more exclusively as female than they did private secretarial positions.

In the second half of the nineteenth century, the business world considered telegraphy to require high skill levels. Ideal telegraphers possessed a specialized knowledge of Morse code, had excellent penmanship, and could rapidly receive and transmit messages. After World War I the teletype machine, which allowed for less skilled and thus cheaper operators, feminized telegraphy. In response, Western Union and others hired larger numbers of women.[76]

Unlike secretarial work and telegraphy, clerking maintained a relatively high level of male participation between 1870 and 1920. In 1920 men still constituted 68 percent of the office clerks in Philadelphia. The career of George W. Stevens highlights the possibilities of upward occupational mobility for male clerks in the late nineteenth century. In 1876, when Stevens was sixteen, Strawbridge and Clothier hired him as a cash boy. Prior to the large-scale introduction of pneumatic-tube systems in department stores, cash boys functioned as the intermediaries between customers and a centralized cashiers' desk. Soon Stevens clambered his way up the occupational ladder, becoming a stock boy and then the time clerk. As time clerk he tracked the entrances and exits of all the store's employees and served as paymaster for the cash boys. From this clerical position, which prepared him for management, he sprang into the store's managerial ranks, first serving as head of the wrapping department, where he directed a staff of young package wrappers. Eventually Stevens became assistant superintendent of the main desk and head of the inspecting department, which oversaw cash registers as well as jewelry and silverware packing, among many other delicate matters of supervision.[77]

A myriad of different clerks dealt with many types of information in an office. Time clerks documented how much time industrial employees worked. File clerks sorted, stored, and retrieved the massive amounts of material on which the industrial economy based its predictions for future business and assessed the profitability of past practices. Bank clerks processed daily transactions involving widely ranging sums of money. Shipping clerks managed individual shipments of goods out of Philadelphia's department stores. Other clerks filtered incoming office correspondence.

To provide an adequate description of clerical job responsibilities, let me follow the convoluted path of paperwork in one typical large office. The Philadelphia Department of Public Works received increasing amounts of correspondence as the city grew. To deal with the growing stacks of letters, the department devised a standardized handling system in 1913. For example, if a concerned Philadelphian wrote to the department about a pothole, a clerk opened the letter, read it, marked its receipt in a mail register, stamped it to the attention of the Highway Bureau, and sent it to that bureau. The Highway Bureau answered the letter (an official dictated the reply to a stenographer) and returned it, along with a carbon copy of the response, to Public Works. There, a correspondence clerk wrote a brief cover note to the citizen, included the Highway Bureau's reply, and passed both on to the mailing clerk, who sent them to the concerned Philadelphian. The clerical handling of the letter did not end there, however. A file clerk then filed the original letter and carbon copies of the responses from both the Highway Bureau and the Department of Public Works. Anyone interested in the letter could easily access the file, in which case the filing clerk pulled it and put a special marker in its place. Clerks clearly labeled each file to denote the departments through which the paperwork had passed. This process, multiplied numerous times, provided much of the everyday workload in the department.[78]

As I mentioned earlier, the selling floor formed the second major clerical work environment. Philadelphia's industrial economy provided as much variety in sales experiences as it did in office vocations. Salespeople served small retail interests as well as large ones, such as department stores. Large manufacturing firms also had sales departments. Finally, the selling floor did not have to be a fixed location. Traveling salesmen ("commercial travelers") took the floor with them in portable display cases. Industrial firms created sales departments whose staffs hocked their wares on commission locally as well as nationally. After the mid-nineteenth century, urban-based whole-salers began to use traveling salesmen to take their goods to merchants in the rural hinterlands. Throughout the industrial era commercial traveling remained a thoroughly male occupation revolving around a clearly male road culture.[79]

At the opposite end of the sales spectrum, the large department store held most of its thousands of salespeople under one roof. By 1908 Philadelphia's Strawbridge and Clothier purportedly employed more than five thousand people, most of them in sales.[80] Department stores as urban institutions had their roots in the large dry goods establishments of the mid-nineteenth century. By the 1890s the term *department store* had entered common usage, and these stores had become fixtures in the industrial city's landscape. What separated them from their predecessors was not simply size. Shoppers freely entered these vast temples of consumerism, and stores did not require them to purchase goods. In fact, browsing was encouraged. This policy stimulated impulse shopping. Moreover, no haggling over the prices of the store's goods occurred. While department stores carried an unprecedented array and vol-ume of goods, they also spurred the quick turnover of stock with regular clearances and sales. Finally, as their name implies, department stores were organized into distinct departments that combined various lines of like goods and offered specially trained salespeople to assist customers.[81]

A store's sales staff would have included large proportions of men in the 1870s. This soon changed as employers realized the low cost and high supply of female labor and increasingly decided that middle-class female shoppers better related to saleswomen.[82] By 1890 the typical sales staff was overwhelmingly female. Men worked in these establishments, but segregation ruled the department-store sales environment. Men dominated management. Even the selling floor itself had distinct gender boundaries. Susan Porter Benson writes that "men were generally confined to men's clothing, sporting goods, rug, and appliance departments, while women sold most other items; among the few departments in which men and women sold together were silks, shoes, and men's furnishings."[83]

Department stores employed a two-track promotional system in which bosses rarely promoted saleswomen into management, yet male employees, especially clerical (nonselling) workers, experienced occupational mobility. Most of the individuals inducted into the Strawbridge and Clothier Quarter Century Club were men who had never been part of the sales staff. Of the twenty-nine new members in 1909 and 1910, only five had been saleswomen at least at some point in their careers. Only two had moved beyond the position of saleswoman in their long stints at the store.[84] These two had experienced minimal upward mobility: they had risen to become heads of stock in their departments.

Management expected all salespersons, whether male or female, to act subserviently in front of customers and to spend long hours selling merchandise. Bosses assessed fines for any breaches of written rules. In many instances the act of selling demeaned salespeople. However irritating or rude the customers might be, the salesperson had to "drown dignity, hide irritation and be blind to imposition."[85] Strawbridge and Clothier expected saleswomen to act as "'I Will' Girls." Bosses encouraged saleswomen to say "I will" not only to unpleasant tasks (such as fitting customers, making exchanges, dealing with stock, and coping with returns) but also to the supposedly nicer duty of selling.[86] In this atmosphere John Wanamaker's legendary platitude that the customer is always right particularly annoyed saleswomen.[87]

An 1894 study of working women in Philadelphia and Pittsburgh done by the Pennsylvania Bureau of Industrial Statistics (PBIS) took statements from hundreds of women. The testimony revealed that work conditions in Philadelphia's retail establishments varied greatly. Some women seemed satisfied or even happy with their employers. They felt justly compensated and reveled in the comfortable accouterments that their employers provided—lunchrooms, decent breaks, and good vacations. Nevertheless, most places of business, particularly large department stores, required salespeople to stand constantly. The PBIS discussed the existence of a state law mandating the provision of seats for employees' use during slack periods. Employers quickly realized that officials could not effectively enforce the law and took advantage of this. Stores either ignored the legislation or provided the chairs but refused to allow their sales personnel to use them. Supervisors fired women who challenged these illegal work conditions. One saleswoman from the millinery department of a Philadelphia store complained to the PBIS, "There are about thirty ladies employed in that department, and no seats are provided for them to sit when not busy. They are obliged to either stand or walk all day, and week after week. There is one chair, which is usually occupied by a customer."[88] Idle time between sales was to be filled by arranging stock.

Saleswomen complained about other hardships, too. Several stores on North Eighth Street kept their front doors open during the winter, "freezing their miserably paid salesgirls." Workers complained about the stagnant air, which likely grew stifling in the summertime. Some smaller establishments lacked sanitary bathroom facilities. Furthermore, saleswomen ranked among the worst-paid people in the lower middle class. They routinely protested about the pittance they collected. Many worried about how to make ends meet. Paying for rent, carfare, food, and leisure stretched their meager earnings too thinly. Of the over five hundred Philadelphia saleswomen surveyed by the PBIS, 60 percent received seven dollars or less per week. In addition, saleswomen toiled long hours. The PBIS found that a little over half typically worked ten-hour days. These women routinely complained that excessively long periods of toil undermined their health and well-being. They craved lengthier lunch breaks and dreamed of more time off on the weekends. Peak shopping seasons, such as Christmas, meant longer hours and dealing with many more customers for the same pay. To top things off, employers occasionally played favorites among their female workers, paying some more than others or treating them more humanely.[89]

Given these conditions, the PBIS wondered why women wanted to work in department stores. Its researchers reasoned that sales work had less drudgery associated with it than domestic work.[90] Additionally, it was safer and much cleaner than most factory jobs. Other aspects of the workplace at least partly ameliorated difficult conditions. Strawbridge and Clothier, like many other larger department stores, offered areas for relaxation to its employees. By the early 1900s the store had an assortment of employee amenities, including a dining room that served hot meals to its saleswomen.[91] In 1910 the firm built a roof garden above the female employees' dining room.[92] Management allowed women to take lunch and afternoon tea at the garden, where they could recline on steamer chairs and settees and read. A heavy canvas that kept out direct sunlight yet allowed for a comfortable breeze sheltered the garden. The store also staffed an employee hospital for short-term ailments.[93] For more serious health problems, in 1880 management established the voluntary Strawbridge and Clothier Relief Association, which provided relief to sick employees (both men and women) and death benefits.[94] The association charged a fifty-cent entrance fee along with a twenty-five-cent monthly assessment. Occasionally the organization did not collect the assessment if sicknesses in the store proved light for a month. Strawbridge and Clothier helped fund the association by contributing fines levied for workers' infractions of house rules. Employees who fell ill could receive five dollars a week for fifteen weeks, if necessary. Co-workers delivered the money and checked on the sick person. When death occurred, the deceased's family earned one hundred dollars. Employees served as the organization's officers and board members. Finally, Strawbridge and Clothier offered its personnel paid vacations.[95]

Clerical workers who dealt with the public toiled in environments architecturally designed to convey specific meanings to the clientele they served. Department stores and banks provide the best examples of this phenomenon. Philadelphia had clear shopping and banking districts in the late nineteenth and early twentieth centuries. Lined with giant department stores, including Gimbels, Litt Brothers, Wanamaker's, and Strawbridge and Clothier, Market Street, east of Broad Street, functioned as the city's shopping hub. In 1912 John Wanamaker opened a new store next to City Hall, replacing a nearby older structure. The renowned architect Daniel Burnham designed the twenty-four-story structure.[96] Strawbridge and Clothier had continually expanded since opening in 1868, buying up properties on Market and Eighth streets. Whether a department store was architecturally a single unit, as was Wanamaker's, or patched together from older buildings and new additions, as was Strawbridge and Clothier, its primary function was to entice customers. Owners built stores to inspire consumption and sumptuously decorated them. For customers, the shopping experience started before they even entered. Stores installed large plate-glass windows for display. Specially hired decorators concocted elaborate displays behind these windows. These display windows allowed customers to browse before entering. In short, they drew people into the store.

The stores' interiors were meant to overwhelm customers with their grandeur. As early as 1887 the *Philadelphia Press,* a local newspaper, ran a front-page story that characterized Strawbridge and Clothier as a "business palace."[97] That year the firm renovated its store. The main aisle of the refurbished emporium stretched across an entire city block, and skylights supplemented by electric lights illuminated the floor below.[98] Seven elevators drew customers upward to more shopping. If any of the predominantly middle-class female customers tired, they could rest in armchairs in the ladies' parlor close to the Market Street doorway, where a maid served their needs and an ample supply of magazines provided diversion. On the sales floor one could choose silks by looking at them under gas or electric light to determine how they would appear at home.

The staff had no such amenities, but by 1889 the store's saleswomen enjoyed their own separate sitting room, lavatories, and parlor far away from the customers' lounging areas. On the one hand, workers toiling in this sumptuous space could not help but feel that they were different from blue-collar workers. On the other, they could not help but notice their segregation from middle-class shoppers. Bosses allowed them contact with shoppers only in formal selling areas. They did not share leisure space with them inside the store. Saleswomen envied the segregated perks that customers received. Work on the selling floor reinforced the notion that saleswomen held lower-middle-class jobs. Their work space clearly was not working class, yet their bosses did not allow them to partake in its strictly middle-class corners.[99]

Banks, too, courted customers with their architectural designs.[100] The second half of the nineteenth century saw a commercial banking district emerge in Philadelphia on Chestnut Street between Fourth and Fifth streets. During the same period banking escalated significantly in Philadelphia's residential neighborhoods. Many of the city's banks conveyed grandeur, permanence, and security through the construction of massive stone facades. Inside, themes of security influenced the work lives of a bank's staff. Architects placed executive offices near the banking room to allow management easy supervision of tellers and cashiers enclosed in cages. The cages separated the bank's employees from one another as well as from customers. Unlike that of department stores, the banking workforce was largely male from 1870 to 1920.[101] Just as department-store saleswomen toiled in a segmented world, however, bank clerks found themselves laboring in an environment that distinguished them from both customers and management. Like their counterparts in the store, bank clerks could not help feeling the class distinctions of their workplace.

Gender segregation permeated the clerical work space in large offices, which distinguished clear male and female work areas based on a sexual division of labor.[102] For example, typing pools in sizable business establishments were often mostly female and placed in rooms dedicated solely to that activity. Nevertheless, although formal rules and structures may have separated the sexes in bigger workplaces, much informal contact between men and women still occurred, as it certainly did in many smaller offices. Female stenographers served male bosses. Male and female stenographers often worked alongside each other, as did male and female clerks, even though gender influenced their positions in the office hierarchy and their potential advancement. "An Every-Day Stenographer," a short story serialized in the *Peirce School Alumni Journal,* describes a small office connected with a steel mill. A male and a female stenographer who work in this office meet and fall in love. Although the story mimics the typical thematic style of office romance that pervaded turn-of-the-century national stenographic journals, it suggests that gender lines in small and medium-sized offices were not rigid.[103]

The story also reinforces Sharon Hartman Strom's argument that women in the industrial office were "sexual objects in a workplace that was increasingly conscious of the female body and the need to both contain and display it."[104] Turn-of-the-century popular culture often objectified women office workers. In short fiction they regularly married the boss or male co-workers.[105] Occasionally women were blamed for the changed sexual dynamics of a mixed-gender workplace. An anonymous commentator from Strawbridge and Clothier argued that "men respect a woman as a comrade and fellow worker; but they deplore and even dislike the so-called business girl—whose mind is on boys, her clothes; and obviously studying what impression she is making on the men about her." Another author suggested that hard-working stenographers who developed good relationships with their male superiors ran the risk of becoming the butts of office jokes and rumors suggesting that they wanted to wed the boss.[106] On one level the commentary is naïve, for it suggests that all men viewed office or store life as solely about work. They did not deign to treat female co-workers as sexual objects. On another level the commentary insidiously inverts reality by arguing that the behavior of "the so-called business girl" invited objectification and that men supposedly dismissed such women. Especially in the small or medium office where male and female workers constantly interacted, women had to negotiate treacherous waters of objectification, discrimination, and occasional harassment.

Women influenced the predominantly male office world when they first entered it. A column in the *Peirce School Alumni Journal* from 1896 argued that women's behavior in the office differed from men's. It suggested that women, socialized to act according to Victorian feminine norms, could accomplish more than men. Women were more apt to make requests in nicer tones than men. They purportedly were more successful than men in asking office boys and messengers for favors.[107] The column contributor viewed office women as typical Victorian nurturers or caretakers. In the eyes of contemporaries, their cheeriness and cordiality rendered the gruff masculine workplace more congenial. Another article stressed that women's service in the office world was of equal if not greater value to employers than men's work and deserved equal remuneration. The article described a male boss who had recently hired women in his office for the first time as commenting that his male and female employees seemed significantly different. The women imparted a new atmosphere to the office. While the supervisor deemed the women's work of equal caliber to men's, the workplace behavior of his newly hired office women diverged vastly from the male office veterans. He proclaimed, "My [female] book-keeper and stenographer do not smoke my cigars, nor any other person's; they do not keep the office floor strewn with torn paper and other odds and ends under the impression that it looks business-like, as their [male] predecessors did; they neither whittle nor whistle, and they do not fall ill, or bury one of their relatives every time a base ball team comes to town. I tell you, women in an office go ahead of men every time in my estimation."[108] Some Victorian employers dealt with the presence of women in the office by assuming a protective, if belittling, role. They felt compelled to create a moral atmosphere to protect supposedly fragile and naïve women and so increasingly regulated the behavior of male and female employees. In part, the spatial separation of women from men in larger offices was a reaction in this vein.[109] These attitudes revealed a paternalistic point of view reminiscent of the Peirce Employment Department's approach to the welfare of women hunting for work.

Many employees undoubtedly bought into management's gendered definitions of particular office or sales jobs as either masculine or feminine. In 1899 Millicent S. Renshaw, a Peirce graduate and trained stenographer, alluded to the connections between Victorian sensibilities about femininity and stenography's definition as women's work: "Women, for physical reasons, must choose those occupations which do not require arduous manual labor. They are quick, apt and possessed, as a rule, of an almost infinite amount of patience and capacity for endurance. Stenography, being light work and requiring the qualities just enumerated, is a profession upon which women are, therefore, peculiarly fitted to enter."[110] At the very least, Renshaw's prose suggests that men might be a bit too aggressive to take dictation. She limits the potential scope of women's employment based on the arduousness of the work involved. In essence, the role of a woman in the public sphere should be limited to office helpmeet. William R. Merriam, a former governor of Minnesota speaking at Peirce's commencement ceremonies in 1902, stressed that no one in the audience expected that "any ambitious young man would entertain the idea of being a bookkeeper or stenographer all his life." Understanding both sets of skills was "one of the best stepping stones to positions of greater responsibility." The majority of men entering the clerical world probably concurred with Merriam and would not have desired such employment if their jobs were defined in the same terms as women's work was.[111]

As mentioned previously, gender's impact on the workplace extended into the realms of promotion and pay. Paying men more than women and dangling promotions in front of men proclaimed a sense of masculine superiority in a heterogeneous work setting. In most offices, large or small, two promotional structures existed. Men could climb the corporate ladder from any position in the office. Women could not.[112] Management pitched the most prestigious jobs toward men. For example, men and women served as telegraphers in the same offices, but the higher-prestige, higher-paying jobs—those serving high-volume lines such as press agencies and market reports—went to men.[113] It was not unusual for Philadelphia's business owners to excuse their stinginess toward female clerical workers by arguing that women would never serve as primary breadwinners for their households. Nationally, in the late nineteenth and early twentieth centuries, women in clerical occupations could expect to earn between 25 percent and 45 percent less than men in comparable positions.[114] Many female respondents who filled out PBIS questionnaires in 1894 complained about inequalities between their pay and the pay given to men doing comparable work. A bookkeeper exclaimed to the PBIS that in her opinion, "a woman doing the same work as a man should receive the same compensation. The reason given why they are not is that a man has a family to support. In many instances this is not the case, as he has only himself to look out for, being a single man. I have my mother to support and I think I can say without egotism that I do my work as conscientiously and precisely as a man could. Why, then, should I have such a small salary in comparison?"[115] Clerical women denounced the gender gap in earnings more often than they did their miserable chances at promotion. They likely felt that they were on safer ground doing so, because paying men higher salaries for the same work especially smacked of arbitrariness on the part of management. Also, as I will show in chapters 3 and 5, upward career mobility for men was closely bound to concepts of manhood, and to suggest that office women should have the same chances to climb in the business world would have been a much more daring assault on Victorian gender norms than asserting a desire for equal pay was.[116] Indeed, once jobs such as stenography were defined as low-paying female work, many men refused to take them.[117]

In fact, if they decried anything when discussing remuneration, male clerks complained about their low salaries in relation to the rest of the white-collar world. However, most believed that some sacrifice early in one's career was necessary for rising in the business world. Men took comfort in the fact that even if they made less money than other white-collar workers did, they still out-earned their female counterparts. Men in the offices and stores of Philadelphia also understood their low earnings as a temporary phenomenon, to be righted when they advanced in their careers.

* * *

Philadelphia's industrial-era lower clerical workforce was a complex social group. The experiences that workers in this heterogeneous pool shared in the hiring process, work lives, and the definitions surrounding their jobs clearly set them apart from both the middle class and the working class. The extent to which they felt that difference is unclear, however. The clerical world offered workers mixed messages and mixed blessings. As I showed in chapter 1, from 1870 to 1920 Philadelphia's clerical sector expanded greatly for both men and women. This enlargement of opportunity was a boon to many who in previous decades would not have had the opportunity to work in the white-collar workplace, particularly those of ethnic stock and women. Nevertheless, shortcomings existed as well, and they were suffused by gender issues. Between 1870 and 1920 upward occupational mobility for the male worker declined, yet it remained sufficiently open to entice new men into the white-collar world and keep particular clerical job opportunities typed as male. In essence, where even the slightest semblance of upward career mobility was still possible, men were employed. Women took the remaining positions. For them, the office and sales world offered steadier jobs, steadier pay, and a cleaner, safer environment than did factories. But women experienced discrimination at every turn in the office. At the very least, most clerking women encountered paternalistic superiors who disregarded any ambitions their female workers might have. Women were supposed to find contentment in the stuff of work, taking dictation, filing, sorting, and selling. Long hours doing tedious, repetitive work ended up the lot for many. To some this proved unbearably frustrating, and they vented their discontent in the workplace, a topic I will examine in chapter 5.

3   Pursuing "Noble Endeavor": Educating Clerical Workers at the Peirce School

In a 1915 promotional pamphlet Philadelphia's most prominent business college, the Peirce School, utilized a fictitious student, "Tom Brown," to guide readers through the school and offer information regarding its physical layout, student services, and academic programs.[1] Tom, whom we met in chapter 2, describes Peirce in detailed, glowing tones, but one gleans preciously little about him beyond his gender and his youth. His parents still have "the responsibility of selecting a school which will fit him for something definite."[2] The pamphlet offers nothing beyond this scanty, skeletal information to flesh out Tom's background. Few historical resources exist to trace the profiles of people who contemplated entering the office or sales workforce at some point in their lives. Published census data, unfortunately, cannot describe intergenerational economic mobility—the movement of a family's children into a class status different from their parents'. Study of the Peirce School's student body, however, permits important inferences about this. In addition, examining the rhetoric the school put out regarding white-collar work, as well as its curriculum, can help us grasp some of the formative experiences that clerical workers had.

Two-year business colleges were new institutions in industrial-era urban America, and Peirce was an important fixture in Philadelphia throughout this period. The school prepared thousands of students for office or sales employment. Thomas May Peirce, Chester N. Farr Jr., A. F. Carll, and R. D. Carll founded the school in 1865 as the Union Business College of Philadelphia, named in honor of the victorious side in the Civil War. The founders had witnessed the economic expansion fueled by the conflict and believed that this would continue in peacetime. They surmised that the city's merchants and manufacturers would need legions of workers trained in the most modern clerical methods to fill their growing and modernizing establishments. Years later Peirce recalled:

> When I organized Peirce School, in 1865, I had not the surplus wealth of a millionaire, but I had a clear apprehension of a popular want of large dimensions. I knew from business men that advertisements for help were answered by the hundreds and that rare was the case in which more than one per cent. of the applications rose to the dignity of consideration. I did not have money to found a school and endow it, but I had time, I had youth, I had some degree of courage, and I gave myself to the work of training the ninety-nine per cent. of applicants who wanted to go into business and whose previous preparation did not secure for them even consideration at the hands of an employer.[3]

On September 18 the college opened in Haydn and Handel Hall, north of Center City, and received its first nine students. By 1870 Farr and the Carll brothers had dropped out of their original partnership with Peirce, and he remained the sole director of the institution until his death in 1896. He tinkered with the school's name, over the years calling it Peirce's Union Business College, the Peirce College of Business, the Peirce School of Business and Shorthand, and the Peirce School of Business Administration. In the first decade of the twentieth century, the school boasted that it was the largest business school in the United States, "exceeded only [by] the great universities," and that it had sent 30,000 "highly trained" men and women into the white-collar world.[4]

The institution's name was not the only thing that changed between 1865 and 1920. In 1869, feeling that the school was isolated outside the central business district, the directors decided to move it to the Inman Building, at Tenth and Chestnut streets, much closer to many of the businesses where the school's students hoped to find jobs. In 1881 the college migrated one block east to the Record Building, where it stayed until 1915, when it relocated to its present location, just west of Broad Street on Pine Street. The seven-floor Pine Street building housed a wide array of facilities besides classrooms. The ground floor included the school's administrative offices, a waiting room, a library, and a large assembly hall. Two elevators whisked students, faculty, and staff upward. The floors above sheltered a reading room, a lunchroom, kitchens, a "ladies' cloak-room," a gymnasium, locker rooms, two bowling alleys, and a 300-foot-long indoor track. On the roof the college maintained an open-air play area utilized for calisthenics, basketball, tennis, and other recreation. In the student restaurant individuals dropped an average of fifteen cents a day on food "absolutely pure" and "fresh-cooked every morning." The reading room and library enticed those interested in research and personal edification as well as people who wanted to play chess or checkers.[5]

Developed to train the legions of clerks and salespeople required by industrial America, business colleges increasingly dotted the urban landscape in the northeastern states during the period under consideration here. In 1880 Peirce competed with Crittenden's Philadelphia Business College and Bryant and Stratton.[6] By 1920 the field had widened. Peirce had several local challengers, such as the Wanamaker Institute of Industries, Strayers Business College, the Taylor School, and the Palmer Business School.[7] Recognizing the growth of an educational movement, in 1878 national business-school owners formed the Business Educators' Association to professionalize business education.[8] Nationally, from 1870 to 1920, business-college enrollment steadily grew. In 1871 the nation's private business schools admitted 6,460 students. By 1920 enrollment had expanded to 188,363, but by then public high-school business programs, with a total enrollment above 400,000, had taken over most of the business education in the United States.[9] Still, business colleges trained many office and sales workers for employment in America's growing industrial economy. They proved central to the evolution of the white-collar work world.

Through an open admissions policy and promotional literature laced with the theme of climbing the socioeconomic ladder, Peirce pitched itself to children from both working- and middle-class backgrounds. The school especially emphasized that clerical training and jobs prepared young men to become small-business owners or enter management.[10] In 1865 Peirce required no more than a "fair common school education" of its incoming students.[11] No strict age or exacting academic standards existed, and students simply had to show minimal math and English proficiency on placement examinations.[12] By 1910 the school's criteria had not changed: "The course of study is graded in such a manner that it may be pursued with profit not only by graduates of preparatory and high schools, colleges and universities, but by students who have not finished the course of study in the grammar schools. In the lower departments a general English education is given in connection with a technical training in commercial subjects."[13] In 1912 the "principal academic requirement" at the college was "that the student shall have a desire to learn."[14] These conditions persisted through the 1920s. The flexible requirements show that the school accepted individuals who possessed no more than basic mathematic skills and the rudiments necessary to communicate effectively in an English-speaking environment. After 1880 the business school even offered an "academical" course that helped prepare those who needed to polish their English and math skills. Completion of high school was not important. The college's youngest students began their course work in their early teens. Finally, the school encouraged individuals to apply even if they lacked the resources to cover tuition. If they showed industry and ambition, Peirce might place them at a day job to defray the costs of attending. These students then completed their course work at the school's night sessions.[15] In 1912 Peirce established the Jennie W. Rogers Loan Fund, which loaned money to students who ran into financial difficulty during their courses of study. The school allowed these borrowers to repay the interest-free loans when they were able. By early 1920 forty-four had dipped into the fund.[16]

In its early catalogs and promotional literature, the Peirce School assumed the essential value and desirability of office or sales employment for all sorts of Philadelphians. Under the heading "A Word to All," the college's 1865 catalog asserted that "money is capital and knowledge is power." The text further trumpeted that "a business education is now in the reach of every class in society."[17] In 1906 administrators linked a business education to the preparation of "young men and women for usefulness in life"; it was designed "to stimulate them by practical subjects and business methods to right thinking, noble endeavor, and correct conduct." Students should not simply lead ordinary lives, reasoned the school's administration. The skills taught by Peirce prepared youthful scholars to achieve the extraordinary through "noble endeavor" in the office or on the selling floor.[18] If this moral suasion failed to persuade one to shift his or her class status by going to Peirce and becoming a clerical worker, the school extended baser enticements. According to Peirce, clerical jobs for both men and women proved very "desirable," because they paid decently and were less demanding than was proprietary or professional work. Yet entrance into this field demanded the excellent training that only the school could provide.[19]

In a turn-of-the-century booklet Peirce administrators offered a fictitious morality tale in which "three very successful men of affairs" meet in a Pullman car and discuss their sons' futures. One plans to send his son to college and then give him a job within the man's office. Another has accumulated a trust for his child. The third will allow his son to pursue his heart's desire, the law, only if he first completes course work at a business school. He argues that the "wisest thing" a father can do for his children is provide them with a business education. This booklet assured prospective students that even those from industrial America's upper class could benefit from training in office skills such as bookkeeping, stenography, or secretarial work. Small-business owners, professionals, and even artists, it harped, could not prosper without competence in these areas.[20] Thus, the school lured students from both sides of the collar line with paeans about the solid income, self-improvement, and comfort involved in clerical work. At the very least, Peirce attempted to veneer business education with a sense of middle-class respectability by suggesting that the children of "men of affairs" should attend classes.

Mirroring the broadly two-tiered hiring system in white-collar businesses that reserved jobs with promotion potential for men, the college constructed two ideal images of success, one male, the other female. According to Peirce's promotional materials, a business education extended different opportunities for men and women. For men, Peirce suggested that clerical work acted simultaneously as a blade severing the ties of familial dependency and as a vehicle launching one to greater occupational accomplishment.[21] Rapid career advancement for men emerged as an important theme in the college's early catalogs. School administrators encouraged male students to fix their gazes up the class ladder. The rhetoric about upward striving found in Peirce's promotional literature portrayed clerical work as a first step to individual prosperity and accomplishment. The school celebrated the idea that many of its male graduates ended up, "within a few years," either as proprietors or executives.[22] It neglected to mention what happened to the thousands who only partially completed degrees. Notwithstanding this lacuna, the idealized vision for men in lower-level white-collar jobs consisted of upward mobility. The college provided living models of such success in the student profiles it occasionally included in publicity materials. Peirce placed Harry K. Nield, an 1896 graduate, in a bookkeeping position where he toiled for two years until he gained a managerial job with the Excelsior Baking Company in Trenton, New Jersey. He worked there for five years. In 1903 Nield established his own baking company in Baltimore.[23] As framed by Peirce, this male vision of success changed little throughout the late nineteenth and early twentieth centuries. The school plugged the potential for advancement via clerical work as a salve for the anxieties men might have about their futures. In a society that linked masculine success with the accumulation of wealth while simultaneously witnessing extreme levels of poverty in its cities, the chance of securing prosperity through a brief and relatively inexpensive education must have been powerfully attractive to many men.[24]

Peirce adapted its focus on advancement for men as the occupational structure of the clerical realm feminized. As was discussed in chapter 2, women dominated the field of stenography at the turn of the twentieth century. Nonetheless, in 1900 men constituted a little over one-quarter of the stenographic and typewriting workforce in the city, and well into the century's first decade the school maintained stenography to be a career that offered advancement to men. In 1906 Peirce pitched stenography as "one of the best stepping-stones" for a man seeking employment in a "railroad" or "any large corporation." By 1912, however, the school truncated this vision of stenography. That year, the college marketed its shorthand course mostly to women, declaring, "This course is designed to prepare young women for immediate employment as stenographers and amanuenses." The commentary added, as if it were an afterthought, "It may also be taken by young men."[25] By this decade few men still saw stenography as a stepping stone. In 1920, following national trends, they accounted for only around 9 percent of the stenographic workforce.[26]

For women, Peirce devised a more static image of clerical work: it paid well and offered a clean and safe work environment. No discussions of stenography as a means for women to ascend to the executive suite found their way into Peirce's advertising. The college's literature celebrated female stenographers for performing their jobs competently and efficiently and expected little else. The school envisioned female stenographers as little more than extensions of the office machines they used. It championed their speed and endurance. Letters of reference couched in terms of efficiency appeared in the college's advertisements. One read: "Her steady application to work was of great assistance to us in turning out a prompt transcript of the large amount of evidence daily taken."[27] Presumably, Peirce promoted this vision of clerical womanhood because it reinforced the placement of women in the white-collar workplace while not too aggressively challenging the presence of men in the office or on the selling floor. Most conspicuously, in no way were women to compete with men for advancement. Thus, the school could draw both a male and female clientele.

By the 1910s Peirce sold secretarial work as the plum of all female clerical opportunities. The college clearly classified the private secretary as superior to the stenographer, but its promotional literature applied the same gendered language to both. The school touted this occupation as well-paying, decorous work but never suggested that women might advance up the corporate hierarchy. Peirce described the position of private secretary as conferring "much dignity" on women. At the same time, the college asserted that "women seem peculiarly fitted to fill such posts when properly trained. Their alertness, willingness and loyalty are seldom called into question."[28] Female secretaries come off little better than helpmeets in Peirce's gendered rhetoric. Indeed, while the school slanted its publications almost entirely toward a feminine vision of the secretary, it carved out a niche for young men as well by recognizing that the occasional male secretary enjoyed the potential to enter the ranks of management.

Peirce served a vital role for Philadelphians with blue-collar family backgrounds and little access to informal family- or neighborhood-based employment connections in the white-collar world. The school offered the training that opened the office or department-store door for these individuals. Philadelphia's economic opportunity structure between 1870 and 1920 provides a dynamic setting in which to view mobility across the collar line. The explosion of clerical employment, the significant second-generation immigrant presence in the offices and stores of the city, and the feminization and proletarianization of the clerical world all suggest large-scale movement of workers across the collar line. Analysis of Peirce's student body from 1880 to 1910 enables us to determine levels of intergenerational mobility from the working class into clerking. The school's financial and enrollment ledgers list individuals on the cusp of the white-collar work world. Additionally, the enrollment statistics provide one of the few sources, beyond employers' personnel records and city directories, of information about a broad swath of the white-collar workforce. Peirce's students and their families monetarily and psychologically invested in white-collar futures through enrollment in the business school. Since educational institutions such as Peirce served as gatekeepers to a growing realm of nonmanual employment opportunity in Philadelphia, the changing demography of the college's student body indicates how various segments in the city's population viewed the possibility of obtaining office or sales work.

In 1880 students enrolled in classes in one of four major departments. The departments offered many of the same courses yet emphasized the portion of the curriculum their titles designated. The Business Department slated courses in general business practices, bookkeeping, arithmetic, penmanship, spelling, grammar, and business correspondence. This department also held lectures in commercial and insurance law. The Bookkeeping Department offered the same courses as the Business Department but emphasized bookkeeping. Likewise, the Penmanship Department stressed writing skills. Finally, the Academical Department ran two programs. First, it prepared all students for their final exams. Second, it offered remedial English or mathematics for those who required it.

By 1900 Peirce had pared down its curriculum, rearranging its academic program around two "courses," the shorthand course and the business course. These constituted the central components in the curriculum for the next twenty years. The shorthand course consisted of a preparatory program that tutored students deficient in English skills and focused on teaching students how to take shorthand notes and typewrite. Other subjects included handling correspondence, filing, business ethics, and operating a variety of office machinery. When students completed the course work, they enrolled with the Graduating Department, which prepared them for their final exams. Much of the business course was organized like the shorthand course. It, too, included a remedial program for unprepared students and its own Graduating Department. The business course itself encompassed classes in arithmetic, banking, bookkeeping, auditing, commercial law, correspondence, business management, ethics, political economy, penmanship, English, history, and geography. Peirce emphasized bookkeeping skills in its business course. Like shorthand students, who practiced their skills on actual business machines and rehearsed their note taking and dictation in the classroom, business students received a practical education in all aspects of business management. Whereas shorthand students could rehearse their newly learned skills in a typical classroom setting, however, the college's administration believed that business students could not. Once business students finished their advanced course work, they entered the Banking and Business Department. This department created a microeconomy within the school. Students ran imaginary firms, as well as a central bank, and dealt with the daily rigors of a mock market setting. In an elaborate imitation of life, the Banking and Business Department printed its own checks, currency, receipts, and business forms. Students practiced sales techniques, auditing, bookkeeping, correspondence, and proper etiquette in this dress rehearsal for the real work world. The environment socialized future office workers into the bureaucratic realm. At some point in the first decade of the twentieth century, a secretarial course was added to the school's curriculum. Its subjects included all those taught under the shorthand course with the additions of arithmetic, penmanship, accounting, and commercial law.

From 1880 to 1910 all courses geared classroom work toward individual instruction. Much like students in a one-room country schoolhouse, rarely were all the pupils in a Peirce classroom at the same stage of their education. This variation arose from a an enrollment process that continued throughout the schoolyear. Individuals registered whenever they desired. Students finished their class work at their own pace. The college suggested six to nine months as an adequate time frame for completion of either the business or shorthand program; the secretarial course took between a year and eighteen months. Furthermore, Peirce divided the schoolday into day and night sessions to accommodate both employed and unemployed students. Although no consistent graduation statistics exist for the 1880s or 1890s, based on the graduation rates in later years, fewer than one-fifth eventually graduated. Sticking it out for the duration, however (or more important, paying for a full slate of classes leading to graduation), was not necessary for clerical or sales employment. Many left once they felt they had received enough training to enter the workforce.[29]

From the start, Peirce invited both men and women to attend. The school established a Women's Department in its inaugural year. This department separated the women from the male student body. Female students even entered school through a special entrance. The school's 1865 catalog assured women that in the institution they could "find that attention and privacy, the want of [which] they have found an insuperable barrier to acquiring a business education": "The numerous applications by ladies during the long time we were connected with different institutions, and the fact that business men advertise for lady bookkeepers, is sufficient proof that there is no lack of those desiring to become or of those willing to employ competent lady bookkeepers."[30] In this passage the founders of the college asserted that their inclusion of women made them innovators in the field of business education. They justified the separation of the sexes for reasons of privacy. The 1866–67 academic year saw the development of the school's Ladies Institute of Art. It had a short life, however, lasting for perhaps only one or two schoolyears thereafter. After the 1866–67 schoolyear, in order to streamline the curriculum, the school dropped the separate ladies department and integrated women into the remaining programs. Whether the institution fully integrated men and women or kept them in separate classrooms remains unclear. Photographs in Peirce's promotional materials indicate that men and women shared classrooms by the turn of the century. This followed the model of increased inclusion of women in the clerical realm.

Only sparse enrollment records exist for the college prior to 1893, although complete accounts remain for the 1865–66 class. In Peirce's first enrollment period, 562 students registered for classes.[31] Women made up a tiny 11 percent sliver of the student body. Available statistics from 1866–92 do not include gender as a category, but they indicate that enrollment steadily grew. Records between 1893 and 1920 are more complete (see table 5). By 1920 the school was attracting almost 3,000 students. An interesting dip in enrollment developed in the 1896–97 schoolyear. The college attributed the decline (which persisted through the next two academic years) to Thomas May Peirce's death in May 1896. The administration reasoned that founder and school were so closely connected that potential students lost faith in attending the college without its namesake at the helm. A national economic depression during these years compounded the enrollment decline. Potential students likely feared the risks involved in delaying work and paying to go to a school that had lost its founder during a period of economic crisis. Mary B. Peirce, the founder's eldest daughter, became principal in 1898, and enrollment began to climb again—and women played a part in this. Between 1890 and 1920 women entered Peirce at continually growing rates, paralleling the surge of new jobs in the female clerical sector. In 1893 women constituted about one-quarter

Table 5. Peirce Enrollment, 1893–1920

Enrollment	1893–94	1896–97	1899–1900	1902–3	1905–6	1908–9	1911–12	1914–15	1917–18	1920–21
Men	965	800	960	1,197	1,212	1,199	1,186	1,259	974	1,779
%[a]	74.2	71.2	70.3	66.0	67.0	62.6	62.0	65.5	38.4	59.8
Women	335	323	406	617	598	715	727	662	1,564	1,196
%	25.8	28.8	29.7	34.0	33.0	37.4	38.0	34.5	61.6	40.2
Male day	545	468	470	505	547	545	537	631	336	912
%	41.9	41.7	34.4	27.8	30.2	28.5	28.1	32.8	13.2	30.7
Female day	243	227	258	350	359	446	407	399	842	516
%	18.7	20.2	18.9	19.3	19.8	23.3	21.3	20.8	33.2	17.3
Male night	420	332	490	664	662	653	631	616	619	619
%	32.3	29.6	35.9	36.6	36.6	34.1	33.0	32.1	24.4	20.8
Female night	92	96	148	260	236	264	289	229	639	550
%	7.1	8.5	10.8	14.3	13.0	13.8	15.1	11.9	25.2	18.5
Total	1,300	1,123	1,366	1,814[b]	1,810[b]	1,914[b]	1,913[c]	1,921[c]	2,538[c]	2,975[c]

Sources: Peirce College ledgers, "Student Statistics (Geographically) 1893–1906" and "Statistics of Peirce School, 1889–1921," Peirce College Archives, Peirce College, Philadelphia.

[a]Percentage of total enrollment.

[b]Includes students enrolled in other, minor programs (35 in 1902–3, 6 in 1905–6, and 6 in 1908–9).

[c]Includes students enrolled in summer session (49 in 1911–12, 46 in 1914–15, 102 in 1917–18, and 378 in 1920–21).

of all the students at the college. By 1920 their share of the student body had grown to about 40 percent. With the potential for clerical employment rising for women early in the twentieth century, pursuing a preparatory education seemed increasingly logical. With its academic programs and placement services, Peirce clearly enhanced opportunities for women to enter an expanding white-collar realm.

One deviation from the trend was the 1917–18 schoolyear, when America mobilized for World War I. That year women far outnumbered men at the school. Overall student numbers also skyrocketed even though male enrollment slipped by almost one-quarter. In the years immediately before the nation entered the Great War, as its economy expanded to fill the war needs of allies, men eschewed attending the school in favor of immediate employment. When the United States officially declared war, many Peirce men volunteered for service, as did thousands of other Philadelphians. As men left the workforce to fight, new clerical opportunities opened up for women, and the increased female share of the student body reflected this. For example, as Janet F. Davidson has shown, of the 112 women hired in the Pennsylvania Railroad's treasury department from 1910 to 1920, 96 got jobs during the war.[32] Between 1915 and 1918 the number of women attending Peirce more than doubled with the enrollment of women who had not seriously considered clerical employment prior to the war. The school added classes to accommodate the newcomers.

The war imbued students and faculty with a fervent patriotism. According to the college, loyal Americans included not only those trained to fight but also men and women serving the country in the wartime economy. Patriots brandished both guns and typewriters.[33] Students organized clubs to fashion leather wind-proof waistcoats for soldiers and sailors. Some volunteers collected old leather gloves, furniture covers, and fur coats for this purpose. Others refashioned the materials into the waistcoats. The "Comfort Kit Club" coalesced to supply soldiers with care packs. Students and alumni bought thousands of dollars worth of Liberty Bonds. The school's administration kept current and former students informed about classmates who had volunteered, including those wounded or killed in action. Above Peirce's main entrance hung a flag bearing the number of enlisted male students. In the school's reception room, the administration proudly displayed a German helmet mailed from the front by a former Peirce student. When Peirce veterans returned after the war, the college's Employment Department helped place them in new positions. After the war the rolls at Peirce continued to grow, and the male/female ratio in the student body returned to nearly its prewar levels.[34]

Men and women at the school attended its night and day sessions at different rates. During the 1899–1900 schoolyear equal numbers of men attended day and night sessions, while nearly 65 percent of the women attended the day session. Most night-session students held jobs, and gender-based differences in the percentages partly reflect lingering Victorian mores against women working and paternalistic concerns about the safety of unescorted women attending the evening classes. As women's participation in the clerical workforce grew, more of them attended night sessions. By 1920 about half of Peirce's female students attended night session classes.

Course enrollment also cleaved along gender lines. The secretarial course was devised "particularly for young women," and they formed most of its enrollment. The school recognized that after the turn of the century, businesses had begun expanding their secretarial workforces by multiplying the number of dead-end jobs offering little upward mobility, and few men sought this new form of secretarial work. According to the school, modern secretarial employment required only basic knowledge of accounting, business customs, and terminology, as well as "tact, judgement, and discretion." School administrators reasoned that women easily grasped these matters, while "young men [were] advised to take the entire business course" alongside the secretarial or shorthand course, "for it should be the ambition of every young man to eventually become the head of the business."[35] Business course enrollment was pitched heavily in favor of men. From the 1890s to 1920 only about 11 to 18 percent of those in the college's business course were women. The rolls for the shorthand course during the 1890s, however, split fairly evenly between men and women. The number of women gradually increased from 1900 to 1910; in the 1909–10 schoolyear they accounted for 57 percent of the college's shorthand students. By 1920 women dominated the classrooms in the shorthand course, where they occupied 85 percent of the seats.

The school's curriculum reflected its gendered expectations for students as well as its demographics. The largely male business course prepared students to be active in the business world. The course's mock settings allowed students to perform a dry run of what they were to experience in the outside world. Students played clerical, managerial, and proprietary roles in the department. Assuming various roles helped familiarize them with all aspects of the white-collar work world, gave them practical skills, and encouraged them to see office and sales work as a springboard into management or small-business ownership. Male students rehearsed for career advancement. One student fondly reminisced: "I remember failing but twice in business during my term in this department, but upon purchasing a new capital for the third term the current of trade turned in my favor, and when I graduated I had made $1906.00, and received from Dr. Peirce $19.06 in good coin."[36] Whether the school's founder actually rewarded all the students who flourished in the Banking and Business Department with cash is unknown. Students in the largely female shorthand course received instruction only in packed classrooms, where they labored behind office machines. This encouraged them to see work as a routinized, dead-end endeavor in which they acted merely as extensions of office technology.

I used data for the 1880, 1900, and 1910 classes to ascertain the occupational backgrounds of the students' parents.[37] The enrollment records list students' names and addresses. Because this study focuses on Philadelphia, the samples I used include only city residents. I linked student data to records from the 1880, 1900, and 1910 federal manuscript census schedules for the city,[38] which allowed me to assess intergenerational cross-collar mobility.

The information in table 6 enhances the portrait of Philadelphia's clerical workforce developed in chapter 1. Its boundaries were far from intergenerationally static between 1880 and 1910. Indeed, very few Peirce students had parents who were office or sales workers. Rather, mobility between the blue-collar world and the clerical realm was significant during this era. About 27 percent of the sampled pupils came from blue-collar backgrounds. Most of these had fathers who worked in skilled or semiskilled occupations, with the numbers split relatively evenly between the two categories. The data from 1880–1910 suggest an impressive level of intergenerational mobility between the labor aristocracy in Philadelphia and the clerical realm. In other words, skilled laborers in the city likely had ample opportunity to push their children up the class ladder.

An important corollary must be mentioned at this point. The census enumerators for 1880 and 1900 did not clearly designate individual workers as self-employed or not. Thus, considerable ambiguity arises when one encounters "skilled workers" in the manuscript census for Philadelphia in these years. Does this mean an individual listed as a carpenter was a self-employed businessman or a skilled artisan? The 1910 manuscript census clarifies this matter. Many of the fathers categorized as skilled in the 1880 and 1900 samples had occupations that could be at least partly proprietary. Eight of the fourteen described as skilled for 1880 had occupational backgrounds that reflected class ambiguity. They could have been partly or totally proprietary. A blacksmith, shoemaker, butcher, chair maker, jeweler, tailor, and two carpenters appeared among the fourteen skilled fathers. About the same ratio, nine of sixteen, had semi-entrepreneurial backgrounds in 1900. Three tailors, two plumbers, a blacksmith, a carpenter, a shoemaker, and a fresco painter numbered

Table 6. Sampled Peirce Students Analyzed by Fathers' Occupations, 1880–1910

Students	Fathers in white-collar occupations			
	Professional	Proprietary	Clerical	Total
Entire sample				
Number	37	101	63	201
Percentage	8.4	23.0	14.4	45.8
Men				
Number	26	72	41	139
Percentage	9.2	25.5	14.5	49.3
Women				
Number	11	29	22	62
Percentage	6.9	18.2	13.8	39.0

Students	Fathers in blue-collar occupations			
	Skilled	Semiskilled	Unskilled	Total
Entire sample				
Number	56	49	15	120
Percentage	12.8	11.2	3.4	27.3
Men				
Number	34	27	6	67
Percentage	12.1	9.6	2.1	23.8
Women				
Number	22	22	9	53
Percentage	13.8	13.8	5.7	33.3

Students	Fathers in other categories		
	Unknown	Deceased	None
Entire sample			
Number	52	63	3
Percentage	11.8	14.4	0.7
Men			
Number	35	38	3
Percentage	12.4	13.5	1.1
Women			
Number	17	27	—
Percentage	10.7	17.0	—

Sources: 1880, 1900, and 1910 federal manuscript censuses for Philadelphia; Peirce College ledgers, "1875–1880 Enrollment," "1880–1883 Enrollment," "1884–1900 Night Session Enrollment," "1898–1903 Day Session Enrollment," "1899–1900 Financial," "1909–1910 Night Session Enrollment," "1900–1910 Day Session Enrollment," Peirce College Archives, Peirce College, Philadelphia.

Note: The entire sample includes 439 students, 282 men and 157 women.

[a]Two fathers had two daughters enrolled.

among the skilled fathers. Consequently, unlike Ileen A. DeVault's turn-of-the-century Pittsburgh, Philadelphia most likely did not have a significant, clearly skilled, blue-collar component to intergenerational mobility into the clerical workforce until 1910. Rather, intergenerational movement into lower-level white-collar jobs often began with families of semiproprietary and proprietary backgrounds until the twentieth century's second decade. This resulted from Philadelphia's economic base, which was geared toward small-scale production and small-business ownership. Unlike Pittsburgh, Philadelphia was not economically dominated by a single heavy industry. Relatively few individuals from professional or unskilled blue-collar families attended Peirce, indicating that clerical futures for members of these groups were either undesirable or unattainable. The data thus suggest that business colleges were important gateways that allowed young people to move into the office or store from other positions on the socioeconomic ladder.

Between 1880 and 1910, however, most students had white-collar backgrounds. Just under one-quarter of the sampled pupils had family involved in small businesses, and they formed the largest nonmanual-worker group. In many cases proprietary families chose to prepare their children for the expanding office or sales opportunities available in Philadelphia. Coupled with the previously cited information, this further complicates our portrait of the class backgrounds of industrial-era office workers. Membership flowed into the clerical realm from rungs above and below on the class ladder.[39] The fact that both skilled blue-collar employees and small-business owners led insecure occupational lives explains this phenomenon. Small businesses often failed, and industrial America increasingly relied on unskilled workers, displacing or replacing skilled workers. Skilled workers also suffered periodic bouts of unemployment. Craftsmen and proprietors thus sent their children to Peirce to stabilize their futures.

Coming from a proprietary background could have affected students in several ways. Growing up, many of these sons and daughters worked alongside family members in the small-business setting. In the workshop or store, students were from an early age inculcated with basic skills such as bookkeeping and clerical management of paperwork, as well as sales techniques. The craftsman's shop or grocer's storefront provided countless lessons that were applicable to the clerical work world. Students with proprietary backgrounds came to Peirce to take advantage of the vast magnification of clerical opportunity that Philadelphia experienced between 1870 and 1920. They and their families realized that among the nonmanual-labor sectors of the economy, office and sales work were expanding quickly. Families took advantage of the growth by encouraging their children to enter safe, comfortable, relatively secure jobs.

The argument that these students may have been compelled to attend the college to maintain the family business seems less plausible. Business colleges flourished because clerical opportunities were expanding, not because proprietors wanted to train their progeny. They gave students transferable knowledge and skills that could be applied in a variety of occupational settings. A small-business owner's children could more effectively learn the nuances of the family business at home. A proprietary family that sent its children to business school to better prepare them for future ownership of the family firm would have been wasting time, money (tuition), and human resources (the potential labor of the student). This line of thought bolsters the notion that students from proprietary backgrounds attended Peirce to take advantage of changes in the industrial nonmanual workforce and become clerks for at least part of their work lives.

Gender offers another angle from which to view the occupational backgrounds of Peirce's students. Proprietary work played a smaller role in the occupational backgrounds of Peirce's women than it did in that of the school's men. Families owning small businesses apparently preferred sending their sons rather than their daughters to business college. They perceived the office and store as more masculine realms that offered advancement or training for small-business ownership to young men. The large-scale feminization of the clerical workforce in the early twentieth century, however, made it markedly easier for blue-collar parents to see their daughters working as stenographers or clerks. Between 1880 and 1920 the female student cohort at the college exhibited greater upward mobility from the blue-collar realm than did the male counterpart. This was especially true in the early twentieth century, a fact that underscores the connection between women employed in light manufacturing and the mechanized office.

Many of the women who rushed to fill the expanding office and sales sector came from working-class backgrounds that exposed them to other women entering the paid workforce at certain points in their lives—primarily when youthful and single. This exposure accentuated the link between women working in factories and those working in offices. In other words, the working woman of the early twentieth century was often not a denizen of the middle class liberated of her class's mentality regarding gender interaction. Rather, she was frequently someone who had extensive exposure to women toiling in the manual industrial world. She and her family quite possibly perceived work behind a desk or a sales counter as a way of avoiding the hazards of the factory floor. If Peirce's female students saw women laboring outside the home, however, they did not draw immediate lessons from their mothers. Students' mothers overwhelmingly did not labor outside the domestic arena. Only one mother in the 1880 sample held a job beyond her home's threshold: Leila Magee, an Irish immigrant and widow, ran a store. Most likely Magee did not venture beyond her home to enter her work world. Little had changed by 1900. Four mothers toiled in the paid labor force. Two held manual jobs—one worked as a housekeeper; the other, as a dressmaker. The two remaining wage earners occupied white-collar positions. One ran a dry goods store, and the other taught school. Both were widows. By 1910 thirteen mothers worked outside the home, and eight of them were widows.

It is important to recognize that children of widows constituted 14 percent of the sampled pupils. Coincidentally, Ileen A. DeVault found that between 1890 and 1903, 14 percent of the students in Pittsburgh School District's Commercial Department had widowed mothers.[40] DeVault reasons that widows who enrolled their children in this program must not have been in dire financial straits, because they gave up one potential laborer to school. This must have also been the case at Peirce. Indeed, families had to pay tuition at Peirce, whereas Pittsburgh's public schools were free. This fact bolsters the notion that widows in the Peirce samples had a modicum of financial security.

The Peirce student samples from 1880 to 1910 indicate three general trends in nativity (see table 7). Native-born Philadelphians who had native-born parents formed the largest proportions of the school's enrollment. They provided about half the enrollment. This figure approximated the segments of the clerical workforce that native Philadelphians held in 1900 and 1910. In 1900, 54 percent of clerical jobs in the city went to nonethnic-stock Philadelphians, whereas they held 51 percent in 1910. Additionally, native-born students with native parents represented about the same proportions of both the male and female student cohorts in all three samples. At the other end of the nativity spectrum, the Peirce samples are underrepresentative of foreigners' participation in jobs on the selling floor or in the office. The foreign-born made up a tiny sliver of the college's enrollment from 1880 to 1910, around 7 percent. This reflects about half the foreign-born participation in the clerical workforce during these decades, which hovered around 12 percent. The discrepancy might be explained by the possibility that many such immigrants found employment in workplaces controlled by their own ethnic group. A German-born clerk might more easily fit in a German-owned corner grocery than in Strawbridge and Clothier. Peirce, an institution dominated by the native-born, posed weighty imagined or real barriers for many foreign-born individuals seeking preparation for office or sales employment.[41]

Table 7. Nativity of Sampled Peirce Students, 1880–1910

Sample	Foreign-born	Native-born, foreign parents	Native-born, native parents	Mixed nativity	Unknown	Total
Total						
Number	29	125	221	63	3	441
Percentage	6.6	28.3	50.1	14.3		
Men						
Number	18	69	146	47	2	282
Percentage	6.4	24.5	51.8	16.7		
Women						
Number	9	58	75	16	1	159
Percentage	5.7	36.5	47.2	10.1		

Sources: 1880, 1900, and 1910 federal manuscript censuses for Philadelphia; Peirce College ledgers, "1875–1880 Enrollment," "1880–1883 Enrollment," "1884–1900 Night Session Enrollment," "1898–1903 Day Session Enrollment," "1899–1900 Financial," "1909–1910 Night Session Enrollment," "1900–1910 Day Session Enrollment," Peirce College Archives, Peirce College, Philadelphia.

Finally, second-generation individuals constituted an impressive presence in the college's classrooms and corridors. From 1880 to 1910 they made up between one-quarter and one-third of the enrolled students. This was just under the share of the city's office and sales workforce held by second-generation students—32 percent in 1890 and 36 percent in 1910.[42] Between 1880 and 1910 children of immigrant parents made up larger segments of the female student body sample than of the male one, which suggests that ethnic women enjoyed greater movement into the clerical workforce than did their male counterparts. In other words, an office or sales job was something more desirable or attainable for ethnic women than for ethnic men. Ethnic men may have found their way into the blue-collar workforce more easily than did their female counterparts.

The German and Irish immigrant segments of the student samples approached the proportions these groups embodied in the city's general population in 1880 and 1900.[43] In 1880, 23 percent of Peirce's student body was of Irish stock. Theodore Hershberg and his associates found that 27 percent of Philadelphia's population was Irish stock in 1880.[44] This is an astoundingly close match. The Irish provided almost 15 percent of the 1900 student sample. During this year 21 percent of the city's population were Irish. In 1910 the student body was again 15 percent Irish, the same as in 1900. The leveling-off of Irish enrollment figures parallels a decline in the numerical significance of the Irish as a segment of the city's population after the influx of New Immigrants in the late nineteenth and early twentieth centuries.

German-stock pupils constituted 15 and 12 percent of the student samples in 1880 and 1900, respectively; German-stock individuals accounted for 16 percent of the city's population in 1880 and 15 percent in 1900. By 1910 they made up 12 percent of the enrollment. The Germans at Peirce thus approximated their percentage of the total population more closely than the Irish did. The Germans and Irish were among the most significant ethnic groups in the social and cultural fabric of Philadelphia, and their presence at Peirce supports this.

By 1910 Jews accounted for almost 11 percent of the college's enrollment. Unfortunately, the 1880 and 1900 manuscript censuses do not consistently recognize individuals of Jewish background, making it is difficult to determine their presence in the Peirce samples. Nonetheless, the 1910 figure resulted from increased immigration levels from central and eastern Europe. Also, as Joel Perlmann has exhaustively detailed, Jewish immigrants and their offspring cherished a tradition of learning and often came from commercial backgrounds, two factors that mesh nicely to explain the significant Jewish presence at Peirce in 1910.[45]

Altogether, then, one would have had an excellent chance of encountering ethnic students in the college's classes at any point from 1880 to 1910. Yet diversity went only so far, for Peirce served an overwhelmingly white student body. This poignantly mirrored the status of minorities in the office and sales world. Only one student from the samples, Edward T. Clark, was African American. The census and enrollment records indicate that Clark lived with a sixty-eight-year-old white woman, Adeline Thompson, and her sixty-two-year-old sister, Anna Clark, paid for half a week of penmanship classes in the middle of March 1880. The manuscript census contains no information specifically about him.

* * *

The Peirce School institutionally encouraged the blurring of ethnicity and helped forge a new white-collar identity, especially among its ethnic and blue-collar students. Its promotional literature successfully drew many students across the collar line. Recently, historians such as Miriam Cohen have argued that American ethnic history has not emphasized intergenerational change in immigrant identities. Rather, for the most part, ethnic historians have focused on the continuity of ethnicity and community cohesion and strength.[46] The potential that enrollment in Peirce and clerking offered for transforming the identities of immigrant-stock individuals suggests a radical reassessment of industrialization's impact on the lives of immigrants and their children. Clerical work in Philadelphia drew thousands of second-generation immigrants. Perhaps work in the office or on selling floors encouraged the children of immigrants to Americanize their identities; accept more

mainstream, middle-class norms of behavior; and emphasize class over ethnicity. From 1880 to 1910 Peirce also facilitated mobility across the collar line
for a quarter of its students. Thus, the Peirce samples confirm that significant
mobility occurred across the collar line in the early history of industrial-era
white-collar work. Business schools served as quintessential conduits for
intergenerational occupational mobility. Business colleges and commercial
high-school programs trained the masses of clerical workers that industrializing America needed. Peirce and its sister schools socialized students into a
white-collar culture and helped them forge a white-collar identity. Men and
women from blue-collar backgrounds learned the proper ways to behave as
well as what gendered expectations to have for their futures.

4 After Hours:
How the Clerical Workforce
Entertained Itself

When the workday ended, clerks, bookkeepers, stenographers, secretaries, and salespeople found a multitude of ways to amuse themselves in the City of Brotherly Love. The leisure experiences of clerical employees were in many ways as important to their history as their work was. Prior to the 1890s the men who dominated Philadelphia's offices and stores devoted most of their free time to same-sex activities, such as fraternalism. But new forms of entertainment began to emerge with the new century. A broadly based commodification of leisure began to transform the ways that urban Americans played. New business ventures emerged to entertain people. The turn of the century was the heyday of the amusement park and vaudeville theaters. Various types of motion-picture venues arose in this period as well. All these entertainment outlets formed major components of the budding commercialized leisure economy (or entertainment economy) that catered largely to white-collar workers. This chapter illustrates the participation of clerical workers in this leisure economy during the late nineteenth and early twentieth centuries and builds on the work of scholars such as Kathy Peiss and David Nasaw.[1] Doing so ties lower-level white-collar workers, a social group of rising significance in the industrial order, to the development of modern leisure patterns. Nasaw has pointed out that white-collar workers at the turn of the century "were the critical element in the construction of the new commercialized 'night life.'" Significantly, "their work was increasingly regimented, concentrated, and tedious, creating a need for recreation."[2] Particularly after 1890 office and sales employees participated in a complex world of entertainment influenced by a variety of important factors. Youth played a big role in the clerical workforce's recreation. The office workforce was young, and the new world of commercialized play was geared toward young people. Youthful, white Philadelphians flocked to sites such as Willow Grove Park (an amusement park) or B. F. Keith's Eleventh and Chestnut Theater (a vaudeville house). Sport also appealed to youth and vigor.

Gender combined with youth to shape key aspects of the clerical workforce's leisure pursuits. This somewhat replicated their workplace experiences in two important respects. First, while the office and selling floor feminized, the new leisure economy provided unprecedented mixed-gender venues for clerks and salespeople at play. The rise of commercial entertainment helped undermine the Victorian notion of separate spheres regarding gender.[3] Male and female office workers began to spend more of their spare time with members of the opposite sex. Like New York's Coney Island, Philadelphia's Willow Grove Park and the amusements at Atlantic City catered to a white-collar crowd including both men and women. But there was more to these leisure activities than just an intermingling of the sexes. Second, much as women and men faced different gender-based expectations at work, clerks played according to gender-based mores. This especially applied to athletics. Indeed, a great deal of office and sales workers' leisure seems to have depended on their sex.

Even as their urban environment was providing them new ways to play at the turn of the century, clerks and salespeople were enjoying increasing time off from work. Their employers offered them regular vacations, and they often had their evenings and their weekends free. Unlike typical blue-collar workers, they possessed the time to participate in the new entertainment economy. In addition, the clerical workforce enjoyed a fair amount of spending money. At the low end of the white-collar pay scale, the earnings of saleswomen might have been paltry when compared to the wages of skilled male workers, but many lived with their families and paid no rent. Some of their pay could be devoted to other things, and inexpensive leisure outlets abounded. Vaudeville houses, for example, charged between ten and thirty cents a ticket.[4]

With respect to leisure activities, clerical workers acted as both consumers and producers. At one extreme, clerks and salespeople participated in highly commodified, public activities that required little creative effort and organization on their part. Vaudeville impresarios, movie-house operators, motion-picture stars, professional athletes, and amusement-park owners and employees were all part of the human apparatus that concocted these amusements. In the most commercialized forms of leisure, clerks participated only as spectators who purchased admission to spectacles that drew droves of other urbanites. Still, as a central pool of customers, clerical workers played an indispensable role in commercial entertainment. The money they paid for admission to urban theaters, amusement parks, and professional sporting events fueled this segment of the urban economy.

Other leisure pursuits consisted of less direct forms of consumption and less public activities in which clerks acted as producers, yet these, too, were connected to the emergent leisure economy. A great many clerical workers spent money on hobbies such as chess. Producing their own venues for play, they formed amateur athletic clubs, purchased the necessary equipment, and poured hours of their own time into organizing these activities. Clerks and salespeople created leisure clubs based on a variety of affiliations. Some derived membership simply from common interests in particular activities, such as cycling or playing baseball. Additional groups coalesced around institutional affiliations such as school or the workplace. Peirce School graduates formed their own alumni association, and Strawbridge and Clothier employees created numerous groups organized around specific leisure pursuits. Of course, the leisure economy's tendrils reached to various degrees into all these forms of recreation. As a case in point, the Peirce Alumni Association regularly organized its own dances. It rented halls, hired musicians, and arranged for catering, thus relying on diverse facets of the leisure economy. Alumni forged their own cycling club, which required members to purchase bicycles and cycling costumes. These roles of production and consumption were not distinct in the leisure activities of the city's clerks and salespeople. Even in the least commercialized forms of entertainment, such as private parties, people often sang songs accompanied by a piano or a phonograph and read from sheet music—all products of the leisure economy. After work a bookkeeper could go on a date to see a vaudeville production and be inspired to join an amateur acting troupe. Clubs did not limit their activities to the invention of their own amateur leisure activities, however. Organizations occasionally facilitated their members' direct participation in commercialized recreation by sponsoring trips to movies or to theaters.

Between the end of the Civil War and the rise of the leisure economy in the 1890s, the major outlets for play available to Philadelphia's overwhelmingly male clerical workforce were fraternal organizations and all-male beneficial societies. These groups adhered to Victorian sensibilities regarding the separation of the sexes and were driven by their members' common interests. Evidence suggests that the city's clerical workforce participated in fraternalism. Between the end of the Civil War and the 1920s, fraternalism constituted a major social movement involving millions of Americans. On a national level the fraternal movement, especially among larger groups such as the Freemasons and Odd Fellows, consisted predominantly of nonmanual workers—a sizable proportion coming from the office or storefront. During the 1870s and 1880s nothing quite paralleled it as a leisure outlet, and it remained popular even after the rise of commercial recreation. The Odd Fellows, Freemasons, Knights of Pythias, and other such fraternal orders claimed an estimated five million members nationally in 1897. Amos H. Hall graduated from the Peirce School in 1866, and the school placed him in a bookkeeping position. The same year he was initiated into the Odd Fellows. Hall climbed both the employment and fraternal ladders over the next thirty years. Other Peirce graduates also joined fraternal organizations. Two specifically clerical all-male beneficial societies formed in Philadelphia shortly after the Civil War, and both had antecedents in New York City. The Bookkeepers' Beneficial Association (BBA) emerged in 1874 and lasted past the turn of the century. This group primarily dispensed death benefits for its members, and by 1900 the monthly membership fee was fifty cents. Upon the death of a member, his fellows each contributed an additional dollar. The deceased's family received five hundred dollars as a benefit. But the BBA underwrote leisure activities as well, throwing annual banquets and regularly sponsoring lectures "of interest to office men" for the edification of its membership. Even though women had entered the bookkeeping ranks the turn of the century, the association remained strictly male.

The Philadelphia Bank Clerks' Beneficial Association (BCBA) formed in June 1869 and lasted at least into the mid-1880s. Regular dues and assessments had netted the organization total assets of $21,338.49 in 1884. It admitted various bank employees from the city, ranging from watchmen to clerks and tellers. The association attracted individuals from bank management as honorary members. In 1884 the BCBA paid out between $600 and $640 to each of the families of members who had died that year. Although it is unclear whether the group sponsored entertainments or leisure activities, BCBA meetings furnished an environment in which the city's bank employees could mingle. Bank clerks and tellers could use their membership for social and professional contacts. It was a true citywide organization. Forty-one banks accounted for the regular membership rolls in 1884.[5] Groups such as the Freemasons and occupationally based beneficial organizations such as the BCBA and BBA persisted into the twentieth century, alongside more commercial ways of spending leisure time.

As the nineteenth century drew to a close, clerical employees increasingly organized their own leisure activities, which generally fell into two broad categories, amateur sport and nightlife entertainments. Late in the century, for example, the Strawbridge and Clothier Department Store's employees began to develop their own recreational organizations with varying influence from the store's management. Initially store managers held a patriarchal view regarding their workers' play. Management tried to heavily control the content of the recreational outlets it provided to its sales and clerical workforce in the early 1880s. Gradually, after the turn of the century, the role of management diminished as it turned to providing venues for play rather than dictating content. The store's clerical workers created their own leisure organizations well into the twentieth century.

It is nevertheless important to note how the store's owners first acknowledged the importance of play in their clerks' lives in the early 1880s. Management's interest in the spare-time activities of employees began in April 1882 when Strawbridge and Clothier started a series of periodic "entertainments." These regular gatherings persisted into the early 1890s. They consisted of amateur and professional talent performing a variety of material; the acts included orchestras and bands, opera companies, instrumental soloists, Shakespeare scholars, humorists, and cartoonists, who all put on elaborate shows before large crowds of store workers. The gatherings occurred in large Center City performance spaces such as the Academy of Music. The initial series of entertainments in 1882 sanctioned the pursuit of recreation by store workers and reified the idea that the contented worker was one who knew how to spend free time appropriately. The first event was held in Philadelphia's Association Hall, and 1,500 people attended (800 employees with their guests). Strawbridge and Clothier workers performed for this initial gathering. In later programs professional entertainers shared the stage with employee talent. The store owners covered the expenses for the extravaganzas. They rented halls and hired the necessary acts.[6] The store superintendent, Clarkson Clothier, left no doubt regarding the purpose of the entertainments when he addressed the audience at the first one. The gatherings aimed to elicit employee loyalty. He observed:

> It is desired by this as well as by other means to foster that spirit of fidelity to the house that is now so largely prevalent among you; to round off the rough edges of every-day business life, and to make all feel that in your connection with Strawbridge & Clothier there are bright spots by the wayside that are pleasant memories to gild the monotonous experiences: and when in the hereafter you may glance back through the vista of receding years, you may find that in your experiences at Eighth and Market streets [the location of the store] you have passed some of the brightest and happiest hours in what I hope may prove to be bright and happy lives.[7]

Clothier continued by discussing how everybody seemed to get along well in the workplace. Petty jealousy did not exist in the store, he said. The superintendent tied this harmony to the employee happiness the entertainment was supposed to generate. To Clothier, good loyal work and healthy, employer-directed leisure pursuits went hand in hand.[8]

Philadelphia newspapers saw this early version of welfare capitalism as evidence that Strawbridge and Clothier was "a liberal firm" and clearly de-lineated these entertainments as programs the store devised to please and placate its employees. The events were meant to control radical sentiment among workers, to limit the influences of socialism, labor activism, "and the other clap-trap humbugs for making everybody hate a man who has more money than himself." Journalists stressed that no other retailers in urban America provided such extravagant entertainment. Some of the material in the shows was quite cerebral. A February 1883 extravaganza began with a lecture and slide presentation by an adventurer who had traveled throughout Egypt and elsewhere in the Middle East the previous year. In a lighter tone, a magician and a ventriloquist with his "family of blockheads" wowed the gathered clerks after the Egypt talk. In one function in March 1883, store clerks provided all the merriment. The program consisted of employees who enthralled the crowd with instrumental performances, singing, and dramatic recitations. Another evening's diversions focused on the Boston Symphony Orchestra, which regaled the standing-room-only crowd at the Academy of Music.[9] These productions helped set the stage for Strawbridge and Clothier's workers to actively engage in leisure pursuits. Even though the store abandoned its management-directed formal entertainments by the turn of the century, employees understood that their bosses encouraged them to play during their time away from work. And over the next four decades Strawbridge and Clothier workers created a myriad of their own leisure groups under management's approval.

In February 1892 seven Peirce alumni gathered to establish the mixed-gen-der alumni association. They formed a committee that by the beginning of June 1892 had drafted an invitation to all Peirce alumni announcing a meeting to develop a leisure organization. About two hundred graduates assembled at the school one evening in the middle of June to create the association. Another formal committee composed bylaws at the gathering, while the rest of the attendees discussed the club's formation. The bylaw committee returned before the end of the evening with a mission statement and the rudiments governing membership, dues, and office holding in the associa-tion. The mission statement asserted that the object of the association would be "to promote social intercourse among the graduates of Peirce College of Business and Shorthand and to aid the faculty in further popularizing [the pupils'] Alma Mater."[10] From the start the alumni association was primarily geared toward recreation. Annual dues started at one dollar. Membership had reached 345 by the end of the first year. During the 1910s the association had over 1,000 members, about one-third of them active. In 1913 the organization held $3,700 in bank accounts. Between 1892 and 1913 it spent about $18,000, a hefty sum, mostly on amusement that included a wide range of activities including lectures, bicycling, and dances. Many of its members participated while still young, employed as clerical workers, and having relatively few responsibilities. A few stalwarts remained active in the organization as they aged, began families, and (for some) moved into proprietorial, professional, or managerial occupations.

Although the alumni association was closely affiliated with the Peirce School, it did not take directives from the college. Unlike an employee organization created under the paternalistic, benevolent eye of an employer, this group enjoyed complete autonomy in its leisure pursuits and raised and spent its own money. The alumni occasionally asked the school for help—say, by providing facilities for a banquet—but these involvements were minimal. The association also spawned smaller groups that pursued specific pastimes; for example, a bicycling club formed in the 1890s.

Both the workers at Strawbridge and Clothier and the members of the Peirce Alumni Association delighted in sports and physical recreation. Throughout the 1890s and into the early nineteenth century, the city's office and sales workers heard much discussion of exercise and its benefits, which set the stage for their involvement in amateur sports. Advice columns both local and national championed the idea that exercise is critical to maintaining physical and mental health. Most of the discussion was directed toward men. In Philadelphia an anonymous turn-of-the-century commentator suggested, "Too many of us spend all day in hot, stuffy, poorly ventilated offices, and as a consequence, when evening comes we are tired, weary and not too companionable."[11] Exercise became part of clerical training at Peirce School. In 1915 the school opened a gymnasium in its new location on Pine Street. The gym incorporated an indoor track, a locker room, and a rooftop exercise field. Initially only male students received gym privileges. The school hired William J. Herrmann, "considered to be the leading exponent of physical training in Philadelphia," to supervise activities and special gym classes.[12] Herrmann was the director of his own physical fitness institute located at Eleventh and Chestnut streets. In the 1910s he advertised separate classes for men and women. Herrmann aimed his male physical-training classes toward "run-down" and "overworked" sales and office employees as well as professionals. In addition, the institute offered a self-defense class titled "Manly Exercise"; Herrmann's Physical Training Institute pitched this course to the "weak," "obese," "timid," and "delicate." For women, it extended lighter exercises for "health, strength, grace, figure, vigor, enduring powers, poise, carriage, and expression."[13]

The Peirce Alumni Association directly connected physical fitness to the masculine work world, stating that a "'sound mind in a sound body' is a trite phrase, but one fraught with meaning. The boys who are taking the physical-training work [at Peirce School] are clear-eyed and vigorous. They stand erect and look the whole world in the face. We venture the prediction that these young men will go further in business life than their fellows who neglect the proper care of their bodies." A former student who had risen from the ranks of office work to become a business owner told male clerks who dreamed of emulating his success that he believed in "all good, clean, healthful athletic sports, such as tennis, golf, automobiling, yachting, etc. Recreation is necessary for both body and mind. It helps to smooth out the rough, troublesome, perplexing problems that come to all in this strenuous life."[14] Women were conspicuously absent from these observations, but by 1916 the school had created separate gym classes for them. Other discussions of exercise occasionally included women. As the backlash against corsets gathered steam after the Civil War and as concerns regarding women's reproductive health emerged, commentators encouraged women to perform calisthenics and gymnastics.[15] In 1912 Thomas Martindale urged Strawbridge and Clothier's saleswomen to walk regularly. Martindale, an English immigrant who accumulated significant wealth as a businessman, was a proponent of strenuous living. In the early 1870s he had started his own grocery store in Oil City, Pennsylvania, where he met the needs of families working in the local oil fields. In 1875 Martindale sold his Oil City store and moved to Philadelphia, where he opened a dry goods emporium that he controlled until his death in 1916. Throughout his later years he enjoyed enough wealth to indulge in big-game hunting and to author several books on the subject. His rags-to-riches life story and his enthusiasm for the outdoors garnered him notoriety in Philadelphia.[16] Martindale was an avid walker and expounded on its health benefits. He contended that, especially in the winter, workers in the "human beehive" of the office or department store built up poisonous bodily secretions that springtime walks could purge. Coincidentally, he also urged women to avoid high-heeled shoes (ostensibly on the selling floor and when they were exercising) because they precipitate lower back pain.[17]

Social commentators encouraged the city's male clerical workers to engage in the "strenuous life," a phrase championed by Theodore Roosevelt, who first formulated this notion in two speeches in 1899 and 1900. Roosevelt worried that American men had grown too effeminate and sedentary. He helped redefine masculinity at the turn of the century by arguing that men had to incorporate healthy doses of activity into their lives. That activity ranged from making war and hunting to playing football or baseball.[18] Men who had recently returned from adventures around the globe treated Peirce alumni to lectures along these lines. Antedating Roosevelt's paeans to the strenuous life, John M. Justice, a Peirce graduate, presented a talk titled "A Summer with the Eskimos" in April 1896.[19] In January 1916 the association heard Thomas Martindale deliver a talk entitled "Alaska and Its Big Game." Apparently, Martindale felt equally comfortable advising women or discussing masculine topics. To the alumni association president who introduced him, Martindale embodied what it means to be a "true man." He was a success in the business world and led an active, masculine life. Martindale gave a general lecture describing Alaska and exhibited numerous trophies, including caribou racks, polar bear pelts, and mountain sheep fleeces. The show hit at Roosevelt's notion of the strenuous life and encouraged the male audience to incorporate active recreational pursuits into their lives.[20] Aptly, Martindale died at age seventy-four while in northern British Columbia on a hunting expedition.

For male urban clerks who could not readily embark on arctic hunting forays, organized amateur team sports offered an easier way to engage in the strenuous life. As a part of American culture, sports antedated the emergence of the leisure economy. By the end of the nineteenth century, however, sporting activities had commercialized and become even more popular. Baseball reached mass audiences as professional leagues emerged. Countless male white-collar workers attended professional games. Baseball clubs even scheduled games to coincide with office work schedules.[21] This brought baseball to the attention of growing numbers of male office workers. Manufacturers also increasingly mass marketed and advertised sports equipment. The popularization of sports as an adult pastime began after the middle of the nineteenth century, when a positive sport creed developed in America.[22] The sport creed especially viewed athletic activity as a healthy outlet for sedentary male workers in the office world and was promulgated by popular magazines read by the middle class. Within the realm of sport, bastions of same-sex leisure persisted even as other activities proffered by the leisure economy increasingly attracted mixed crowds. In fact, strenuous competitive recreational activity helped separate male office workers from their female counterparts as the office world feminized. Consequently, from 1890 to 1920 athletic leisure largely remained divided along gender lines.

Social reformers also took up sports as a panacea for the supposed ills of the industrializing city. Conceivably, sports could integrate immigrants into

American society by mixing them with native-born players on teams. At one level, teams encouraged cooperative effort and alleviated the atomization of the bureaucratizing world. On another level, organized sports emphasized competition and reinforced the masculine ambition encouraged in the white-collar workplace. Additionally, muscular Christianity influenced the way late nineteenth-century Americans viewed sports in quasi-moral terms. Boston's Thomas Wentworth Higginson and other American proponents of muscular Christianity, a doctrine borrowed from Great Britain, argued that physical exercise is moral, healthy, and manly as long as it does not involve vice-riddled activities such as gambling, drinking, card playing, shooting billiards, and frequenting prostitutes. These vicious activities had been associated with preindustrial notions regarding sport.[23]

At midcentury many employers openly opposed their workers' indulging in athletics. Bosses saw sports as wasteful and draining. Steven M. Gelber notes that "in 1859, the directors of the Farmers' and Mechanics' Bank of Philadelphia forbade their clerks from being members of cricket or boating clubs."[24] He stresses that in the middle of the century many employers specifically discouraged baseball among their workforces. But change was afoot. By the last two decades of the nineteenth century, employers had accepted the sport creed. They gradually caught on to sports' positive possibilities for their workforces. Many companies performed a complete about-face and heavily sponsored employee baseball teams. Workers responded by creating clubs on their own. The city's Bank Clerks' Athletic Association formed in 1887. This association supported a wide range of activity, from lacrosse to cycling. It even spawned a baseball league in which individual firms fielded teams.[25] In late 1893 and early 1894, clerks in the Philadelphia and Reading Railroad Company created an athletic association. Like the Bank Clerks' Athletic Association, the Philadelphia and Reading Railroad Athletic Association offered its two hundred members a wide array of athletics, because, as its program said, "a clerk who sits in an office all day is one, above others, who should take such recreation."[26] Association members avidly pursued baseball, football, cricket, and tennis.

Beyond simply exercising and indulging in athletic competition, clerks at the Philadelphia and Reading Railroad used their athletic association as a forum in which they solidified companionships forged at work, reinforcing friendships struck within individual offices. Three of the organization's ten officers served as clerks with the railroad's auditor of merchandise traffic. One of them, W. W. Smith, entered the auditor's office in 1891. He initially played first base for the association's baseball team and served as its captain and manager, but work pressures forced him to pare back his coaching responsibilities. The baseball team's right fielder and another club officer, Henry Forster, worked alongside Smith in the same office. He had been there since the mid-1880s. The association's business manager, George M. Heins, joined the railroad in 1892, clerked in the same office as the other two, and helped found the football team. These three likely chatted about association matters during work and on their breaks in lunchrooms nearby the Philadelphia and Reading Railroad's massive and new terminal complex in Center City. Additionally, the association fostered brotherhood that bridged structural boundaries within the corporation. The remaining seven association officers came from different departments within the railroad. This fraternization had the support of the company's management. The railroad let the clerks establish recreation grounds near its Tabor Street Station in the McCartersville section of North Philadelphia. It also discounted fares from work to the Tabor Street Station for association members. It is easy to imagine clerks from different offices within the corporation meeting after work in the mammoth depot of the Philadelphia and Reading terminal to catch a train to the Tabor grounds for a game of baseball.

The Strawbridge and Clothier management gradually accepted sports as legitimate leisure activities for employees. No evidence indicates that the store ever openly opposed sport, but in the late 1800s it did view athletics as child's play. In the 1880s and 1890s the only sporting activity the store endorsed occurred at periodic picnics it sponsored for its hundreds of cash boys and other very young male employees, including wrappers, stockkeepers, and some sales personnel. Beginning in 1879 Strawbridge and Clothier threw annual picnics held on or close to the Fourth of July. The picnic on July 4, 1884, was typical. Early that morning three hundred boys (in 1882 there were two hundred; in 1887, five hundred) gathered outside the store at Eighth and Filbert streets. Adult chaperones marshaled the young workers into seven military-like companies. Each company had a special designation, and each boy received either a red or sky-blue ribbon with a company designation emblazoned on it in gold letters. They pinned these to their shirts. A single adult male chaperon led each of the companies in precision drills that the kids had rehearsed after work during the four previous days. Strawbridge and Clothier hired the twenty-two-piece State Fencibles' Fife and Drum Corps to lead the boys down to the Broad Street Railroad Station, where they boarded a special train that conveyed them to Sharon Hill, just outside the city. From the Sharon Hill stop they proceeded to Isaac H. Clothier's nearby home, where activities and food awaited. The adults planned an elaborate track and field meet. Boys ran organized footraces of various lengths for prizes ranging from baseball bats and Indian clubs to penknives (the store

had used fliers and word of mouth to announce these races to the boys over
the previous few days so that they could practice their skills). Strawbridge
and Clothier also provided baseball and football equipment, as well as the
implements for quoits, a game similar to tossing horseshoes. After the games
the boys slaked their thirsts and gorged on mountains of refreshments. The
three hundred quarts of milk and two hundred quarts of ice cream no doubt
appealed to the youngsters. A specially hired train conveyed the kids back to
the city at 6:00 P.M.[27]

Strawbridge and Clothier openly and prominently bolstered employee
athletics after the turn of the century. The store's male staff were most involved in competitive athletics. In the first decade of the twentieth century,
management encouraged male workers' involvement in baseball, basketball,
and bowling. This support culminated in May 1910, when the store purchased
a city block in West Philadelphia bounded by Sixty-second, Walnut, and
Locust streets on three sides and Cobb's Creek Boulevard on the fourth. The
store refurbished the bleachers, grandstand, baseball diamond, and two tennis
courts that already stood on this 5½ acre property and added a stable and
garage for its delivery service.[28] The top floor of the structure was reserved for
employee athletic use. It housed men's and women's locker rooms, showers,
and dressing rooms. It also held a gymnasium, as well as tennis and basketball
courts.[29]

Employees responded by creating the Strawbridge and Clothier Athletic
Association that same year. Its initial membership totaled 327 people—188
men, 81 women, and 58 boys and girls. The association's annual dues in 1912
amounted to one dollar for men, fifty cents for women, and twenty-five cents
for youths between sixteen and twenty-one years old. Anyone younger than
sixteen paid no dues.[30] The association scheduled regular events such as
baseball games and track meets held on the athletic fields. On Memorial Day
1911 the athletic association sponsored a track meet that drew twelve hundred
spectators who witnessed men, boys, and girls (but no women) compete in
a variety of events before a rainstorm ended the meet.[31] By 1912 store management had custom-fit the gymnasium with new equipment that could
accommodate gymnastics, boxing, fencing, and wrestling.[32] No other store
in Philadelphia developed comparable facilities, bragged employees.[33]

Of the organized amateur team sports that played a central role in the
leisure lives of male clerical workers, the most popular was baseball. The
game held some connections to the work world for clerks, bookkeepers, and
other office workers, because, as Steven M. Gelber has noted, it "emulated
business in its specialization and division of labor, its structural integration,
its emphasis on speed, and quantifiable production."[34] Nationally about

two-thirds of city dwellers who played the game as amateurs in the late nineteenth century were white-collar workers. In the 1880s and 1890s many urban areas, particularly in the Northeast, saw "commercial" baseball leagues develop. These leagues comprised teams of various firms that competed against one another.[35] Commercial leagues persisted into the early twentieth century. Between 1900 and 1920 Strawbridge and Clothier teams participated in both storewide competition and intercompany games. A 1906 issue of *Strawbridge & Clothier Store Chat* prominently mentioned baseball. Several departments created baseball teams that year. The bookkeepers, under the team name A. M. Truitt, went undefeated in a tournament, winning eighteen to twelve and ten to nine against the credit department. They clobbered the delivery department twenty-six to five. Some teams were organized along occupational lines—the bookkeeping team, for example—whereas others were pooled from the entire male staff of a department and included clerical workers as well as department managers. Intrastore rivalries emerged. The wholesale department boasted that if it created a team in 1909, "no outsiders [would play] in any position."[36] This suggests fierce competition, and some store teams must have brought in ringers to win games for them. Teams also formed across department lines, as did the Eureka Giants, who competed in 1907. A 1907 game illustrates the different types of team organization. By a score of fifteen to five, Strawbridge and Clothier's jewelry department trounced the Wanamaker's team, which consisted of players drawn from across the department store's staff.[37]

Intrastore play in 1908 saw an interesting twist on the class dimensions of the game. Strawbridge and Clothier's Tuesday Field Club, constituted of the heads and assistant heads of the store's many departments, sponsored a summer baseball series on Tuesday and Friday afternoons at the Stenton Athletic Club on Twenty-fourth and Tioga streets. Male employees from the store's various departments formed two teams for the series. The teams, the Executives and the Merchandisers, likely included managerial employees. On June 23 the Executives pummeled the Merchandisers twenty-five to eighteen. The Merchandisers never really threatened after a big first inning by the Executives. The series continued throughout the summer. On September 5 the Executives won the championship in a sloppy twenty-nine to twenty-eight slugfest. The same day the two teams celebrated the end of the series by playing a second, "theatrical" game in costume. They joked that the "Ancient Britons" played baseball this way. Most of the combatants dressed in workingmen's garb—overalls, boots, and aprons. A "bricklayer," "smithy," and a "baker" played.[38] The two umpires, adorned as knights, wore breastplates and helms. The game's class inversion seemed quite comical, especially to the Executives, most of whom posed for a postgame photograph that later ran in the *Strawbridge & Clothier Store Chat.* The article alongside the photograph mused that the smith's "straight form showed that he never stooped to that kind of work." The theatrical whitewashed baseball's origins by emphasizing an ancient Anglo-Saxon lineage for America's pastime. The game's participants and spectators must have understood these class and racial messages even if they bore humorous overtones. Play that day expressed the department-store workers' notions that they were definitely not working class and that baseball should be strictly a white game. Although the participants might not have toiled as bookkeepers or clerks in the store, the two contests that day drew a sizable crowd of spectators who did.[39] The theatrical game's messages particularly resonated with any clerical employees who attended. They may have missed the game, but the readers of the *Strawbridge & Clothier Store Chat* would certainly have picked up the messages.

During inclement weather white-collar men turned to indoor sports, including bowling and basketball. Prior to the 1920s social commentators linked bowling to gambling and the preindustrial bachelor leisure subculture, for saloon basements housed many early alleys. Bowling was clearly a man's sport. Working-class, clerical, and professional men all bowled in leagues.[40] In the early twentieth century Strawbridge and Clothier men participated in the city's Commercial Bowling League, which comprised employees from "many leading commercial and manufacturing houses in Philadelphia." A bank clerks' league existed as well. Teams composed of drug clerks, insurance company employees, and Pennsylvania Railroad workers also competed in citywide play.[41] In 1909 the commercial league held its competition during the spring, and the "Clover Club of S&C" handily won the championship. The Clover Club repeated in 1910 by beating the American District Telegraph Company in two out of three games in the final round.[42] In 1915 even the Peirce School bragged of two lanes on the fifth floor at its new Pine Street address.

Basketball, too, enjoyed popularity. By the winter of 1909 Strawbridge and Clothier workers had created their own basketball league. They rented a hall on North Broad Street for their games and charged ten-cent admission to their roundball contests on weeknights. Nine all-male teams from various departments challenged one another to games. Once ironed out, the schedule accommodated the seasonal demands and rhythms of store work. For example, the transfer and delivery department team could not play matches during the Christmas rush.[43]

Although the occasional women's basketball club sprang up at Strawbridge and Clothier, athletic coverage in the in-house magazine emphasized men's teams. It also stressed competition ("friendly rivalry") and the pursuit of league titles all within the context of manhood. The store's sportsmen were, it said, audacious, well-trained, and ambitious both at work and at play. Supposedly, the proper athletics for women did not elicit rivalry but focused on the maintenance of good health, much as Thomas Martindale's platitudes about walking suggested. When seventy-five women formed a gym class at the store in 1912, the employee magazine crowed that "a great deal of benefit will be derived through the light exercises and healthful games the members of this association will indulge in."[44]

The only major mixed-gender sporting pastime in which the clerical workforce participated was cycling. Both amateur baseball and bowling demanded relatively minor levels of consumer activity—purchasing uniforms and equipment. Cycling required larger expenditures for bicycles, bicycle repairs, spare parts, and clothing, as well as for food and lodging on longer trips. In the 1890s urban America experienced a cycling craze. Men and women went mad for the two-wheeler. Alumni from Philadelphia's Peirce School created their own cycling group, the Peirce Alumni Cyclers, in 1897. Members of the club, which lasted only about a year, used the bicycle to explore the picturesque environs of parks and suburbs that lay at the city's frontiers. While scorching along the roads and trails in these border regions, clerical employees also utilized the bicycle to investigate more ethereal but very significant frontiers involving gender and class.

Incarnations of the bicycle before the 1890s failed to gain popularity because of their prohibitive cost and their dangerous instability. The most popular model before the 1890s was the "ordinary" bicycle, whose American debut occurred at the Centennial Exhibition in Philadelphia. The ordinary sported a gigantic front wheel that ranged in diameter from forty to sixty inches and a tiny rear wheel.[45] The cyclist sat above the large wheel. As its shape might indicate, successfully riding the ordinary demanded much practice, patience, balance, and tolerance for pain. It still earned a loyal following among hardy middle-class men who did not mind the toll it took on both the flesh and the pocketbook. They enjoyed the speed and independence of cycling.[46] After 1887 American manufacturers distributed the mass-produced "safety" bicycle, which looked much like today's bike. It had two equally sized wheels, a diamond-shaped frame made of steel tubes, and a chain drive. Further improvements included pneumatic tires and lighter construction. The safety cost less than its predecessor, and as bicycle manufacturers improved production techniques, prices fell even further. Because the safety exacted less sacrifice from the body and pocketbook, millions of people owned bicycles by the mid-1890s. As the safety's name implies, its riders mastered this metal beast much more quickly than they did the ordinary.

Members of the Peirce Alumni Association interested in cycling constituted their own club in the late summer of 1897.[47] These clerical workers followed the example of the more elite city cycling organizations that flourished in the early 1890s. The alumni created an elaborate club complete with a constitution, a board of governors, and a membership that soon approached one hundred.[48] In the early fall the Peirce Alumni Cyclers procured a clubhouse at 3118 Diamond Street, near Philadelphia's huge Fairmount Park, in the northwestern section of the city. The city's cycling enthusiasts loved traversing the park. The Peirce cyclers declared Diamond Street to be "one of the most popular cycling thoroughfares in the city."[49] They considered the clubhouse ideally situated as a waypoint for funneling them out of the urban landscape and into Fairmount. These bike enthusiasts felt they needed a specific gathering place or staging area where their members, who came from all over the city, could coalesce before venturing out into the greenery of the urban periphery.

For their first cycling excursion, or "run," the cyclers gathered in the city and sallied into Fairmount Park. The first run occurred on an early autumn evening, and bike lanterns guided club members along the route. The large group that embarked from Center City was evenly divided between men and women. A long line of couples started out around 8:00 P.M. and made its way up Broad Street toward Girard Avenue. The trip from Girard Avenue to Fairmount's Valley Green Inn, on the east side of the park, took about an hour. Valley Green was a former roadhouse that had ceased serving alcoholic beverages when the Fairmont Park Commission acquired it in the early 1870s. No mishaps occurred along the route that likely snaked along the scenic banks of the Schuylkill River on East River Drive (today's Kelly Drive) and down another picturesque road tracing the banks of the Wissahickon Creek, which took the cyclists deep into the park. At Valley Green brightly colored Japanese lanterns illuminated the trees along the slowly moving creek. Then, under the warm light of the lanterns, the cyclists gathered for refreshments at a long table surrounded by benches. A cartload of watermelon soon arrived. According to the *Peirce School Alumni Journal*, "It was, indeed, a pleasant spectacle—the groups of rosy-cheeked girls, so attractive in their cycling costumes and the young men, who looked becoming in their short trousers, all beaming with that good nature which is characteristic of healthy and moderate indulgence in cycling."[50] The watermelon quenched thirsts and provided for high jinks as the snack degenerated into a good-natured food fight, and club members smeared rind into their friends' faces. Soon thereafter the evening wound down, and everybody headed home. This initial run embodied key themes involved in the cycling club's recreation. It particularly involved mixed-gender play. Cycling also immersed these clerks and salespeople in high levels of consumption. Through these consumer activities, they tried to affect the trappings of middle-class professionals and small-business owners. Indeed, the very act of maintaining their own club was an attempt to ape the leisure patterns of those above them on the class ladder. Finally, all the cyclers' jaunts took them to the city's green fringes.

As already mentioned, the Peirce Alumni Cyclers included both men and women from the clerical world. This mirrored the changes revolutionizing the way young adults in urban America spent their spare time at the turn of the twentieth century. The Peirce cyclists used the bicycle as a vehicle that breached gender boundaries in the realm of sport. The mixed-gender nature of the club also reflected the increasing presence of women in the workplace. The cyclers' first run to Valley Green highlighted the possibilities of mixed-gender leisure activity for the clerical workforce. (As I will discuss later, intergender contact occurred at more commercial leisure sites, too, including amusement parks, variety theaters, and dance halls, where clerks and salespeople abandoned the mores of the workplace.) Women and men on cycling excursions interacted in an atmosphere that sanctioned play and loosened standards regarding everything from dress to comportment. Specifically, the cyclers saw fit to engage in a watermelon-throwing melee during their first jaunt. Such activity allowed men and women to playfully touch, become disheveled, and act in ways strictly forbidden by the formality of the office or selling floor. In the new world of mixed-gender leisure pursuits, white-collar employees celebrated release from the constraints of the office. The cyclers, of course, did not dispense with all their society's mores. Gender equality was out of the question. Men controlled the cycling experience, and unattended women received male "chaperons" for the club's runs.[51] In this vein, the Peirce Alumni Cyclers offered advice directed toward their female members:

A FEW DON'T'S TO THE LADIES.

—Do not scorch [ride fast].
—Don't ride in front of the pacemaker.
—Try to keep in line as much as possible.
—Always ride with the partner assigned to you.
—Don't go out on a run without seeing that your tires are inflated and in good condition.
—Don't go out on a run without putting some graphite on your chain. This will save a good deal of worry and energy.
  (The above also apply to the gentlemen.)[52]

In other words, women had to arrive prepared and avoid being too aggressive or independent. They could not switch partners, even if conversation grew tiresome on the ride. Indeed, the list implies that the women constantly required male guidance. At the same time, following the list's suggestions would have minimized the problems male chaperons might have encountered. For example, it seems to suggest that only men could handle racing. If a female cyclist ran ahead of the pacemaker, she might subsequently tire and slow down her chaperon. The club made male chaperones responsible for emergency repairs as well. Male cyclists clearly viewed women as the weaker sex at play.

Nevertheless, the club's membership was split evenly between men and women. Nationally, women formed 25 to 30 percent of bicycle purchasers in the mid-1890s, and many cycling clubs that formed during the craze included both men and women. In important ways, cycling challenged Victorian mores regarding a woman's place in society and sport. It gave women the freedom to explore the public realm more easily and aggressively.[53] It offered them the opportunity to engage in sports with men, a rarity in the late nineteenth century.[54] Female cycling outfits also challenged fashion traditions. Women increasingly wore loosely fitting clothes and bloomers both on and off their bikes. Their attire masculinized as the cycling craze matured.[55]

For the Peirce Alumni Cyclers, contact between men and women was not limited to runs. Both sexes were involved in all facets of the organization's life, particularly activities centered in the group's clubhouse. In this they were hardly unique, for members of the cycling clubs that dotted the urban landscape in the 1890s did much more than ride bikes. These groups invented their own complex organizational lives, relying on local resources ranging from their own treasuries to the excursion sites available to them. In addition, they formed their own social spaces in clubhouses, where they held dances and parties on a regular basis.[56] In November 1897 the men and women of the Peirce club's furnishing committee decorated the clubhouse the group had recently rented. The committee spread a carpet in the parlor and decorated its walls with pictures of Thomas May Peirce (the Peirce School's founder) and his widow, Mary. The club held a lecture entitled "Patriotism of American Poets" to defray the costs of renting the new space and decorating it. The event, which cost twenty-five cents to attend, drew hundreds of alumni and their guests.[57] Individual members donated books for the clubhouse's library. The house was envisioned as a place for socialization during both winter and summer (when extremes in weather did not allow for cycling). During the winter of 1897–98 the alumni planned weekly entertainments at the site. The organization encouraged members to bring family, friends, and dates to clubhouse functions.[58] For the first major event, a "package party," each of the partygoers brought a wrapped gift. The alumni held an auction of the gifts as the central event of the evening. Partygoers had no idea what each wrapped package contained, which made bidding interesting and fun. All the proceeds went to the organization.[59]

The cyclers filled March 1898 with foul-weather clubhouse activities that involved both genders and a great deal of play. In fact, women cyclers planned all the events. They exercised quite a bit of control in the domestic arena of the clubhouse, while men dictated the tenor of outdoor runs. The cyclers staged "entertainments" each Friday. For the first, a "novelty party," the women devised games in which male cyclers had to perform traditionally female domestic activities such as sewing. Women brought rags, pins, buttons, thread, and other sewing supplies and devised competitions in which men had to show their prowess at timed activities such as sewing buttons and threading needles. Good-natured fun was the rule for the evening—especially, as one commentator put it, for the "gentlemen who were victims of the torture at the hands of the fair sex." Of course, one must assume that the women cyclers derived a great deal of pleasure having the upper hand in a sex-typed play activity, a role completely different from the one they held in the male-dominated office world. The following week's "cobweb party" offered many visitors an innovative game. Prior to the gathering, volunteers unwound a large number of balls of pink string throughout the clubhouse, from "roof to cellar," lacing them around furniture and fixtures, into a complex cobweb of knots and tangles. Participants who chose to play were given the task of untangling and rewinding the balls of string. The quickest finishers of each sex received a prize. A woman finished first, displaying a skill in dealing with knots and tangles that "would have made an experienced sailor green with envy." Again, the cyclists were aware that their clubhouse play involved activities emphasizing domestic skills. One alumnus suggested pointedly that, like the sailor, "the male members who participated in the contest were also green, but not with envy. Of course a lady finished first, but one member remarked that he thought curiosity had something to do with that. (That's unkind.)" The gathering on the third Friday of March involved the club's women showing off their musical talents for the men. Piano solos, recitations, and mandolin performances punctuated the evening. The last week of March saw both men and women cooperate in staging a series of shadow puppet performances. Quite clearly club members knew that, when in the clubhouse, they were in territory controlled by women cyclers. Within its walls, women made the rules, women possessed the special skills that won recognition, and most important, women dictated the nature of mixed-gender play.[60]

The Peirce Alumni Cyclers, by creating their own club, imitated the middle-class cycling clubs that dotted Philadelphia. At play the clerks and salespeople involved in this organization pedaled into an imaginary future in which they envisioned themselves crossing into more lucrative, firmly middle-class occupations or marriages. Cycling was a dress rehearsal for an eventual journey into a new frontier, membership in the middle class. As I mentioned previously, being a cyclist required large expenditures for bicycles, bicycle repairs, spare parts, and clothing, as well as for food and lodging on longer trips. This kept cycle ownership out of reach for most clerical workers until the mid 1890s, when bike prices declined. Even when these prices went down, however, cycling was still quite an investment and out of reach for many blue-collar workers. So, by forming a club and purchasing their own bikes, the Peirce alumni distanced themselves from the working class and allied with professionals and small-business owners.

Nationally, middle-class urban cyclists formed thousands of clubs in the late 1880s and first half of the 1890s. As early as 1892 more than thirty-one cycling clubs existed in Philadelphia. Many had clubhouses located in northwestern neighborhoods close to the city's Fairmount Park. Mostly businessmen and professionals participated in these early clubs. Eleven rather elite clubs with substantial clubhouses formed the Associated Cycling Clubs (A.C.C.) of Philadelphia in 1888. This umbrella association promoted races, publicly defended cyclists' interests, and sponsored cycle shows that encouraged the fad in the city. In February 1892 the A.C.C. held a show in Industrial Hall, where it exhibited manufacturers' and cycle shops' latest goods.[61]

The cycling fad of the 1890s was massive. Saloonkeepers, theater owners, and even producers of luxury goods such as watches, jewelry, and fine suits lamented business losses they attributed to the expanding bicycle craze, as prosperous Americans diverted their money into cycle-related expenditures.[62] In addition, small towns along the roads commonly traveled by urban cyclists touring the countryside complained about increased traffic. Every Sunday in 1896 when conditions permitted, about ten thousand cyclists crossed the Delaware River from Philadelphia to Camden and its southern New Jersey hinterlands. This traffic encouraged taverns to stay open on "dry" Sundays. Southern New Jersey's residents accommodated the cycling crowd's collective thirst in more informal ways as well. Local farmers on Whitehorse Pike sold beer "openly over the tailgates of their wagons," upsetting local churches.[63] Philadelphia's Hart Cycle Company, a retailer, published a clever promotional booklet in 1892. At a basic level, it encouraged bicycle purchases by showing off the latest models. In addition, it listed the asphalt streets leading to Fairmount Park and supplied directions for the easiest ways to get to the park's entrances. The booklet listed cycling clubs in the city as well as important bicycle magazines. The promotional tabulated mileage for trips to places around Philadelphia, including Willow Grove, Bryn Mawr, Chadds Ford, and Gulph Mills. This chart indexed accommodation sites, provided distances from Philadelphia's City Hall, and gave directions. In the early years of the cycling craze, Hart's promotional wove a web of consumerism for cyclists. It connected buying the machine, joining a club, planning an excursion, and obtaining accommodations. This web of consumerism was well set to snare office and sales workers as soon as cycles became affordable for them in the mid-1890s.[64]

In 1896 American manufacturers assembled 1.2 million new bicycles. In the mid-1890s a new high-grade bike cost $125; a new low-grade one cost $50. At century's end more than six thousand bike repair shops existed in the United States.[65] In many ways the marketing of bicycles presaged the marketing of automobiles. Installment buying was available. Manufacturers came out with new models yearly and relied on planned obsolescence to fuel bike purchases. One could obtain a better deal if one waited until model year closeouts in department stores and bike shops. Merchants offered credit for trade-ins.[66] One could also purchase used bikes for as little as $15 by 1896.[67] By mid-decade these incentives had made the bicycle obtainable for clerks and salespeople. What had been a fairly elite pastime gained a wider following. In the 1890s Americans spent tens of millions of dollars on bike purchases, maintenance, cycling outfits, maps, and accessories such as bells, lanterns, and tire repair kits (Fairmount Park cycling rules required riders to provide lamps for their vehicles, and each bike had to have "a bell with a spring attachment which [could] be distinctly heard at a distance of thirty (30) yards—sleigh bells being inadmissible.")[68] The Peirce Alumni Cyclers relished the consumption that went along with their pastime. Men bragged to one another about their new purchases, as a bit of gossip printed in the *Peirce School Alumni Journal* suggests: "Blank has a new Columbia, Wills, a Cleveland Tandem and Sinberg, a new Yellow fellow."[69] Special committees reviewed the use of uniforms and hats.[70] And of course, the club spent a fair amount of money on renting the clubhouse and furnishing it.

Middle-class cycling clubs participated in discussions of local political issues, especially road maintenance in their cities. The Peirce Alumni Cyclers followed suit, for they, too, discussed political matters. They shared the interests of the League of American Wheelmen, a national cycling organization formed in 1880. The league monitored road quality for cyclists and continuously encouraged agitation for improvements. The alumni cyclers avidly followed Philadelphia City Council proceedings regarding local road conditions and construction. The club rallied its membership to oppose the extension of streetcar tracks in the Thirty-second Ward, where the clubhouse lay. In this matter they symbolically chose leisure over work, for the city's network of streetcars daily conveyed thousands of workers to their jobs.[71] Their attitudes about the city's attempts to improve streetcar lines around the clubhouse underscored the important place that conspicuous forms of recreation had in the lives of these office and sales employees. The cyclers' protests implied that their leisure pursuits were more important than the daily work routines of thousands of Philadelphia workers. By asserting this, they emphasized the fact that they could indulge in such play. They could purchase and maintain bikes. Their lifestyles and personal budgets accommodated middle-class behaviors. The alumni had ample time off to recreate, and they were organized enough to assert their right to play over the city's need to lay trolley track.

The bicycle gave white-collar workers a taste of independent mobility before the advent of the automobile. The two-wheeler let them go anywhere good roads led when pleasant weather prevailed. Trolley schedules and routes failed to constrain a cyclist's wanderlust.[72] As Gary Allen Tobin has noted, the craze spawned America's first real "tourist service sector."[73] Whether elite or not, clubs and individual cyclists planned excursions beyond the city into the countryside, where they spent their money at local inns, watering holes, and repair shops when needed. They also had to purchase maps and food for their journeys. The bicycle provided riders with a means to venture outside the built-up city on their own terms. They chose their own destinations, controlled the pace at which they rode, and selected the stops they made along the trip. Cycling benefited the flesh, as Frank N. Thomson, president of the Peirce Alumni Cyclers, declared: "The physical being is toned and strengthened in every muscle and tendon" when one sets out on a bike. Riding anywhere would improve a person's bodily condition, but Thompson added that only the careful selection of destination could benefit the senses and the mind. Pleasant landscapes comfort the eye, and cycling in a beautiful environment "affords all the restful recreation born of new scenes and thoughts."[74] This benefit was particularly important to office and sales workers who labored in mundane indoor jobs. It seems fitting that the Peirce cyclists reveled in touring the green bounty of Fairmount Park and the bucolic periphery of Philadelphia.

The club crisscrossed Fairmount's vast acres of greenery, visiting locations such as Hunting Park, Belmont, and the Wissahickon Valley. The park's many trails and beautiful scenery drew thousands of cyclists in the 1890s. At the beginning of the cycling craze in 1891, cyclists made 136,228 trips into Fairmount, according to park guard estimates. This number surely rose throughout the decade. So many cyclists invaded Fairmount that the park's commissioners devised an elaborate set of rules for two-wheeling enthusiasts. Most of the directives focused on maintaining control of the vehicle. For example, cyclists could not raise their legs higher than "three-quarters of the radius of the front wheel above the axle thereof." Presumably this regulation also maintained a minimum level of middle-class decorum.[75]

Additionally, the alumni visited suburban areas on the fringe of the city, such as Bryn Mawr and Fox Chase. As the trip to Valley Green indicates, the club planned activities when they reached their destinations. On an evening in October 1897 the cyclers ventured out to Bryn Mawr, traveling to this Main Line suburb to visit the home of a physician who was friendly with the club. The doctor met the Peirce cyclists at the outskirts of town and escorted them to his home. As they approached the house, the alumni heard strains of piano music on the evening air. Inside an "elegant repast" awaited.[76] The cyclers danced the night away and left just before midnight, finding their way back to the clubhouse by the light of their bike lanterns. The evening's activities emphasized the boundary-crossing nature of bike riding for the club. Its members directly sampled middle-class living by absorbing the niceties of a comfortably appointed suburban home. They engaged in mixed-gender entertainment by twirling about on the dance floor, and they pedaled out of the city, into the suburbs.

In early June 1898 the Peirce Alumni Cyclers held a "strawberry festival" in their clubhouse. Nearly two hundred people attended and danced the entire evening. This was the last major event for the cyclists, however. Several forces caused the club's rather abrupt demise. For one thing, Philadelphia's sweltering summers broiled away their enthusiasm. The summertime heat and humidity rendered riding or even socializing at the clubhouse uncomfortable. Indeed, the clubhouse received little use, and club members realized that it was too remote from their residences and that it cost too much to rent.[77] In September the cyclers decided to quit the lease. These enthusiasts reasoned that the more successful cycling groups in Philadelphia had geographically based memberships concentrated near their clubhouses. Peirce alumni lived scattered throughout the city. Many experienced difficulty cycling from home to the clubhouse or making the trip via streetcars. Indeed, few lived closer than a forty-minute streetcar ride to the clubhouse. It is interesting that the alumni chose to get rid of the domestic clubhouse, where women held the upper hand in leisure activities. The cyclers concluded that they could survive without it—that it served only a secondary purpose. Unfortunately, the loss of a gathering place signaled the club's death. Finally and more broadly, cycling fell out of style throughout urban America soon after the club coalesced. By the turn of the century, the fad had fizzled. It remains unclear exactly why, but the advent of the automobile, the continued improvement of streetcar lines, and the development of subways coincided with the end of cycling as an adult pastime.[78] People found these means to offer more convenient ways to leave the city than did the two-wheeler.

As the winter activities of the Peirce Alumni Cyclers suggest, Philadelphia's office and sales workers created their own nightlife, which included social activities not linked to sports. The city's clerks formed theatrical organizations and choral and instrumental groups, threw parties, and held banquets. Reflecting trends in the public nightlife that emerged in urban America in the late nineteenth and early twentieth centuries, clerical workers invented a largely mixed-gender evening leisure culture, including especially parties and banquets.

Every year after 1892 the Peirce Alumni Association held an annual banquet. Association committees began organizing the event months in advance, planning the menu, preparing entertainment, printing invitations, arranging for speakers, selling tickets, and renting a hall for the occasion. Hundreds of alumni and guests attended these banquets. In 1906 the association voted to suspend rules that permitted only alumni to attend. According to the membership, this allowed female members to bring escorts, a desirable outcome because "the question of getting to the banquet hall and home again [was] sometimes serious."[79] It also allowed men to bring dates. The Reverend Dr. Russell H. Conwell, founder of Temple University, spoke at the 1906 banquet at the city's Majestic Ballroom. Conwell, a proponent of the gospel of wealth, was known for his "Acres of Diamonds" speech, a paean to the pursuits of riches that he delivered countless times in the late nineteenth century. His audience at the banquet listened intently to the address, which specifically focused on advertising. The association also sponsored periodic lectures, such as the Reverend Charles Edward Stowe's presentation on Abraham Lincoln in 1913. After the lecture the alumni listened to an organ recital.[80]

Not all self-created nightlife was so sedentary. The Peirce Alumni Association scheduled annual dances. Attendance usually hovered between 100 and 150. Hired orchestras played, drinks flowed, and couples made turns around the dance floor. The association arranged the 1906 dance at the Rittenhouse Hotel. They decorated the rented hall with potted plants, palms, and flowers. If dancers grew weary or wanted to engage in conversation, they could retire to the divans and easy chairs scattered throughout the hall.[81] Strawbridge and Clothier employees, too, organized similar dances. In 1915 they planned a summer series of frolics under a pavilion constructed on the store's athletic fields. Six hundred employees and their guests attended the first dance in early June, and for the rest of the summer Thursday nights were reserved for the popular social events. The Strawbridge and Clothier Employee Orchestra furnished music for this summer of dancing.[82]

Philadelphia's clerks developed their own musical groups. In 1904 male and female employees formed the Strawbridge and Clothier Chorus, a reincarnation of a chorus formed in 1881. This first, short-lived group had performed at many of the entertainments provided by management in the late nineteenth century but fell apart in the mid-1880s. An all-male group existed briefly in the mid-1880s as well. The twentieth-century chorus was organized specifically to commemorate the twenty-fifth anniversary of the store's employee relief association, but the group developed into a permanent organization numbering over one hundred singers. It performed at various store functions and regularly sang at Willow Grove Park. The group also played benefits. In April 1906 it sang to raise money for the victims of the San Francisco Earthquake. The ensemble thrived in the early twentieth century. Its concerts at Willow Grove attracted immense crowds of employees and general fans.[83] The June 29, 1909, evening concert drew throngs of listeners to the outdoor pavilion. Male singers wore evening attire, while the women wore white dresses that radiated the electric light.[84] The chorus held concerts at the Academy of Music, too. The group rehearsed for many hours, and bonds among members were tight. After the store closed on Christmas Eve 1908, for example, chorus members serenaded H. J. Tilley, a member of store management and the man who rejuvenated the group in 1904. The serenaders delayed rushing home to their families so that they could surprise their leader. They presented to him a handmade pillow stitched with the chorus's emblem. The rest of the chorus's officers also received gifts.[85]

Strawbridge and Clothier's female employees in the inspecting department formed the Clover Mandolin Club in 1906. The first "class" elected officers and a teacher to guide those uninitiated in the stringed instrument. They met every Friday for lessons. After the club had learned several pieces, the entire inspecting department received invitations to formal concerts. The club continued its studies for the length of a schoolyear and then held a graduation, the women forging close friendships throughout that year. On graduation each mandolinist collected a personalized, humorous graduation favor; for example, Rhoda Salmon earned a knife to "sharpen her flats."[86] The club remained active throughout the early 1900s, offering new members a year of mandolin instruction and putting on performances. Membership fluctuated between twenty and forty. It is unclear whether members from previous years continued playing or a complete set of new musicians joined each year.

The commercial leisure economy that emerged in the 1890s was closely linked to technological innovations such as the phonograph, movies, roller coasters, and automobiles. The advent of electricity played a significant role in stimulating the development of nightlife based on commercial leisure pursuits. Electrified trolley lines brought patrons to theaters and amusement parks that relied on electricity to entice patrons with gaudily lit facades and provide their entertainments. The first electric service in Philadelphia sparked to life in 1881. That year, the Brush Electric Company lit Chestnut Street between the Delaware and Schuylkill rivers. Soon thereafter the city's theaters adopted electricity first to ignite their gas lamps and later to provide lighting directly.[87] Electric lights warmly lit streets near commercial leisure establishments. Brighter streets appeared safer and more inviting. The excellent interior and exterior lighting produced by electricity and incandescent bulbs helped revolutionize the city's entertainment economy. In 1880 seventeen theaters existed in the city;[88] by 1913 more than 350 lined the streets.[89]

Between 1890 and 1920 a huge array of commercialized leisure pursuits emerged in urban America. From dance halls to roller coasters, these activities offered office and sales workers many choices. Three types of commercialized leisure will serve to indicate the variety of possibilities available in Philadelphia: professional theatrical productions (ranging from vaudeville to, occasionally, opera), vacations, and outdoor activities pursued at venues such as Fairmount Park and Willow Grove.[90]

Until the 1890s Philadelphians faced limited theater choices. This situation resulted partly from a lack of lighting technology and partly from the city's elite, who tended to dislike professional theater.[91] Prior to the advent of commercialized leisure pursuits and nightlife, the middle classes largely did not attend theater. Their leisure activities centered more on the home. White-collar workers did occasionally venture out to museums, but museums in the late nineteenth century were closer in spirit to present-day carnivals than to museums as we now know them.[92] They involved a great deal of theatricality. A patron at an establishment such as the Arch Street Museum (Ninth and Arch streets) paid to see menageries of strange creatures, mermaids, and multiheaded beasts. Often the museums exhibited people with grotesque deformities. B. F. Keith, who eventually became a nationally known vaudeville theater impresario, received his start in entertainment working in circuses and as an employee of Bunnell's, a famous dime museum in New York. When he opened his own museum in Boston in 1883, Keith publicized as the museum's initial feature attraction an underweight baby that allegedly tipped the scales at one and one-half pounds. At the end of the nineteenth century Keith moved away from the freak-show exhibits of dime museums and became a leading figure in the popularization of vaudeville theater. Keith made his transition from museums to vaudeville in Boston, and he succeeded by applying lessons learned from his earlier career. He knew that the oddities displayed in dime museums were not the only things that attracted the middle classes. Promises of sanitized crowds and propriety enticed them as well. When Keith opened his first theater in 1886, he therefore emphasized affordable ticket prices, performances devoid of any raunchy or off-color material, and comfortable, clean seating. The theater soon attracted white- and blue-collar men and women as well as children. He brought these innovations to Philadelphia in 1889 when he opened the Bijou, a variety theater, at the corner of Eighth and Race streets.[93]

The Bijou's opening marked a watershed for the city, because it helped legitimize variety theater. Prior to the 1880s middle-class tastes deemed variety shows inappropriate, especially for women. Keith and E. F. Albee, his partner, billed the shows at the Bijou as family entertainment. Keith tagged his new theater the "Drawing Room Theater of Philadelphia—High Class, Refined Entertainment."[94] He strove to keep the theater and the sidewalk in front of it clean. Ticket prices ranged between ten and twenty-five cents, and the stage was constantly alive with entertainers. This reflected Keith's innovative policy of "continuous performance," which he had worked out in Boston. Patrons could come and go at will while the acts continued to flow across the stage. With cheap prices and promises of respectability, the partners marketed their theater to the youthful clerks. Moreover, the Bijou offered a perfect setting for gender-integrated leisure, an acceptable destination for young couples on dates. This reflected national trends as vaudeville and variety theater began drawing millions of urbanites; white-collar workers constituted the largest segment of this audience.[95] Not all were equally happy with this newfound respectability, however. Some theatergoers used to more raucous houses initially found it difficult to swallow the Bijou management's expectations for audience etiquette. Before performances during the Bijou's first several months, Albee lectured theatergoers on comportment.

On Christmas Day 1895 the Bijou became the first Philadelphia theater to show a true motion picture. Shortly thereafter movies formed a regular part of the playbill. From the late 1890s until the rise of movie palaces in the 1920s, motion pictures generally played as part of the program in vaudeville theaters throughout the city. The number of these "combination" houses exploded in the 1910s. In 1913 alone seventy combination houses arose in Philadelphia. Additionally, a handful of venues devoted solely to big-screen movies existed on Market and Vine streets.[96] Nonetheless, before 1920 clerks and salespeople most often caught movies as parts of a vaudeville show.

The Bijou was the most famous vaudeville stage in Philadelphia until 1902, when Keith opened his new "Million Dollar" vaudeville house at Eleventh and Chestnut streets. The Bijou went into gradual decline as its surrounding neighborhood became the city's tenderloin district. After 1910 it turned to burlesque.[97] Keith's Eleventh and Chestnut Theater, however, gained immense popularity. As he had done with the Bijou, Keith promoted this theater as uplifting, morally sound entertainment. "High-Class Vaudeville," the "Home of the Wholesome Shows," read publicity materials.[98] Clerks flocked to this type of venue. Brilliant white terra cotta adorned the theater's facade, and the immaculately clean gold-and-scarlet decor overwhelmed patrons once inside. Catering to the needs of patrons at Keith's, a "small army of ticket-sellers, doormen, check-room boys, messengers, footmen, and matrons, in distinct uniforms[,] were placed at strategic spots throughout the theater. During performances, beknickered ushers passed up and down the aisles bearing 'distilled ice water.'"[99]

Like the Bijou, the new theater featured continuous performance. Monday through Saturday two daily marathon shows were run. The first started at 1:00 P.M. and ran for four hours. The second finished at 10:30 P.M. Keith's had no break between individual acts, and patrons came and went as they pleased. Many cut out during the films the theater screened.[100] The shows were astoundingly eclectic. A typical bill had twelve acts ranging from acrobatics to one-act plays. In 1910 the "Home of the Wholesome Shows" included lectures, dancing, strongman acts, trapeze acts, ethnic comedy, and blackface minstrelsy.[101] Keith's drew entertainers including Will Rogers, Charlie Chaplin, the Marx Brothers, and Al Jolson before their movie fame. Harry Houdini also appeared at Keith's in the 1910s.[102] As the career trajectories of Chaplin and Jolson suggest, the city's vaudeville houses remained popular until the rise of feature movies in the 1920s.

Most clerical workers did not regularly attend operas or serious dramatic theater. It was too expensive. In special circumstances, however, the Peirce Alumni Association arranged for group discounts to theaters frequented by wealthier turn-of-the-century Philadelphians. Between 1909 and 1915 the association organized reduced group rates for its members to shows at the Metropolitan Opera House on North Broad Street. This huge and lavish structure, built by Oscar Hammerstein, opened in November 1908 and held about four thousand people. It originally bore its founder's name—Oscar Hammerstein's Philadelphia Opera House. It quickly ran into financial trouble, however, and Hammerstein sold the house to the prominent Philadelphia financier E. T. Stotesbury in 1909. The new owner renamed it the Metropolitan. Operas played in the house off and on until 1920, when it was again sold and used as a movie palace and vaudeville theater.[103] The Met's management encountered difficulty filling the cavernous halls with patrons. For its first "opera party" in 1909, the alumni association received half-price tickets on four-dollar seats (Hammerstein must have desperately needed patrons), and 190 members seized the deal.[104] After 1910 the alumni association acquired discounts through Stotesbury, who had been one of Peirce's first students.[105]

In the 1910s the association also occasionally landed discounts to serious dramatic presentations. In 1917 its members saw the famous actor John Drew in William Makepeace Thackeray's *Pendennis* at the Broad Street Theater.[106] Each alumnus or alumna paid roughly half-price for a pair of two-dollar seats. The Broad Street Theater, located at Broad and Locust streets, had been built to draw crowds to the city for the Centennial Exhibition. Its architecture mimicked a mosque, but no one could confuse it for a house of faith. Its minarets were painted in gaudy primary hues. Inside, even the box office looked like a minaret. The theater, originally intended to be temporary, stood until 1937. In the late nineteenth century it became the playhouse for the wealthier classes in the city as they increasingly accepted "legitimate" theater.[107] These excursions by clerks into more elite entertainment venues exhibited their longing for movement up the social ladder.

Commercialized leisure pursuits involved more than just nightlife, however. Many office and sales workers also went on vacations, taking full advantage of the time off they received from their employers. Clerical employees were among the first industrial-era workers to secure regular vacations. By 1909 Strawbridge and Clothier was offering one week of vacation annually to those employees who had one year's service; after three years the yearly vacation increased to two weeks.[108] The department store also shortened its Saturday hours in the summertime, which accommodated weekend getaways. Managers in Philadelphia businesses believed that vacationing was good for the white-collar worker. One small-business owner from the city promoted the ways taking a trip could expand the business acumen of men. He urged "young men to take vacations and visit other cities in order to broaden their knowledge as to how this world is made up of different people. The best investment a young man can make, if he has not been outside of his town, is to take a trip to some other big town where they 'do things.'"[109] Strawbridge and Clothier believed that "vacations make better workers." The firm considered getting away from work to be vital to increased productivity. Time off gave workers a chance to recharge their minds and bodies. The store urged workers to spend their free time sensibly, which "means something quite different from racing off to some gay 'resort' and living for a week or two in a continual whirl of late hours and excitement. It means rest; it means quiet; it means extra sleep and cheering intercourse with friends and relaxation of whatever sort best recuperates mind and body."[110] Some clerks and their managers imagined that bosses and workers in the city's offices and the stores formed a "community of interest" that believed in the value of vacationing—it gave them the opportunity to return "refreshed, and with increased physical and mental activity begin another year with renewed interest." Despite the paeans to vacationing uttered by many clerks and bosses, some saleswomen allegedly abused their time away from Strawbridge and Clothier. Some took in extra work, such as typing, to increase income. Others used vacations to cover sicknesses or medical procedures. The store advised saleswomen not to fritter away vacation time by making dresses in preparation for going out. Furthermore, bosses emphasized that nightlife activities were excellent ways to squander one's vacation time and were to be avoided at all costs. Many workers failed to heed their employers' wishes. In their own ways, they used their vacations to get away from their often tedious jobs.[111]

The readers of the *Peirce School Alumni Journal* were treated to regular features detailing the vacations of former students and teachers at the college or the interesting trips of acquaintances. Those who regularly perused the journal's contents learned about some of the faraway places and peoples described in the more ambitious travel narratives. The pages of the *Alumni Journal* carried travelogues describing in awestruck terms extravagant trips taken by former students and other adventurers to distant places throughout North America and the rest of the world, including the Hudson River valley, Chicago, Salt Lake City, Yosemite, the Klondike, Alaska, Cuba, Hungary, Austria, and Africa. The American West received a great deal of treatment. The author of one such tale, Harry S. Sheppard, resigned his job as a private secretary in 1894 to spend a year traveling throughout North America, and he regaled alumni with his stories. His printed recollections of San Francisco's Chinatown were filled with relatively tolerant, intriguing details about Chinese religious observances and the community's New Year celebration.[112] Not all accounts depicted their subjects in as kindly a manner. In fact, two former students told their own tale of a trip to San Francisco's Chinatown. Unlike Sheppard's report, their story was full of racist imagery. The duo suggested that Chinese faith comprised simply the idolatrous worship of "hideously carved figure(s)" and suggested that Chinese immigrants living near the Golden Gate were hopelessly deluded for leaving offerings in front of the statues—"water or tea placed before the Joss, of course[,] evaporates, but the Chinaman believes his God drinks it." The duo reserved their harshest images for their description of an opium den:

The opium smoker is probably the greatest curiosity—a dirty, sickening room, 8x15 without any ventilation, will hold ten to fifteen smokers on shelves. The outfit consists of a small lamp, pipe and a small box of opium. John Chinaman lies on his shelf, takes a little raw opium on a long needle, cooks it by skillful manipulation over the light (it then smells like burnt peanuts), puts it in the bowl of the pipe, which he turns over the fire, and inhales until all the opium is exhausted, when he then exhales the smoke. The process constitutes one "joy" or "pill" and he repeats it until under the influence of the drug. It takes twenty-five or thirty "joys" to put John in dreamland, but one or two would be sufficient for an average man.[113]

Their comments reflected the Americans' emerging fascination with urban vice districts and, more particularly, opium smoking, which became the stuff of sensational newspaper tales in the late nineteenth century.[114] While these authors sought to impress with their brazen storytelling, the preponderance of narratives astonished readers with images of natural wonder. Jennie W. Rogers told of giant redwoods, glaciers, and the thousands of seals perched on the rocks of the Golden Gate.[115] Most office and sales workers could afford only closer destinations, such as Atlantic City, but these articles surely fed their curiosity and wanderlust.[116]

At the turn of the century "the shore"—the New Jersey and Delaware coastlines—lured many of Philadelphia's vacationing office and sales workers. Resort towns dotted the coast and enticed the clerical workforce with their sand, nightlife, and surf. Strawbridge and Clothier management noticed the shore's pull on its employees and attempted to manage their play. In 1909 the store purchased a large beach house in Wildwood, New Jersey, a resort town, and arranged for groups of workers to spend their vacations in it. Initially management intended that the house be used by the young girls who labored in the store, and it charged each vacationer three dollars a week for rent.[117] Strawbridge and Clothier quickly decided to open it to all female employees, probably because the younger ones did not show enough interest to justify limiting its use to them. In 1910 the store opened part of the summer vacation season at the home to all its workers, male and female.[118]

The structure, a four-level Victorian-style house, sported a two-story porch that wrapped around it and afforded a vista of the seashore. The living room held a piano, and the dining room contained mission-style furniture.[119] The edifice was close to Wildwood's boardwalk and main pier. Both lured vacationers with a wide array of entertainment. If vacationers required greater excitement, they could stroll to the nearby Wildwood Speedway, an automobile racecourse. Exhausted thrill seekers could strain only their eyes and view the course from the house, if they chose.[120] A house matron regimented the vacations of the youngest girls. She strictly monitored play and planned activities to amuse her charges. It is unclear whether the vacations of older women who visited the house were as structured.

In the 1890s the Women's Christian Association of Philadelphia (WCA) had a shore house that the city's working women could use for summer vacations. The house, named "Sea Rest," was in Asbury Park, New Jersey. As long as they were Protestant, workers from any occupation could apply for rooms in the house. Time off at Sea Rest must have been particularly attractive to female clerks who had regular vacations. A potential vacationer had to find a friend with whom to apply, because the WCA accepted only pairs. Moreover, they had to apply in person at the WCA's offices at Eighteenth and Arch streets. The organization required applicants to furnish letters of reference, charged each selected candidate seventy-five cents per day to use the house, and limited them a two-week maximum stay.[121]

The most popular shore destination for Philadelphia's clerks was Atlantic City. From its beginnings in 1855, Atlantic City was designed to be an oceanside summer resort town directly connected to the Philadelphia market. By the 1890s it took only fifty minutes to travel by rail between the two cities. Atlantic City drew its visitors primarily from Philadelphia's thousands of office and sales workers.[122] Besides boasting beaches, boardwalks, and piers, the city offered lively vaudeville and variety houses. Clerks and salespeople who had planned for a vacation could afford the costs of vacationing in Atlantic City. An eight-dollar weekly allowance for food and lodging covered expenses at the turn of the century.[123] The city also had roller coasters and thrill rides dotting its piers and boardwalks. Shore resorts such as Atlantic City and Wildwood allowed clerks and salespeople to mingle with the opposite sex and indulge in the luxuries of the emerging leisure economy.

If Philadelphia's clerical workers wanted to enjoy the outdoors for only part of a day or an evening, they had closer venues. Willow Grove Park and Philadelphia's municipal Fairmount Park attracted thousands of office workers and salespeople. Amusement parks and public parks refashioned nature for the urban public's enjoyment—to relieve the tedium of urban life. In the former, paved paths provided easy access to wooded areas and open spaces. Manicured lawns replaced open fields. Plant life and wildlife were strictly managed. Police patrolled the parks to control visitors' behavior. For their part, amusement parks provided commodified versions of the outdoors that melded technology with nature. They transformed natural settings into mechanized pleasure lands. Amusement parks reinvented their landscapes and even mechanized nature. Roller coasters and other thrill rides, as well as Ferris wheels, offered artificial hills superimposed on their natural surroundings. Some rides even featured elaborate internalized landscapes when cars plunged riders into dark tunnels.

Willow Grove Park, owned by the Philadelphia Rapid Transit Company, opened Memorial Day 1896 a handful of miles outside the city. The amusement park drew massive summer crowds throughout the early 1900s, with 3 million people visiting it in 1903. A significant portion of Willow Grove's guests likely toiled in offices and department stores.[124] This and other amusement parks provided environments in which patrons suspended social realities. Adults acted like children and transgressed time-honored social norms. Couples clutched one another on rides. Park dance halls and pavilions provided other venues for interaction between men and women.[125] As discussed previously, the Strawbridge and Clothier Chorus regularly performed at Willow Grove's pavilion. The pavilion was a focal social space, and park management did not charge admission for concerts there. One had to pay only the twenty-cent streetcar fare to get to the park. Prior to World War I nighttime summer concerts there attracted thousands of Philadelphians.

Visitors disembarked from streetcars at the park's special terminal. A tunnel led from it to the music pavilion. Inside the tunnel program boys greeted the crowds, which during daytime often included whole families. Many intended to spend the day at the park, picnic, and catch the concert. A natural tree-lined enclosure helped form the pavilion. A bandshell sat atop a hill that sloped toward a lake. The pavilion accommodated only a small portion of a typical audience. The rest sat on benches lining the hillside down to the lakeshore. To sit in the pavilion, men had to wear ties and jackets. Women also had to don formal attire. Guards stood at the end of each row to keep patrons quiet with warning taps on the shoulder. Listeners who wanted to flout the rules could do so more easily beyond official seating but still within earshot of the concert.

The crowd pleaser John Philip Sousa conducted at Willow Grove from 1901 to 1924, but the park featured many other attractions as well. It contained a bicycle racetrack where regularly scheduled races were held at the end of the nineteenth century. In fact, the world record for the mile was set at Willow Grove in 1898. Roller coasters, too, enticed park patrons. The oldest—the "Nickel Scenic," as Philadelphians affectionately called it—was built in 1896. Its slow ride provided beautiful views of the park. Before the widespread use of automobiles acclimated people to high speeds and rendered the slow ride boring, park-goers could not get enough of the Nickel Scenic.[126] In addition, the park opened a movie theater in 1899. Altogether, Willow Grove encompassed a smorgasbord of entertainment that combined the latest technology with a bucolic setting.

Public parks antedated amusement parks as outdoor spaces specifically designed for leisure. As the Peirce Alumni Cyclers' excursion along the Wissahickon Creek to the Valley Green Inn shows, clerks readily used Philadelphia's Fairmount Park. In July 1906 Sarah J. Hornberger, the head of the toilet goods department at Strawbridge Clothier, treated her fifteen saleswomen to a trip into the park. They played games, ate supper, and listened to a band.[127] The park had its origins in the gardens surrounding the city's large waterworks, which were planned and built in the 1810s and early 1820s on the Schuylkill River. In 1855 a city council act officially inaugurated the park. Twelve years later the Fairmount Park Commission was formed to direct further land purchases. By the late 1800s Fairmount Park was the largest municipal park in the United States, a status it still retains. Fairmount afforded white-collar workers many options for leisure pursuits, such as open fields for picnicking, space set aside for sports, countless pedestrian trails for hiking, waterways for boating, and a zoo. I will focus briefly on the Wissahickon Valley, a long gorge cut by the Wissahickon Creek, for we have proof that salespeople and office workers utilized it for leisure.[128]

Between 1868 and 1873 the Fairmount Park Commission acquired most of the Wissahickon Valley within city limits. Its roughly 1,800 acres brought the park's total acreage to around 4,000 in the early 1870s.[129] In the colonial and early national periods the creek had been a hub for water-powered mills. By the mid-1800s the creek's notoriety as mill center had long passed. The park commission immediately razed most of the remaining mills along the creek.[130] The commission thus wiped out the industrial legacy of the Wissahickon Valley to transform it into a managed forested landscape. The commission did not return the outdoors to pristine natural conditions, however; rather, it transmuted the area into a huge adult playground.

Prior to the park commission's purchase of the valley, the area abounded with taverns and roadhouses that catered to a largely male working- and middle-class clientele. The area's watering holes were known for their catfish, chicken, and waffle dinners. To drum up customers, one even kept its own menagerie comprising monkeys, two black bears, and an assortment of smaller animals. When the Fairmount Park Commission purchased the Wissahickon land, it mandated that all roadhouses and taverns on the property stop serving alcohol. This drove all but the Valley Green Inn out of business.[131] Most were demolished. The Log Cabin, for instance, was destroyed and replaced by a picnic ground; thus, in a striking re-creation of this space, an open, managed natural space patrolled by police supplanted the roadhouse that had dispensed intoxicating beverages and harbored unknown, potentially unseemly elements in its dark recesses. The picnic area appealed to the middle-class sense of propriety appreciated by clerks and salespeople. Moreover, the indoor, largely male social space was changed into an outdoor venue ideal for mixed-gender interaction. In response to the leveling of these taverns, businesses sprang up along the creek just outside park territory to serve hungry, thirsty, and exhausted park visitors who had not planned on picnicking.

The valley extended considerable leisure opportunities to its patrons. Park management limited a wide, well-kept path along much of the valley to nonautomotive traffic. It was perfect for cycling or strolling. Hiking and bridle paths stemmed off this main trail. Beautiful scenery abounded, as did ample picnic grounds. The Fairmount Park Guard patrolled the area and had the authority to arrest troublemakers.[132] The restored natural beauty of the valley gave Philadelphia's clerks an escape from their city within its limits. Streetcar lines rendered the Wissahickon, as well as Fairmount Park in general, easily accessible. This natural playground supplied much respite from the office or selling floor.

* * *

In the late nineteenth and early twentieth centuries, Philadelphia's clerks produced their own leisure activities through formally organized groups. Clerical employees also acted as individual consumers in the new leisure economy. These distinctions are helpful in understanding how white-collar workers spent their lives outside offices. The atomization that the industrial-era office and department store occasioned through long hours and increasingly mechanized work did not transfer into leisure pursuits. These workers created a rich group life away from the workplace. The Peirce Alumni Association and the many employee organizations formed at Strawbridge and Clothier attest to this. Clerks also avidly consumed leisure entertainments, filling vaudeville houses and amusement parks.

Clerical workers mingled with professionals, proprietors, and managers in the leisure organizations they created. Both salespeople and managers were active in the same clubs formed by the Strawbridge and Clothier workforce. Clerical workers, proprietors, and professionals likewise mingled in the Peirce Alumni Association. This indicates the enchantment that middle-class life held for clerks and salespeople. Not only did they dream of moving up the occupational ladder, but they also liked spending leisure time with those a rung above. When discounted tickets became available for opera performances or legitimate theater, clerks in the Peirce Alumni Association snapped them up. By attending these venues and thus associating with individuals above them in the social hierarchy, office and sales workers posed as full-fledged members of the middle class. Clerks imitated wealthier Philadelphians' other pastimes, too (for example, by embracing cycling). They even went on vacations to Atlantic City, mimicking the globe-trotting travels of their "social betters." It is thus quite interesting that, as the following chapter discusses, masquerade played a significant role in the leisure lives of people toiling in the stores and offices of Philadelphia. Copying the play of those higher on the social ladder fueled their dreams of social climbing.

Gender played important roles in the leisure pursuits of clerks, as it in other aspects of their lives. Their recreation included both same-sex and mixed activities. Male clerks used sports, especially baseball, to affirm masculine bonds and friendship while their workplaces feminized. Male teams promoted the competitive nature of sports, which neatly matched the initiative and ambition men were supposed to display in their occupations. A team's climb up the rankings in a league nicely matched a young man's scramble up the career ladder. Athletics for women, however, revolved around maintaining good health. Just as social commentators discouraged ambition for female clerks, athletic competition among women was out of the question. Regardless, like male sports teams, all-woman leisure organizations such as the Clover Mandolin Club affirmed same-gender friendships that had developed in the workplace. But gender's impact on the recreation of clerks was more complex. As consumers in the new leisure economy, these clerks learned to spend free time with members of the opposite sex in vaudeville houses, movie theaters, public and amusement parks, and mixed-gender clubs such as the Peirce Alumni Cyclers. Their play often mirrored the nation's transition from Victorian ideals to more modern scruples. Philadelphia's clerks, involved in both mixed- and single-gender play, straddled the Victorian world of separate spheres and the modern world that featured men and women playing together while away from work.

Strawbridge and Clothier rotunda, 1898 (reproduced by permission of the Hagely Museum and Library, Pictorial Collections)

Strawbridge and Clothier saleswomen and customers at hat counters (reproduced by permission of the Hagely Museum and Library, Pictorial Collections)

Strawbridge and Clothier Mandolin Club Minstrels, 1910 (reproduced by permission of the Hagely Museum and Library, Pictorial Collections)

"Elevator Courtesy," from *Store Chat,* Jan. 15, 1910, p. 27 (reproduced by permission of the Hagely Museum and Library, Pictorial Collections)

"Elevator Courtesy," from *Store Chat,* Jan. 15, 1910, p. 27 (reproduced by permission of the Hagely Museum and Library, Pictorial Collections)

"A Thoughtless Action," from *Store Chat,* Dec. 15, 1915, p. 12 (reproduced by permission of the Hagely Museum and Library, Pictorial Collections)

Karl Graff, of Strawbridge and Clothier's telephone service, from *Store Chat,* Feb. 15, 1910, p. 60 (reproduced by permission of the Hagely Museum and Library, Pictorial Collections)

Employees at Wildwood, N.J., beach, from *Store Chat*, June 10, 1914, p. 115 (reproduced by permission of the Hagely Museum and Library, Pictorial Collections)

Employees at Wildwood, N.J., vacation home, from *Store Chat*, July 15, 1912, p. 185 (reproduced by permission of the Hagely Museum and Library, Pictorial Collections)

Strawbridge and Clothier baseball team, 1910 (reproduced by permission of the Hagely Museum and Library, Pictorial Collections)

5 Workplace Virtues, Rebellion, and Race

In the late nineteenth and early twentieth centuries, clerical workers were constantly bombarded by messages regarding the nature of the ideal employee. Beginning in high school and in business colleges, and later when they entered the workforce, their teachers and employers reiterated models of ideal behavior in numerous ways. The content of classroom lectures and workplace sermons has been lost to us, but important sources describing these expectations have survived. Advice columns in employee magazines dispensed detailed images of the model worker. The pages of the *Strawbridge & Clothier Store Chat* contained mountains of information regarding the quintessential salesperson. The *Peirce School Alumni Journal* likewise preached to its readers about comportment in the workplace. Using *Store Chat* and the *Alumni Journal* allows us to reconstruct the paragons of deportment bandied about in the clerical world. Teasing out the actual behavior of clerks on the job is a bit more tricky, but in this regard, too, these publications are some of the best materials on which to draw. According to these sources, the model clerk exhibited several essential traits commonly discussed in the late nineteenth century. The most important of these virtues—loyalty to the firm, industriousness, thrift, and temperance—reflected themes that had been peppered throughout the exhortations of moralists and bosses since the times of Benjamin Franklin and were still prevalent in popular success manuals of the day.[1]

The ideals absorbed by Philadelphia office and sales workers profoundly influenced their lives. Taken together, the workplace virtues encouraged men and women in the office or store to view their tenure there as preparation for future endeavors. Nonetheless, the vision of the model worker was deeply affected by gender dynamics in the workplace. Essentially, men and women acquired different versions of the ideals, versions that diverged over ambition. Whether it was received by men or women, however, the image of the virtuous worker proved popular among clerical employees. There was little collective opposition to these ideals. Instead, disgruntled men and women in the office and on the selling floor turned to more individualistic forms of rebellion, breaking work rules and sometimes embezzling company funds. Moreover, these powerful workplace ideals reached beyond work. For example, many employees indulged in blackface minstrelsy as both performers and consumers during their time away from their jobs, an activity through which they forged a notion of whiteness that referred both to workplace ideals and to the racist content of the minstrelsy they imbibed. In fact, through minstrelsy, the traits of the exemplary worker became white traits.

In 1882 the Strawbridge and Clothier store superintendent Clarkson Clothier addressed his workers at a store-sponsored concert. He emphasized that workers and management should strive "to foster that spirit of loyalty to the house that shows itself by clear cut thorough work."[2] Good work clearly indicated devotion to the firm. The message persisted at Strawbridge and Clothier throughout the early twentieth century. In 1906 a list of ideals published in *Store Chat* ranked loyalty to the store and oneself first. This formulation of loyalty, which connected self and store, considered the individual worker's best interests to be the same as the business's.[3] The relationship oddly yoked individualism to obedience: what was good for the store and management was good for the individual worker. Workers quickly comprehended that keeping their mouths shut at work offered one of the best ways of displaying fealty to the store. Throughout the city's white-collar workplaces, bosses encouraged employees to use discretion when discussing their jobs with co-workers or people outside the office. Office and sales workers often had their hands on sensitive information that crossed their desks or counters as dictation, budgets, or memoranda. Painfully aware of this, employers sought to hire individuals who could be "implicitly trusted" and were "proof to temptation."[4] These attitudes encouraged an air of secrecy in the office or on the selling floor. Workers had to know what not to divulge. To err on the side of caution and say nothing regarding one's job seemed the best rule. When the *Peirce School Alumni Journal* published a list of twenty useful hints about appropriate workplace behavior, three of the top four hints dealt with loyalty. Bosses demanded respect from their underlings. Employees had to be "mum" about "matters passing through [their] hands," and "silent about all office business."[5]

Managers and advice columnists also maintained that hard work conferred not only ample earnings but also pleasure. An employee should not "rejoice at having secured an easy position." Rather, these authors suggested, good workers looked for jobs that taxed their talents to the utmost. Commentators considered easy jobs stultifying.[6] In addition, they asserted that success did not occur instantly; the people toiling in the office and on the selling floor had to devote years of labor to achieve it. The ideal employee struggled to exceed management's expectations, ventured commentators. In the large stores and offices, where "the temptation to become a clock-watcher [was] very great," clerks and salespeople had to do something to distinguish them-selves.[7] Industriousness seemed the best thing to set oneself apart from more ordinary counterparts.

Thrift was also important in the conceptualization of the ideal clerical worker. Bosses and commentators urged Philadelphia clerks to practice self-denial when it came to their monetary resources. Overindulgence in luxuries and frills spawned evil.[8] In particular, loose personal spending habits might encourage workplace theft. Model workers not only avoided squandering their pay, however; they actively strove to save money. Bosses told their sub-ordinates that today's austerity would pay off during periods of misfortune or old age. Ideally, thrift meant a habit of saving fixed amounts at regular intervals.[9] Strawbridge and Clothier went further, however, advancing be-yond simply editorializing about thrift. It implemented programs designed to nurture frugality in its workforce. In 1884, following the suggestion of two workers, the store created a voluntary savings fund for its employees.[10] Men and women deposited money with the fund, which was invested with the store and earned interest. They could borrow money and take out loans through the fund. Additionally, in 1907 Strawbridge and Clothier created a pension fund from which members who had worked in the store for fifteen years or more could receive aid after retirement or infirmity. Employees regularly contributed to the fund, and the store donated $35,000 in 1912.

Items in *Store Chat* and the *Peirce School Alumni Journal* also celebrated temperance and delineated proper behavior for men and women in their private lives. In a unique display of passion, one Strawbridge and Clothier employee, F. Estella Paine, devised a distinctive temperance-themed costume for a Halloween party held at a Center City YWCA in 1909. Paine won first prize in the costume competition for her ensemble, which was based on the *North American*, a Philadelphia newspaper that had a policy of not printing liquor advertisements. To make her costume, Paine had pleated copies of the paper into a full, empire-waist outfit. Dozens of copies of the paper's masthead adorned the top portion of the outfit, while a panel reading "I Am a NORTH AMERICAN Girl Because THE NORTH AMERICAN Does Not Print LIQUOR ADS" ran down its entire front. In addition, the young woman carried a bundle of *North Americans,* a trumpet, and a bearded mask whose whiskers bore the slogan "We Print No Objectionable Advertisements." An engraving of her outfit ran in the Strawbridge and Clothier employee journal.[11] Another antidrink commentary aimed at Strawbridge and Clothier employees came from Fr. Joseph L. J. Kirlin, a Catholic priest from Philadelphia. He denounced intoxicating beverages and assured that combining "business and 'booze'" led to unemployment.[12] For Peirce graduates, letters toward the end of a list entitled "The Alphabet of Success" and published in the *Alumni Journal* warned:

> *T*ouch not, taste not, handle not intoxicating drinks.
> *U*se your leisure for improvement.
> *V*enture not upon the threshold of wrong.
> *W*atch carefully over your passions. [emphasis added][13]

The alphabet laid out a clear message regarding alcohol. Letters *U, V,* and *W* also suggested to office and sales workers that improper leisure activities (beyond venturing into the saloon) meant certain downfall. Behavior dubbed immoral by mainstream society, such as premarital sexual contact and involvement in prostitution, surely stood on the "threshold of wrong" and were to be avoided by controlling one's passions.[14]

All in all, then, turn-of-the-century commentators encouraged self-sacrifice and moderation in the private lives of workers. Model employees, they said, should labor beyond the workplace to preserve the personal character deemed critical to success on the job; idleness, however, would lead to perdition. Consequently, workers were encouraged to spend their free time cultivating their minds and bodies.[15] Above all, however, as one writer said in a modern-sounding turn of phrase, the ideal clerk has "learned to resist all temptations to throw either money or time away. He has learned to say NO."[16] Success meant "sacrifices in personal pleasure many, many times."[17] Any form of dissipation or bawdy entertainment outside the workplace impugned one's character, harmed one's chances at fortune, and most important, sapped one's concentration and energy at work. If this was not enough, the publications also featured observations about all these ideals written by renowned national figures, such as Marcus A. Hanna and Andrew Carnegie, as well as prominent Philadelphians, such as the financier Edward T. Stotesbury, traction magnate Peter A. B. Widener, and Temple University founder Russell H. Conwell—people many clerical workers admired as extremely successful examples of these very traits.[18] These champions of capital were the heroes of the virtuous employee.

Nevertheless, no universal model of the ideal worker covered both men and women. Commentators bent the virtues along gender lines, fashioning versions of manhood and womanhood that workers were supposed to emulate. Authors expected both men and women to spend only a brief period in the clerical world. Virtuous male employees exhibited ambition while loyally serving the firm. They hoped to quickly climb out of office or sales jobs and into more respectable positions. The idea of remaining subservient on the selling floor or in the office represented a degree of gender-typed failure to many men, largely because this was what commentators expected of clerking women during their careers. As Judy Hilkey has noted, Gilded Age success literature masculinized willpower, and it formed a central component of ambition. Weakness and passivity were seen as female traits.[19] Male clerks in the city were advised to "aim high" and dream of becoming "a bank president, railway superintendent, officer of a corporation, partner in a prominent firm, or the like."[20] Focusing their gaze up the class ladder and exercising ambition allowed men to separate themselves from the women working alongside them.

For men, ambition and loyal service were not seen as antithetical. Rather, they reinforced each another. Supposedly only when striving to better himself could a male clerk best serve his employer and learn how to be a manager or a small-business owner. A model male clerk might start out as an errand boy or telegraph operator, but he dreamed of the boardroom. Merit, not favoritism, elicited promotion from employers in this ideal vision.[21] Archetypical office men did not worry about salaries, for earnings naturally increased with hard work and ambition. Luck did not factor into ambition; one made his own luck.[22]

The depiction of the ideal office man as ambitious was not new to the industrial period, for ambition underlay the entire system of apprenticeship in the preindustrial office world, but the preindustrial office had coupled ambition with the notion that today's clerk would become tomorrow's business owner. In the industrial period ambitious male office workers dreamed not only of possible proprietorship but also of climbing the corporate ladder and entering management. Incorporation altered the dreams of men. Being a sales manager, chief bookkeeper, or department head, while not too far removed from run-of-the-mill office drudgery, allowed the men who filled these positions to be more assertive than did laboring as a bookkeeper or filing clerk. Even though they still reported to higher-ups, these managers directed and evaluated the toil of common office employees. They set the pace of work, enforced rules, and to some degree were involved in hiring or firing decisions. Nevertheless, the ultimate dream of being one's own boss—a partner in a firm or the sole proprietor of a business—endured.

Business ownership or executive status involved all sorts of decisions, testing an individual's business acumen and drawing on a wide variety of talents in areas including marketing, purchasing, accounting, and managing interpersonal relationships among important clients. William G. Berlinger, who graduated from Peirce School in 1886, serves as an example of a virtuous male clerical employee who displayed just such virtues. When he finished school, he possessed the fine penmanship to become a bookkeeper but passed up an opportunity to work as one, accepting instead an office boy position in one of the city's large rug manufacturing and sales firms. His qualities of "energy, initiative, and application[,] which indicate sterling business ability," earned him increasing amounts of responsibility on the job. He quickly became the head of the company's delivery and shipping department, where he learned "to perform other duties that were valuable in enabling him to gain a broad and comprehensive grasp of the business." He also served as a salesman both in the store and on the road. By 1910 he was vice president.[23] For male clerks, ambition and the workplace ideals of loyalty, industry, thrift, and temperance meshed well. All these principles reinforced upward striving: the loyal man had the boss's ear; hard work showed initiative; and the thrifty and temperate worker did not dissipate his earnings or energies but remained focused on climbing the corporate ladder.

At the same time, the clerical workers who contributed to and edited *Store Chat* and Peirce's *Alumni Journal* expected women to find contentment at work while they waited for the offers of marriage that would sever their connections to the work world. Virtuous women on the selling floor or in the office supposedly found fulfillment in terms much more circumscribed than those under which men operated. They ostensibly discovered happiness in the basic hard work and responsibilities of their jobs. For them, ambition couched in terms of the rapid career advancement favored by men was contrary to success in the workplace. Idealized female stenographers did not dream of becoming management. Rather, they set their sights lower and focused on improving their work skills, to "bring their speed up" and effectively transcribe technical terms.[24] At most, the desires of the idealized female office or sales worker stretched toward matrimony and directly linked womanhood in the office with marriage. The office trained them well for wedded life, argued authors in *Store Chat* and Peirce's *Alumni Journal.* Exposure to the workings of the business world better prepared single women for managing home finances. Because an office or saleswoman had more contact with the ostensibly dangerous outside world than did a woman who went straight from childhood into marriage, she had learned to better appreciate the meanings of "love and protection" and her husband's "little attentions."[25] On a more mundane level, she learned the "true value of money" and of thrift regarding her husband's earnings. She also came to "appreciate home life and all that a comfortable, restful home means to [her husband,] who has been battling with the world all day for her bread and butter."[26] In a vision vastly diverging from the one available to men, the idealized female clerk or salesperson had no ambitions besides being satisfied in her work and preparing herself for domestic bliss. Sweating over the selling counter or office desk laid the groundwork for good fortune in the home, and one should not aspire to more. An upward-striving ex-saleswoman who left Strawbridge and Clothier remarked that she subsequently made more money as a stenographer in a large law firm, a position many women perceived to be far superior to working on the selling floor. She nevertheless discouraged her former department-store co-workers from following her, because she believed that there were real problems with stenographic work that quite possibly outweighed the potential material benefits:

> The fact is the average stenographer really has more than one employer—there being several men in the office, as a rule, for whom she works. She is given instructions and work to do, in the presence of a number of people, and amid a great deal of confusion, which is extremely trying on her nerves. When she leaves the office at night she doesn't leave all business behind, but is continually thinking of and worrying over dictations and instructions she has tried to take during the afternoon (in the midst of excitement and confusion) and wondering if she can do it accurately, and have it ready by a certain time in the morning. A Department Store girl when she is finished at night, leaves all business cares and worries behind her, and is free until the morning.
>
> Do you draw a lesson from these facts, my sisters?[27]

The lesson, of course, was that her career-oriented fervor was not necessarily a model to emulate. Highly stressful jobs involving decision making and a high-pressure environment were to be avoided. In this context, loyalty, industriousness, thrift, and temperance took on vastly different meanings than they held for men. None of these virtues was coupled with career advancement for women. They were supposed to understand these traits as simply reinforcing their subservience to their bosses, principles that would ensure that their stints in the working world would be harmonious, if unambitious. Loyalty and hard work turned saleswomen into the "I Will Girls" alluded to in chapter 2. Thrift helped female clerks economize and live further on the salaries they earned. Overindulging in alcohol did not ruin one's chances at climbing the corporate ladder. Rather, it wrecked a woman's reputation at work.

Occasionally, however, women who exhibited what would have been seen as masculine ambition were rewarded. A female Peirce graduate was such a good stenographer that her company decided to retain her at the sizable annual salary of $1,300 even after she married. She accepted. Another woman rose from clerical worker to partner in a manufacturing interest in only ten years. This was certainly impressive, but the partnership agreement required her to continue to do the ordinary office work of managing the company's books and correspondence.[28]

The paltry amount of union activity among lower-level white-collar workers before 1920 suggests that the vast majority of office and sales employees identified with their employers. Clerks aligned themselves more closely to management than did their blue-collar counterparts. The upbeat tone of most of the articles and personal columns in Peirce's *Alumni Journal* went beyond simple promotion of the school or the achievements of individual graduates. Clerical positions for women, for example, were championed for the status they allegedly embodied.[29] Working in such jobs required tact, education, and style. The scores of stories that celebrated the individual business achievements of male graduates reflected the hopes of many of the journal's male clerical readers who saw themselves as future business owners, managers, or professionals.

The differing gender-based views of ambition surely complicated matters. Because office men especially focused their career aspirations up the corporate ladder, they were unlikely to see female secretaries and stenographers as comrades. In fact, much like skilled blue-collar workers, they likely perceived women employees as a threat, depressing wages in the white-collar workplace. Whether male clerks attained their loftiest goals was often irrelevant. Even those who moved only one rung up the corporate ladder were apt to side with their bosses. Some flaunted any little power they accrued through promotion. In 1894 a female typist in Philadelphia complained that many lower-level managers, such as chief clerks or department heads, "abuse [their authority] when the opportunity offers." She explained that, "being governed by the desire of personal aggrandizement, and the desire to stand well with the employer," such mangers were "often harsh and arbitrary to the employes [*sic*]": "The [business owner] selects his managers for their business ability, but if he would occasionally investigate the courses of these men it might have a very beneficial effect and conduce to the comfort of the employes [*sic*]."[30] Few unions existed among clerical workers between 1870 and 1920,[31] and organizing was most difficult for saleswomen. The Retail Clerks' International Protective Association, the most significant clerical union, did not encourage their participation. Bosses quickly fired dissenters, and the female clerical workforce experienced particularly rapid turnover.[32] Oftentimes disillusioned women simply quit their jobs and found others. A 1894 survey of over five hundred saleswomen in Philadelphia found that 54 percent had changed sales jobs at least once in their short careers.[33] The male workforce, too, saw a regular reshuffling of its ranks, but in a different direction. Between 1870 and 1920 enough men received promotions to fuel the mobility dreams of their brothers in the office and stores of Philadelphia. As mentioned in chapter 1, in 1905 the RCIPA blamed its tiny membership rolls on the fact that most male clerks dreamed of becoming small-business owners.

Rather than quit their jobs, some clerical workers who harbored grudges about poor pay and bad working conditions found other ways to challenge the established norms of the workplace. They rejected the images of the ideal employee. Usually these acts of defiance were concealed and to a great degree individualistic. In a 1908 *Store Chat* article Elbert Hubbard described the two kinds of employees he saw in every business. Individuals whom he categorized as "the Bunch" desired a "maximum wage" for "minimum service." They were "apt to regard their employers as the enemy." People with this mentality failed to work their required hours, overindulged in food and drink, overspent, and stayed away from the job at least one day a week. Hubbard provided no name for the second variety of worker, but these people adhered to work rules and led lives of moderation and exercise. They also worked hard and formed "no cliques" in the workplace.[34] Levels of workplace defiance varied along a sliding scale of degree and scope. Insubordination was usually hidden, occurring when the boss's back was turned. More rarely it involved direct confrontation with one's supervisor. Typically individuals acted alone in their rule breaking, but occasionally groups were involved. Finally, defiance could be measured according to how much it hurt employers and whether it was illegal. Flouting a dress code or committing petty theft was fairly insignificant, but embezzlement proved to be another matter altogether.

In large workplaces, when managers were absent or not looking, many employees simply ignored burdensome rules, such as those that forbade department-store salespeople to talk with one another or sit down during business hours.[35] Some saleswomen resorted to stealing as an act of irreverence or compensation for their paltry pay rates. To preclude such acts, bosses reminded new salespeople of management's vigilance. Supervisors purported to know workers' abilities by assessing their sales volume. In 1909 Strawbridge and Clothier ominously warned its new hires of management's watchfulness: "Systems are in operation in every Department, as well as at

Headquarters, keeping a record of your errors, and your claim and right to promotion from time to time will be measured by these records." In its next breath management warned that it monitored personal behavior as strictly as it policed productiveness, saying: "Should you be inclined to group with fellow members for the purpose of gossip, and should that be recognized by those who have supervision of your work as being characteristic of your service, it will as positively work to your detriment as though you were making errors in excess of what might be considered a normal ratio; in fact, gossiping and grouping beget a carelessness and indifference which interferes with your ability to give satisfactory service."[36] Reading between the lines suggests that the store had regular problems with the personal behavior of its sales staff. The stories in *Store Chat* that focused on breaches of the rules confirm this. A simple act like gossiping or sitting down on the job took on rebellious overtones.

The pages of *Store Chat* anonymously criticized infractions. Employee commentators who believed that they possessed the idealized traits of the model clerical worker described store management as godlike, omniscient, and standing in perpetual judgment. The ideal of "unquestioning obedi- ence" to supervisors was juxtaposed to descriptions of a young man stealing matches from the firm, an errand boy watching a parade on Broad Street instead of delivering an important message, and a female stock clerk not tabulating her inventory sheets correctly during a big sale. The store warned that workers could not successfully conceal their transgressions. Manage- ment would inexorably uncover abuses, to the great disadvantage of the guilty employee. Alongside any possible punishment loomed "the loss of self-respect on the part of the one who awakes to a realization of the fact that he or she has willingly, knowingly transgressed one of the first laws of God and man—obedience."[37]

While these passages were meant to strike fear into the hearts of employ- ees, many, particularly saleswomen, resented them and defied management. Susan Porter Benson has detailed the love-hate relationship that many sales- women had with their work.[38] Female department-store employees developed retail skills on their own and felt indignant about management's attempts to instruct them in the science of selling. Many saleswomen envied the con- spicuous consumption of their middle-class female customers but disliked the condescension shoppers often exhibited. In collegial departments the saleswomen formed close bonds and many times competed with other sell- ing areas in the store. Nonetheless, as their bosses feared, numerous sales- women were clock-watchers. Bored with their jobs, impatiently waiting for the workday to end, these employees flouted rules to make their work lives more interesting. They chewed gum while on the selling floor (an infraction of store policy). They treated customers with aloofness and sometimes turned their backs on difficult ones. In addition, some women let their private lives influence their sales. When depressed or upset by outside factors, they did nothing to hide it.[39]

A few women acted out their dissension in groups. During the second half of 1909 and early in 1910, Strawbridge and Clothier had problems with saleswomen crowding out customers or making them uncomfortable on store elevators. Management began allowing workers to use public elevators in the early 1900s but emphasized that salespeople had to yield to customers and do everything to make them feel at home, but many workers ignored or outright rejected these stipulations. In particular, management decried the "flying wedges" that saleswomen formed on their way into elevators. Customers leaving the lifts had to barrel through these wedges like football players to make it to the all-important goal—the selling floor. Once in the elevator, saleswomen apparently did not mind pushing customers to the back and loudly gossiping and giggling. Management found it particularly "objectionable" that workers discussed their "vacations, fellow employes [*sic*], and personal matters," all the while using slang. Their elevator behavior demonstrated the irreverence that some saleswomen had for the store's rules as well as for customers. When elevator doors shut, saleswomen must have felt relieved to be out of the direct gaze of management and in a place where they could reject the idealized vision of the obsequious female clerk promulgated by their bosses.[40]

Insolence in more intimate office settings most often transpired on an individual scale. The Fourth Street National Bank suffered from two significant incidents of employee insubordination in the late 1890s. The incidents were especially strong, criminal assaults against the ideal of loyalty to the firm. In 1897 Fourth Street National realized that George DaCosta, hired in 1886 when the bank opened, had gradually embezzled $12,000 and then fled. DaCosta had repeatedly shifted money from several accounts to cover his tracks. In cases such as this, banks had a way of recouping some or all of their losses. When hired, a new employee posted a bond with a surety company; in case of a broken contract, the bank claimed the bond. Fourth Street National did this in the DaCosta case when the bank could not catch its thief, snatching instead the $15,000 bond his parents had raised for him. DaCosta's overall motivations behind the embezzlement remain unclear, especially given the fact that his peculation did not even cover the bond. Be that as it may, his actions exhibited a complete disregard for the lending institution's policies and the image of the ideal employee.[41]

In February 1899 the Fourth Street National hired Gustave A. Meyer, a multilingual Austrian immigrant, as a clerk in the foreign exchange department. By the end of October 1899 he began hinting to his colleagues that he planned to leave, mentioning both Florida and California as destinations. He kept to himself a plan to steal sixteen blank letters of credit. Meyer left the bank on October 30 and never returned. At the end of November the runaway clerk or an accomplice forged several of the checks in Bombay, India, to obtain a large amount of money, $3,000 of which was wired to an accomplice in New York. The bank hired the Pinkerton Detective Agency to track down Meyer,[42] but it never unearthed his whereabouts.

These two incidents of employee defiance exhibited a great degree of secretiveness. They were not isolated. Embezzlement—or defalcation, as it was widely termed in the nineteenth century—occurred regularly in the industrial-era office. The *New York Times* ran hundreds of articles about lower-level white-collar workers who had stolen from their employers between 1870 and 1900. In the summer of 1879 twenty-three-year-old George Seltzer, a bookkeeper for the Philadelphia stock brokers Musgrave and Company, unsuccessfully attempted to pilfer $2,525 from work. He forged his boss's signature on two checks, cashed them, and absconded to New York, where city detectives tracked him down and locked him up in the Tombs, the municipal jail. Five years earlier Seltzer had started his career as an office boy with the firm. He worked diligently and so thoroughly earned the trust of his superiors that they quickly promoted him through a succession of jobs. Laying aside any qualms, the youthful bookkeeper rationalized his peculation as an emergency loan. In his desk he left a note addressed to "Dear Mr. Musgrave," stating that he had "borrowed" the money to help him though a period of financial difficulty and that a woman lay "at the bottom" of his problems. Although Musgrave did not believe Seltzer, the young man's explanation matches a popular rationalization among embezzlers: "I am just borrowing the money and will return it." This type of reasoning no doubt allowed Seltzer to minimize the criminality of his deeds and made it easier for him to steal. He probably relied on heady doses of rationalization to neutralize any social controls that might have kept him from stealing. He likely convinced himself that he could get away with a deed that was not so bad, simply some concealed borrowing. The bookkeeper set aside work rules, his boss's expectations, and his own reputation for honesty and hard work. In a similar case, Samuel Entwittle, a clerk with the flour dealers E. Lathbury and Company, ran into trouble when he stole $5,000 dollars from his employers. Entwittle did this to pay for the high life he led, which drained his moderate salary.[43]

Other embezzlers tilled their stolen fortunes into speculative ventures. In the early 1880s the bookkeeper William P. Pierson teamed with his assistant to bleed about thirty thousand dollars out of the American Baptist Publication Society in Philadelphia. Pierson, who saw himself as "working like a slave for a small salary," maintained that the duo planned to borrow the money, speculate, make their fortune, and return the loot. With some initial success, they poured stolen capital into transactions involving mining interests, oil stocks, glass manufacturers, and natural-gas wells. They were "infatuated with the fabulous gains promised by investment in Florida lands." The two hoped that casting a wide net would yield the best catch. Pierson even started his own grocery store, which he unloaded just before getting caught. The bookkeeper used his earning to furnish his house elegantly, purchase a horse and carriage, and entertain extravagantly. The horse and carriage did in the duo. In early May 1886, while out for a spin, Pierson was thrown from it and broke his leg, incapacitating himself and keeping him away from the office, where his deceit was quickly revealed by others poring over the books.[44]

As the DaCosta, Meyer, and Pierson cases suggest, embezzlement often entailed a great deal of planning and thought. Typically these were not crimes of passion. At the heart of the matter, office thieves simply desired to make easy money. Exaggerated levels of ambition surely lay behind some embezzlements. Office thieves felt compelled to pilfer so they could realize their dreams of material gain and believed that their current situations somehow thwarted their desires.[45] Defalcation most often involved men who regularly handled large sums of money or credit. Although a clear knowledge of their bosses' schedules and the workings of the office no doubt encouraged wayward clerks to formulate plans for seemingly flawless heists, temptations such as open cash drawers, unlocked safes, blank checks, and easily imitated signatures must have preyed strongly on clerks who had little self-control. An editorial in the Philadelphia *Evening Bulletin* noted that one embezzler's annual salary of $1,500 "was a small one in consideration of the fact that half a million dollars annually passed through his hands." Nevertheless, it went on to suggest that this disparity was not enough to push one into crime. Rather, such excessive temptation combined with a dishonest nature to yield disaster.[46]

Embezzlers were almost always male employees,[47] probably because male clerical workers were usually the ones who handled sizable transactions in a business. Office women less frequently held jobs where the temptation to embezzle was great and therefore did not face such lures. Also, in a twisted way, masculinized notions of ambition drove many to steal. These were the overambitious in the office. Covetous of material gain and unable to wait for promotion and higher salary, they tried to illegally jump-start their socioeconomic ascent. They abandoned the workplace virtues described previously and chose to violate the trust of their employers. By making off with vast sums of cash, they also rejected the steady industriousness that the model worker so cherished, trying instead to "get rich quick." The impetus for peculation often included a disregard for the other elements of the employee paragon—temperance and thrift. Many office thieves led private lives of abandon in which they spent freely. People like Entwittle and Seltzer ran up huge debts by indulging in luxuries. Paying off their saloon tabs, jewelry bills, and gambling adventures necessitated theft, not thrift.[48]

In other situations especially bold workers openly challenged the authority of their superiors in face-to-face confrontations. Unfortunately, little evidence remains of the sharp interchanges that occasionally punctuated business. "An Every-Day Stenographer," a short story drawn from the *Peirce School Alumni Journal,* suggests the flavor of one of these incidents. The male protagonist, a stenographer named "Merritt Ames," confronts his boss, "Mr. Cobb," when the boss forces him to stay after work for extra dictation. Ames refuses to work the extra time and offers his resignation. Taken aback, Cobb relents and tells Ames to return in the morning and finish the dictation.[49] The importance of the story lies in its implicit lessons. On the surface it seems odd that the *Peirce School Alumni Journal,* which celebrated loyalty to one's employer, would run such a rebellious story. However, the tale emphasizes that some employers themselves violated the relationships implied in the image of the idealized worker. Cobb is a grasping, ruthless boss who overworks his underpaid employees. He violates their trust and abuses their loyalty. Openly challenging his authority is an affirmation of the idealized worker. The story reveals the existence of appropriate times and ways to rebel against perceived workplace wrongs—and implicitly judges secret rebellion and collective resistance to be dishonorable. Rather, a manly confrontation of individuals was the preferred recourse. This individualization of conflict helps to explain the lack of unionization among clerical workers, especially men. Their dreams of eventually moving into management or small-business ownership allied them too closely to their bosses to contemplate collective resistance or unionization. Protest, if necessary, became a contest between two individuals—the overreaching boss and the aggrieved male worker—over their divergent understandings of the workplace virtues. Otherwise, it had to be shunted into veiled, behind-the-scenes deeds. Collective action meant challenging the individualism underlying the dream of mobility out of the clerical workforce. And sacrificing this dream remained too difficult for most employees.

The idealized image of the clerical worker had ramifications beyond the job, too, via its intimate ties to the ways that these employees viewed race. Although historians have begun to elucidate the experiences of clerical workers, the impact that race had on their lives has received scant treatment.[50] Race profoundly touched the work and leisure lives of Philadelphia's clerks and salespeople. They derived a distinct set of racial precepts regarding their status in society from their daily toil and their experiences at play. The office world and selling floor were largely white environs in the early twentieth century. Of the city's almost 80,000 office and sales workers at the turn of the century, only about 1 percent were African American. This proportion changed little in the next twenty years. During those two decades native-born whites who had native-born parents made up just over half the clerical workforce.[51] An additional third were the children of white immigrants. Many of these workers used racial stereotypes while at play, reinforcing the notion that white-collar work was for whites only.

The burgeoning commercialized leisure economy of the industrializing city deployed its delights to seduce unmarried clerical workers during their time away from work. Commercialized pleasure activities such as going to vaudeville performances, movies, and twirling the night away at dance halls provided young clerks and salespeople with powerful messages about gender, sexuality, and importantly, race. Many of the city's office and sales employees watched professional minstrels sketch out stereotypical depictions of African Americans in local blackface theaters and vaudeville houses. Going a step further, personnel from Philadelphia's stores and offices imitated professional minstrels by forming their own minstrelsy clubs. Clerks and salespeople, male and female, smeared themselves with burnt cork and acted racist parts for their fellow workers' entertainment.

Blackface minstrelsy, with its supposedly realistic impressions of blackness, served as a perverse morality play for white clerical workers. Blackface stereotypes represented the inverse of the workplace virtues previously discussed. The humor that white-collar workers derived from minstrelsy exuded the notion that African Americans did not belong in a modern, regimented, urban society that presumably offered reward only through sober toil. The racist imagery of blackface bolstered the notion that African Americans were unfit for clerical work. The content of minstrelsy consequently appealed to office and sales personnel, many of whom who led lives in constant flux. Laughing at bigoted parody, male and female clerical workers could set aside their anxieties about upward occupational mobility and concerns about gender politics in the workplace. Furthermore, the warped depictions of blackface characters offered the American-born children of immigrants toiling in office and sales jobs common ground with their native white counterparts. At its heart, blackface allowed a variety of clerical workers—men and women, ethnic-stock and native—to at least temporarily minimize their differences and develop a shared sense of racial identity. They found comfort in an understanding of whiteness as the opposite of the caricatures they viewed on the minstrel stage.

As Matthew Frye Jacobson has so aptly put it, "race resides not in nature but in politics and culture."[52] Blackface was not simply entertainment or an element of American popular culture unrelated to what happened beyond the threshold of the theater. Throughout the nineteenth and early twentieth centuries, the minstrel stage served as an arena in which actors and audiences tinkered with the intertwining concepts of race, class, and gender. Scholars have linked blackface minstrelsy most often to white, working-class, male audiences, especially in the antebellum period.[53] These workers used minstrelsy to forge a common sense of whiteness and hide cleavages within the working class.[54] Clerical workers used blackface for purposes similar to those of antebellum mechanics: to minimize differences among themselves. Whether audience members were blue- or white-collar workers, both repudiation and attraction lay at the heart of the blackface experience for whites. On one level, performances loaded with stereotypes negated the humanity of African Americans and mocked their efforts to succeed in society. Clerks in the audience and on stage clearly understood that they were nothing like the nasty caricatures they observed. On another level, however, whites were drawn both to laugh at performances and to strut on stage themselves. David R. Roediger and Lewis A. Erenberg have stressed that antebellum minstrelsy and popular post–Civil War "coon songs" allowed white audiences and minstrels to "project onto Blacks values and actions that aroused both fear and fascination among whites."[55] At the core of all this lay the belief of many whites, both actors and spectators, that the caricatures authentically portrayed African Americans and black culture.

Professional minstrel depictions of blacks grew more vitriolic during the latter nineteenth century.[56] This trend continued into the early twentieth century. Antebellum minstrelsy had typically drawn its demeaning plots and tunes from a stilted image of plantation life, but blackface in the post–Civil War period, when slavery no longer distinguished blacks from whites, often ridiculed the aspirations and lives of urban African Americans. Turn-of-the-century minstrels spent quite a bit of stage time disparaging the upward striving of blacks, with the image of the strutting urban dandy eclipsing the plantation slave on stage.[57] The dandified role subsumed many antiblack stereotypes, including the buffoon, the intemperate laggard, and the razor-wielding punk. In addition, the rise of social Darwinism in America helped intensify minstrelsy's nastiness at this time. As African Americans from the South increasingly migrated to the urban North in the early twentieth century, antiblack sentiment increased among northern whites. For example, in the late nineteenth and early twentieth centuries, the United States, particularly its urban areas, experienced a "coon song" fad. The bigoted content of these popular songs (as well as the racist caricatures scrawled onto countless song sheets printed for public consumption) tapped into the same animosity that fed social Darwinism and the eugenics craze, both of which validated racial discrimination as a matter of science. James H. Dormon argues that roughly between 1890 and 1910, the popularity of coon songs "underlay a major shift in white perceptions of blacks[,] a shift whereby existing stereotypes came to be either confirmed or embellished and indelibly encoded as part of the semiotic system of the period."[58] Clerical workers' interest in minstrelsy was part of this transformation as well. For many whites, the invidious images of African Americans laced throughout popular culture blurred into reality.

A tale full of racist humor that ran in a 1911 edition of *Store Chat* replicates several of the conspicuous themes in minstrelsy performances and hints at the shift to which Dormon alludes. In the racist parable, a black wife calls a doctor about her sick husband. According to the wife, the husband has fallen ill for no apparent reason after he spent what is billed as a "typical day" in the park. The typical day for this stock character involves overeating, heavy drinking, tumbling off of two amusement-park rides, and getting into a razor fight. The wife cannot understand what is wrong with her husband and urges the doctor to visit. In ostensibly serious tones, the story's introduction claims that it "is really one of the most characteristic tales of the colored race ever printed. It is more than that, however; it actually points a moral of importance to all of us." Salespeople derived a common racial identity in opposition to the story's stereotypical depiction of African Americans as violent, clumsy, ignorant, overindulgent dandies.[59] The tale depicts dissipation as "characteristic" of African Americans. Stereotypes are posed as reality for the white clerks perusing the story. The husband in the story cannot stop eating, drinking, fighting, or causing scenes in general. He wastes precious time and money on excessive leisure. He is unruly, obstreperous, and loud. The husband's shenanigans disrupt household life, render him unemployable, and call into question his role as provider within the household by impugning his dedication to family and employer.

Another narrative from a 1904 edition of the *Peirce School Alumni Journal* exhibited similar racist overtones. The demeaning plot is about a white man who hires an African American valet. The white man soon thereafter purchases a pair of "loud, checked trousers," and his valet covets them. The valet contrives to spill grease on the pants and thus inherit a pair of unlaunderable hand-me-downs. The black character's boss implores him to wash the pants. As a matter of course, the servant fails to even attempt this. His employer questions the valet:

"Did you scrub them well?"
"Yes, sah."
"Did you try a hot iron and a piece of brown paper?"
"Yes, sah."
"Did you try ammonia?"
"No, sah. I ain't done tied 'em on me yet, but I knows they'll fit me."[60]

The racist humor involved in the slanted accent of the black dandy and in his confusion about the word *ammonia* suggests incompetence. His loyalty and trustworthiness are questioned. The interchange reminded Peirce alumni that blacks did not belong in their work world. Together, these two stereotype-laden tales concocted a loathsome vision of blackness, but this vision did not stand alone. The traits of laziness, duplicity, drunkenness, and buffoonery developed in these stories were the polar opposites of the virtues laid out for clerks and salespeople within the context of work—industriousness, loyalty to the firm, thriftiness, and temperance.

The workplace ideals emerged in a overwhelmingly white work context and came to be associated with whiteness. As I discussed in chapter 1, African Americans seeking office or sales jobs found little success in Philadelphia during the first two decades of the twentieth century. Like those elsewhere in urban America, the city's privately owned white firms seldom hired African Americans as clerical workers. White employers dreaded that their white customers and clients would refuse to be served by African Americans. When noticed by whites, African Americans were viewed in rather unflattering terms. In 1909 a white employee at Strawbridge and Clothier highlighted the burden of responsibilities he faced on the job and at home as the chief thing differentiating him from African Americans working in the store. According to this man, black workers could be unremittingly happy-go-lucky because their allegedly simple lives failed to provide them with any real worries. The white employee believed that black workers in the store abided by the mantra "don't worry, smile."[61]

The leisure pursuits of clerical workers reinforced the lessons about race that they gleaned at work. Specifically, besides watching minstrel shows, white office and sales clerks performed in blackface in Philadelphia. These shows were freighted with intertwining, complex messages rooted in class, gender, and race. Whether engaged in amateur minstrelsy or watching professional acts, however, employees laughed and shuddered with the same breath, all the while reinforcing a common racial and occupational identity. On stage they tinkered with traits foreign to the ideal office or sales worker. It was safe to be deceitful, slothful, profligate, savage, and simple under a layer of burnt cork in the imaginary realm of play. Meanwhile, acting like the stereotypes in the everyday white world of the sales floor or office was out of the question.

Blackface performance had been a traditionally male endeavor prior to the late nineteenth century. Male actors cross-dressed to play female roles. That made the all-female Clover Mandolin Club's minstrelsy distinctive. Women at Strawbridge and Clothier's formed this group in 1906 to teach one another how to play the mandolin.[62] The group, which involved dozens of women, presented annual concerts to exhibit the members' talents. For their performance in the spring of 1910, the club decided to put on a "minstrel show and dance" at Dawson's Grotto. Twenty-four women in blackface and fine white dresses played their mandolins and performed sketches. A small band accompanied them. As did professionals, the mandolinists organized their minstrel show to focus on three stage personalities: an interlocutor, "Bones," and "Tambo." The interlocutor was the master of ceremonies. For this role, the mandolinists employed a man costumed in blackface and a white suit. In typical minstrel acts Bones and Tambo (whose stage names sprang from their instruments, bone castanets and tambourine) served as the central comedic figures, utilizing ham-handed racist comedy to rouse the audience. Two department-store women played these characters for the mandolinists. They wore the most makeup, featuring exaggerated white lips. Additionally, soloists and choruses exhibited their vocal and instrumental prowess.[63]

The concert was not a one-time event for the club. In 1912 its members once again staged a minstrel show, this time at Mercantile Hall in Philadelphia. On this occasion thirty-eight "young ladies took part in black-face." The mandolinists' show combined antisuffrage sentiments with their racist repertoire in a number called "Woman's Suffrage Parade."[64] This skit likely sprang from themes embodied in a "stump speech" published in an 1881 guide to amateur minstrelsy. The guide offered the speech as an example of stage-ready performance material to dilettante blackface actors. The speech, titled "Female Suffrage," was meant for a cross-dressing male thespian but was easily adaptable for women. In it, the blackfaced character, dolled up to look like a "woman's rights champion," assails men: "My dear, *dear* sisters! We are here this evening to discuss, recuss, and *cuss* the men generally." The monologue descends from there into a sweeping assault on men.[65] Professional male minstrels had a long tradition of using blackface to criticize women who dared to break with Victorian gender mores.[66] Applying burnt cork to their visages and cross-dressing allowed male minstrels to satirize women willing to challenge men in the political realm, a traditionally masculine arena. The mandolinists utilized the same guise.

The mandolinists' performances likely reassured the men in the audience (and those reading write-ups of the shows in *Store Chat*) that the store's women were not as threatening as women suffragists. This soothing display catered to white-collar men, who were no doubt highly insecure about their workplace status and upward mobility as increasing numbers of women entered department-store and office employment. The mandolinists not so subtly implored their male counterparts to believe that saleswomen were not as emasculating as suffragists supposedly were. Although they might work together on the selling floor, there was no need to feel that women competed with men. In fact, they could find common ground in lambasting women perceived as overly aggressive. The general context of each show was equally reassuring. The performances constructed a burnt-cork version of store life that emphasized male authority figures. The male interlocutor filled the role of masculine management, controlling the pace of performance and occupying center stage. A handful of men (not wearing burnt cork) conspicuously occupied the seats of the accompanying band in front of the minstrel stage. With the numerous women mandolinists, they conspired to titillate the audience with a bigoted production. In this blackface imitation of the gender dynamics on the selling floor, men and women toiled together harmoniously and pleased their "customers" with skits and songs. Men filled pivotal roles in the store and on stage while women largely constituted the ranks of the chorus, which symbolically duplicated the selling staff.

Although the mandolinists featured antifeminist and bigoted stage material, they did not lampoon their society's mores about dress appropriate to their gender and class. The women minstrels wore demure white dresses, not the mismatched gaudy clothing of "wenches" portrayed by traditional male, cross-dressing performers. The mandolinists' masquerade thus involved a complicated layering of gender, class, and racial issues. Their message included the incongruity of seeing blackened skin against the clothing of young, white female clerks. This must have struck the crowd in the packed houses they played to as farcical. *Store Chat* described the show in the spring of 1910 as "most pleasant."[67]

Provided they performed in conventional attire, the members of the Strawbridge and Clothier Mandolin Club seem to have been all too ready to impugn things, such as black culture and suffrage activists, that mainstream American society deemed strange. Susan Porter Benson has shown that saleswomen prided themselves on having a sense of fashion or stylishness. It was an important element in the on-the-job self-identity of women who worked in department stores.[68] The mandolinists' white dresses reminded audiences that the women possessed the good taste of department-store clerks. Social mores did not allow white women in blackface to act or dress lasciviously, as did the cross-dressed wenches of the professional minstrel show. Their skin may have been painted black, but the audience knew that whiteness lay underneath, emphasized perhaps by the delicate white fabric of the dresses. The content of their minstrel performances proved more intricate, therefore, than were the broad parodies staged by antebellum all-male troupes. By "blacking up" and yet simultaneously dressing in middle-class attire, the mandolinists mocked the upward striving of African Americans. In both performances the alternating layers of whiteness and blackness they depicted on stage informed their audience and themselves that they all shared a common racial and occupational identity. Their minstrelsy insinuated that African Americans could never be part of their exclusive, white occupational world, a powerful message to all involved in the show. As David R. Roediger has noted, "The simple physical disguise—and elaborate cultural disguise—of blacking up served to emphasize that those on stage were really white and that whiteness really mattered."[69]

Young men working at Strawbridge and Clothier also engaged in minstrelsy. Fourteen of them formed the Argyle Minstrel Club in 1912. The club first met in the gymnasium on the store's athletic fields in West Philadelphia. Three older male employees taught the teenaged minstrels-in-training, only four of whom had stage experience. The group performed at a Philadelphia Knights of Columbus hall in April 1912. The production required several busy weeks of rehearsals to familiarize the newcomers with acting. The club prided itself on its original material, especially jokes. Its show included twelve songs, physical comedy, jokes, and sketches. The evening finished with a sketch, entitled "Wanted, a Valet," whose characters were two "applicants," "Lewis Lewis" and "George Washington Congo."[70] The former's name was clearly demeaning. The latter, an insidious transformation, substituted the scientist George Washington Carver's last name with *Congo.* For whites in the audience, the Congo symbolized the most primitive and savage setting possible, and the name captured white scorn for African American aspiration and achievement.

The minstrels drew the lines between white and black, civilization and barbarity, all too clearly. The Argyle club's stage work sketched out clear concepts of class. Blackface characters applied for menial jobs as servants. For these young men, African Americans who dreamed of advancing beyond skilled employment into the white-collar realm were laughable. The blackface production surely bolstered them against any doubts about beginning careers in a clerical world that offered shrinking levels of advancement. If nothing else, the minstrels could cling to the notion that they held jobs beyond the reach of black Philadelphians. This may have alleviated a bit of their anxiety about their own shrinking chances to climb the social ladder by reminding them that they had achieved some level of exclusivity in their social status.

Additional amateur blackface troupes arose among white-collar workers in Philadelphia. Strawbridge and Clothier's lower-level management partici-pated in blackface minstrelsy. Floormen formed the Heed Club's minstrel group in 1910, and in June of that year they gave an elaborate stage perfor-mance that was highly choreographed and backed by a small orchestra.[71] Students at the Peirce School developed their own blackface minstrel group in 1911. In June of that year the "Ham and Egg Club" performed for fellow students, alumni, teachers, and guests at a rented hall in Philadelphia (a dance followed). The all-male troupe's performance was a huge hit. In a poignant minstrel twist, the student performers used their blackfaced alter egos to subvert white authority and throw "good-natured 'knocks'" at faculty members attending the show.[72]

The Ham and Egg Club emerged in an institution that prepared thousands of young men and women to become clerical workers in the late nineteenth and early twentieth centuries. Peirce trained people for all types of office and sales work. The fact that faculty and alumni came to and enjoyed the club's performance indicates that the school's administration approved of the show's content. Minstrelsy was viewed as something appropriate for clerical workers and their formative development while in school. The club's racist extravaganza was popular no doubt in part because it helped solidify a school-based identity among students and reinforced camaraderie among faculty and graduates. The performance particularly assisted students in the development of a mutual identity fixed in a sense of whiteness, especially important at Peirce, which, much like the city's clerical workforce, had a substantial population of second-generation immigrants. As Matthew Frye Jacobson has shown, in the latter half of the nineteenth century and the first two decades of the twentieth, the Irish, as well as the New Immigrants from southern and eastern Europe, were not considered as white as the descendants of western Europeans. Jacobson writes that these years "witnessed a frac-turing of whiteness into a hierarchy of plural and scientifically determined white races."[73] The descendants of Anglo-Saxons ruled this hierarchy, and immigrants such as Italians and Russian Jews held an inferior racial status in American society and culture. The "whiteness" of these newcomers was questioned by a wide range of Americans, especially academicians, politicians, scientists, and social commentators. By using African Americans as caustic comedic material, second-generation immigrants at Peirce and within the general clerical workforce could shore up their status as whites.[74] By laughing at the stereotypes on stage, ethnic-stock individuals publicly affirmed their desire to assimilate or "pass" as white. The irony of putting on a black mask to do so did not trouble many amateur minstrels.

The evidence of amateur blackface minstrelsy among Philadelphia's clerks and salespeople suggests the obvious question: what encouraged them to do it? To be sure, the city's clerical workers readily absorbed blackface acts in local vaudeville houses. Going a step further, they had ample opportunity to learn the medium firsthand at a prominent local minstrel theater, the Eleventh Street Opera House (Frank Dumont, a nationally prominent minstrel and avid promoter of amateur minstrelsy, served as this theater's director in the early twentieth century). Nonetheless, arguing that they simply picked up minstrelsy from the expanding leisure economy and leaving it at that is unsatisfying.

Professional blackface minstrelsy developed into a prominent feature in urban theaters of the antebellum period and remained hugely popular throughout the rest of the nineteenth century. It subsequently became intertwined in the burgeoning commercialized leisure economy of the turn of the century. Actors covered in burnt cork performed in vaudeville houses that white-collar workers frequented, and over the next few decades the racist humor of blackface seeped into American movies and radio. Not only was the new leisure economy laced with racially charged entertainment; it was racially segregated as well. Movie houses, amusement parks, dance halls, and theaters either racially segregated audiences or excluded African Americans altogether. These conventions encouraged mutual racial identification among native whites of western European descent and audience members of various other ethnic backgrounds.[75] The racist humor and segregation evident in vaudeville productions, movies, and minstrel acts reinforced the low status of blacks in American society.

From 1854 to 1911 Philadelphia was home to what locals considered the longest continuously running blackface minstrel theater in America. In a period when vaudeville dominated urban theatrical entertainment, the Eleventh Street Opera House survived because of its widespread popularity and status as a Philadelphia institution. In 1854 the theater opened in a renovated Presbyterian church, and the structure changed little during its long life.

Minstrels applied their makeup in the former Sunday School room, and parts of the ecclesiastical interior survived after the structure's conversion into a theater. Patrons could easily discern where the church's gallery had been transformed into a balcony, for example. Through the years the house went by the names of the leaders of its minstrel troupes, but most Philadelphians referred to it as "the Eleventh Street Opera." Located on Eleventh Street between Chestnut and Market streets, it lay conveniently close to clerical workplaces. Nearby stood numerous office buildings, the Reading Railroad terminal, and several major department stores, including Strawbridge and Clothier. Frank Dumont served as the last impresario and namesake of the house. When the Eleventh Street Opera closed in 1911, professional minstrelsy persisted in the city. Dumont moved his troupe several blocks to the northeast into the old Arch Street Museum structure, which he renovated. Renamed "Dumont's," it thrived until he died in 1919. Another minstrel, Emmet Welsh, took over and ran the theater until 1928.[76]

The Eleventh Street Opera House and Dumont's catered to middle-class standards of audience decorum and behavior, as did the vaudeville houses mentioned in chapter 4. Workers at Strawbridge and Clothier were well aware of the theater. In fact, the children who worked at the store as cash boys and girls were treated to a show there in 1910. Rain had canceled a planned mid-September outing to the Strawbridge and Clothier's athletic fields for the store's young workers, so the adult committee arranging the outing hurriedly concocted an alternative that included a luncheon in the store's restaurant and a trip to the opera house. The committee secured a large block of seats at the theater, where the boys and girls caught a blackface matinee. After the show, the minstrels, in drag, posed for a photograph later run in the *Strawbridge & Clothier Store Chat* above the sarcastic caption: "Seven of the prettiest saleswomen of Strawbridge & Clothier."[77]

Strawbridge and Clothier would hardly have sent the boys and girls to the theater unless both clerks and managers found blackface acceptable. Indeed, many Philadelphians regarded the opera house to be appropriate for even the most impressionable of audiences. In 1899 Dumont remarked that his theater, "noted for the character of its entertainments, is patronized by clergymen, and is a household word among local and visiting pleasure-seekers."[78] A journalist grieving the eventual decline of the theater described going to it as a Philadelphia tradition, appealing enough even for children, as well as those "whose religious convictions kept them away from other show houses." The author lamented, "What Philadelphian is there who does not remember his first trip to Dumont's? Parents seemed to think that it was the place to take a boy or girl for their first glimpse inside a showhouse. And indeed, it was, for nowhere was such clean, wholesome humor, perhaps of the slapstick variety, purveyed. Fully half of Philadelphia's population saw its first show there."[79] The journalist considered racist humor more morally upstanding than the movies or vaudeville.

The opera house was not the rough, masculine, working-class venue that antebellum minstrel theaters were, but neither was it simply child's play. Typical shows at the house began with a "circle" of blackface characters exchanging jokes and singing minstrel songs. The company then performed two or three routines that included short plays written expressly for the minstrel stage, as well as burlesques of current events, legitimate theatrical productions, or local news items. Local politics provided ample material for the minstrels. Nearby locations, such as the Broad Street Station and Wanamaker's in-store restaurant, served as settings for comic sketches performed in the theater.[80] Clerical workers were thoroughly familiar with both these places and must have found the sketches set in them especially comical.

By the turn of the century Dumont had achieved national fame as a popular author of dozens of nationally circulated minstrel songs and skits. His theater showcased the material he wrote,[81] which reflected the transition from antebellum to industrial-era minstrelsy. Much of Dumont's work abandoned the plantation setting in favor of more modern backdrops that were thoroughly familiar to the city's clerks and salespeople. One of his skits even referenced sales work in the urban arena and featured the dandy character. In fact, in the introductory notes to the sketch, Dumont reminds prospective minstrels that they should set their plays within the context of their hometowns—the play "has been localized in various cities by putting on the programme the name of some leading clothing house [such as] 'Scenes at Rogers, Peet, & Co' in New York; Oak Hall in Boston; and Wanamaker's in Philadelphia, etc." Dumont utilized a version of the sketch to draw white-collar workers into the Eleventh Street Opera House. Published in 1889, "Scenes in Front of a Clothing Store" revolves around "Monroe Dickinson" and "Job Hoosick," two "seedy" criminal characters unwittingly hired by a clothing-store owner to serve as living mannequins. As the duo model the store's latest suits, they rob customers passing by. The short piece underscored the notion that African Americans did not belong in the white-collar world, a message that undoubtedly struck a chord with status-conscious white clerks.[82]

Frank Dumont authored two widely distributed volumes on amateur minstrelsy, handbooks that Philadelphia's white-collar minstrels had surely seen.[83] Published in 1899, *The Witmark Amateur Minstrel Guide* built on an earlier volume and offered a comprehensive discussion of minstrelsy for novices. In this volume Dumont actively encouraged the development of amateur minstrel companies throughout the United States. His *Guide* offered basic instruction, including a glossary of stage terms, sample programs, skits, stories, gags, and monologues. The book pitched amateur minstrelsy as an appropriate "vehicle to present the talent of a club, college, school, or association" and even devoted sections to women minstrels. Dumont steadfastly reassured his readers that minstrels wearing burnt cork did not need to fear that the stereotypes they conveyed from the stage would stick to them. After a simple rinse following the show, the performer would revert to a "Caucasian ready to take up the 'white man's burden' instead of the coon's."[84]

Many of Philadelphia's clerks and salespeople clearly understood this duality. They intimately connected whiteness with ideals about work handed to them in the context of a lily-white workplace. This was their "white man's burden." The affected blackness of the minstrel show was an inversion of these ideals and a temporary respite from their "burden." This duality is reflected in a 1914 article from *Store Chat* that applauded Harry L. Sampson's talents as a minstrel. Sampson worked as a salesman in the men's clothing department, but he had fifteen years of blackface theater experience outside the store. The biographical sketch proclaimed that "some of Sampson's best friends would hardly recognize him in minstrel garb."[85] Like the women of the store's mandolin club or members of the Argyle Club, he led a double life. In his predominantly white work world, Sampson absorbed and lived the paeans to hard work, thrift, temperance, and loyalty. In his spare time, on the stage, he flouted these traits, sheltered by the understanding that his inversion of workplace ideals was only mimicry of African Americans.

* * *

The vision of the ideal worker that Philadelphia's clerical workers received affected their lives acutely. The virtues promulgated in the office or on the selling floor influenced their experiences in both the arena of work and the world of leisure. The ideals of loyalty, industriousness, thrift, and temperance focused clerks on the future and encouraged them to see office or sales employment as a way station in life. On the job the portrait of the model worker left little room for collective forms of rebellion. Disaffected clerks and salespeople had to show their distaste for workplace norms by resorting to hidden forms of irreverence. Whether disgruntled employees broke work rules about chatting or engaged in more serious acts, such as defalcation, they undermined the behavioral paradigm of the workplace in private ways. In broader terms, the very nature of this rebellion reinforced the individualism implicit in the ideal of the model worker. A bookkeeper might embezzle thousands of dollars and repudiate the notion of loyalty to his boss, but he did so to get ahead, for his own benefit. In this type of environment, acts of rebellion were fragmented and rarely involved mobilizing support among co-workers.

In the realm of leisure, workplace virtues were conflated with whiteness, and the opposite of this image was associated with blackness. The racial attitudes of clerks and salespeople involved in blackface minstrelsy sprang from the fundamental insecurity of their positions in modern society. They were members of a transitional group who planned on a temporary stint in the office or on the selling floor. Additionally, second-generation immigrants wrestling with assimilation into mainstream society found security in the dehumanization of African Americans. Slathering burnt cork onto their faces allowed these clerks to role-play and safely indulge in behavior that they considered inappropriate for their workaday lives. For them, minstrelsy was a humorous (albeit racist) recreational outlet or release from the tedium of the store or office. The key factor for these amateur minstrels was that the stereotypes embodied in their performances did not stick to them. They were temporary manifestations of the stage to be laughed at and washed away with the burn cork at the end of a show. The whiteness elaborated at both work and at play represented a cord of identity that clerks and salespeople could firmly grasp as they negotiated transitions in their lives.

6   Home and Neighborhood

In the second half of the nineteenth century and the early twentieth century, Philadelphia's residential patterns changed greatly. Large-scale social and economic currents shaped the city into an "industrial metropolis."[1] Forces such as immigration and industrialization drastically altered the residential landscape of the Quaker City. As I have shown, lower-level white-collar workers felt these influences in the workplace, but home was no different. An investigation of the residential patterns of clerical workers in 1870 and 1920 can show how these forces came to alter their housing choices. In 1870 the city was in the early throes of industrialization. By 1920 it had become a mature industrial metropolis. The housing choices of industrial-era office and sales workers fit into two general patterns during this period. First, thousands of clerks and salespeople lived in row houses in typical urban residential settings, either as heads of households or more often as dependents. City directories and the federal manuscript census for 1870 and 1920 allow us to explore these residential patterns. These sources, however, cannot adequately describe the second important facet of clerical residential life. Industrial Philadelphia developed a furnished-room district in the early twentieth century, and many unmarried men and women flocked to it seeking inexpensive rooms to rent. In lodging houses—or furnished-room houses, as they were called in Philadelphia—single office and sales workers led lives of relative independence from family supervision. Their behavior in the furnished-room district challenged societal norms, especially those regarding sexuality.

The 1870s lay in the middle of a thirty-year period during which the social and economic patterns of the mature industrial metropolis emerged. In 1850 Philadelphia still more closely resembled the colonial walking city than it did its twentieth-century successor. People of varying class and ethnic backgrounds lived near one another and close to their workplaces. The Chicago school of sociology's model of concentric urban zones, which features a core of poor or working-class city dwellers and a periphery comprising the better-off, did not neatly fit the city. In fact, the reverse held true—peripheral districts exhibited a working-class flavor while middle-class and elite Philadelphians clustered in the city itself. After the 1850s, as the city industrialized, massive changes began to reshape the city's neighborhoods, and Philadelphia gradually came to fit the Chicago school's model,[2] the process culminating in the early twentieth century as middle-class suburban districts developed. In 1854 the city absorbed all the surrounding communities in Philadelphia County and increased from 2 square miles to 130. Between 1850 and 1880 the city experienced a substantial influx of Irish, German, and British immigrants, known as the "Old Immigrants." Philadelphia started to develop a web of mass transit that connected outlying districts with the central city, and its housing stock expanded because of a building boom that continued in the twentieth century. Its economy began to industrialize. In the thirty years after 1850 the city's population doubled, reaching over 800,000. Simultaneously, its population density declined, largely because new construction in outlying neighborhoods outpaced population growth.[3] Philadelphia was not highly segregated ethnically during this period.[4] Only African Americans experienced significant levels of housing segregation. The Irish intermingled with Germans and native-born Americans. Individual groups did not dominate the city's wards. Rather, occupations had a more significant influence on where people lived. Most individuals lived near their places of work. Neighborhoods such as Northern Liberties, Manayunk, and Kensington contained sizable working-class majorities concentrated around mills. Unlike their blue-collar counterparts, the city's white-collar workers were already moving away from their places of work by the 1860s and 1870s.

After 1854 the residential population in Center City, the neighborhoods that had formed the preconsolidation city and fell within William Penn's original gridiron plan, began to shift. The area between Seventh Street and the Delaware River lost population, while that west of Seventh grew as Philadelphia's population pushed away from the city's historic center. A central business district (CBD) of offices and retail stores coalesced around Market Street.[5] It stretched north to Arch Street and south to Walnut Street. Westward it reached Broad Street, and its eastern boundary was the Delaware River. Some of the district's small business owners and clerical workers bunched in residential neighborhoods nearby, but after the 1850s, as the commercial area expanded, white-collar workers lived increasingly further afield, and some even commuted via streetcar to jobs in the district.

Map 1 plots the home addresses of 620 clerical workers.[6] It shows that the vast majority of Philadelphia's office and sales workers lived in two large residential groupings straddling Center City, just beyond what had been preconsolidation Philadelphia. These concentrations accounted for 77 percent of the individuals sampled. The clerical employees who resided outside Center City were part of the rapid outward push of population reshaping the city. In 1860, 41 percent of the city's clerks dwelled outside preconsolidation Philadelphia.[7] By 1870 the clerks living beyond Center City far outnumbered those inside its boundaries. In 1870, however, very few resided in homes across the Schuylkill River, in what later developed into the streetcar suburb of West Philadelphia. Center City's northern and southern boundaries (Vine and South streets) lay about one-half mile from the city's business district.

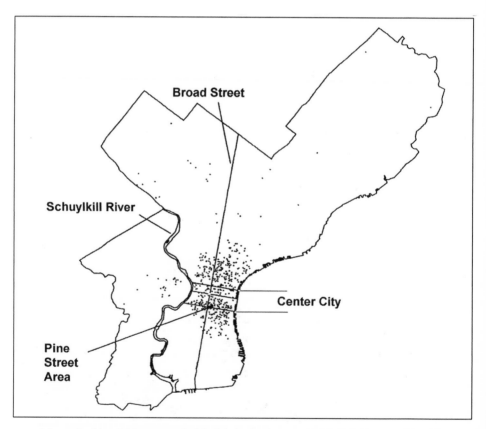

Map 1. Residential Patterns of Philadelphia's Clerical Workers, 1870

Map 2 represents the work addresses of more than 400 individuals sampled for map 1. It shows that most clerical workplaces clustered in the CBD. Specifically, 442 individuals in the sample worked in the CBD. Just over two-thirds of these lived more than a half-mile from work.[8] As early as 1870 clerks and salespeople toiling in the business district either strolled to work or took advantage of the streetcar system that had developed in the 1860s.[9] The streetcars superseded an inadequate and expensive omnibus system that had provided a slow, bumpy, uncomfortable ride. By 1870 five hundred horse-drawn streetcars (horsecars) served Philadelphians. They rode on rails and provided a much smoother, faster ride than the omnibuses.[10] At the very least, horsecars gave thousands of clerks the option to ride to work during inclement weather.

In 1870 the neighborhoods in western Center City and the northern reaches of Philadelphia housed large numbers of native-born clerical workers and

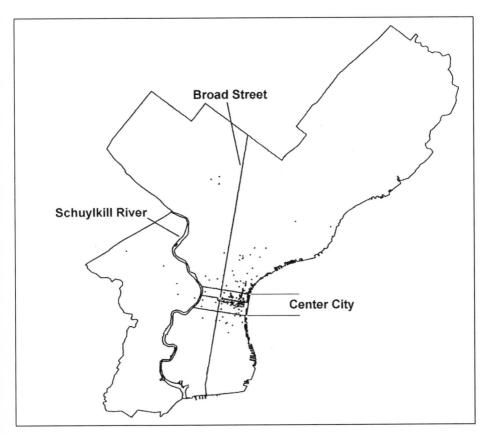

Map 2. Work Addresses of Philadelphia's Clerical Workers, 1870

proprietors.[11] These areas and the city's southwestern periphery absorbed many of the white-collar workers who moved away from the city's core. To shed more light on the residential patterns of office and sales workers in 1870, I examined an approximately four-block-square concentration of addresses (indicated on map 1) in the 1870 federal manuscript census for Philadelphia. This sample stretched west along Pine Street from Twelfth to Ceruse streets.[12] The neighborhood occupied an area within the original boundaries of the city as it was platted in 1681 by Thomas Holmes, William Penn's surveyor. What had been wilderness in the late seventeenth century had by this time transformed into a dense urban residential district. It lay in the path of Philadelphia's white-collar workers as they moved from the older core toward the city's fringes. The residential cluster stood within walking distance of the business district. If the clerks and salespeople living in this part of the city toiled in the business district, they had a daily quarter- to half-mile walk to and from work. The neighborhood was largely residential, its streets lined with row houses. Church steeples dotted the skyline. Three major houses of worship attracted flocks of faithful within the boundaries of the sample, and five others existed less than one-half a block outside it. As for industrial sites, one large shoe factory stood in the neighborhood. An asylum for the deaf and mute occupied the northeast corner of Pine and Broad streets. Although major streets lined with substantial homes crisscrossed the area, some blocks contained side streets and alleyways where cheaper housing was procurable.

Two hundred office and sales employees, many of them relatively young, resided within this area. About four-fifths were male.[13] Regardless of gender, sizable numbers lived with their parents. Exactly one-half of the clerical workers in the enclave were dependents, while one-fifth boarded with other families. The remainder headed households. Two-thirds of the female clerks lived with their parents and siblings, but just under half of their male counterparts did. This suggests that families sending children into the white-collar workforce in 1870 more readily let their sons live on their own. Whatever their gender, the young workers who remained with their families enjoyed little privacy in their crowded homes. Parents or guardians closely monitored their daily lives. Many of them likely felt quite scrutinized between their bosses in the work world and their parents at home. This domestic dependency influenced clerks' work lives as well. Nineteenth-century employers paid entry-level clerks less, because management assumed they lived with family and did not pay rent. This policy especially affected women. With regard to pay, little changed throughout the rest of the nineteenth century. Saleswomen in the city's department stores overwhelmingly lived with their parents. Of the more than 550 saleswomen surveyed by the Pennsylvania Bureau of Industrial Statistics in 1894, about 71 percent lived at home.[14] As more and more single women became office workers or labored on selling floors, it became clear that employers, particularly Philadelphia's retail establishments, reasoned that these employees could live on lower pay.[15]

The dependent clerical workers in this neighborhood came from families of varied class backgrounds.[16] The largest portion, about 29 percent, came from families where the head of the household did not work. Most often this meant families led by widows. Young clerks and salespeople provided much-needed income in such homes—an added burden of responsibility.[17] The sixty-seven-year-old widow Susan Donnelly, for example, oversaw a household in the Pine Street sample. She had six children, five of whom held jobs and lived with her. Two of her children, Margaret (age thirty) and Susannah (age twenty-four), worked as saleswomen. Two toiled at blue-collar jobs—a milliner and an upholsterer. Another labored on a locomotive. Margaret and Susannah probably earned less than their blue-collar siblings, but the two women likely provided steadier income than did their three working-class relatives, who were more prone to periodic unemployment. Margaret's and Susannah's pay likely formed the backbone of the household's income. Families headed by small-business owners composed the second-largest segment, almost a quarter of the sample. (Some dependents worked in their fathers' businesses. Sixteen-year-old Henry Cowan, for example, clerked in his father's wholesale grocery. Most likely the elder Cowan viewed Henry's work as an apprenticeship.) Finally, dependents from skilled blue-collar backgrounds constituted another substantial group, one-fifth of the sample.[18]

Whether the dependents came from skilled or proprietary backgrounds, a quest for economic stability likely motivated many to seek office or sales work. Indeed, the figures just cited reiterate the findings of chapter 3. As the work world industrialized, the labor aristocracy sought the security of clerical or sales work for many of its children. In families headed by proprietors, children often took clerical jobs as security against the fickle small-business world. An office or retail job was seen as a more steady alternative to the unpredictability of small business ventures.

The clerks and salespeople in the Pine Street area were overwhelmingly native-born whites of native-born parents, a group constituting 56 percent of the sample.[19] The Irish (i.e., first- and second-generation) accounted for a third of the clerks in the neighborhood. The minority status of the Irish in this part of the city was typical of the experiences of Irish-stock Philadelphians in the late nineteenth century. Most of the city's Irish resided in neighborhoods where they constituted a distinct minority.[20] Second-generation Irish made up almost one-fifth of the sample, which suggests that they constituted a sizable segment of the office and sales workforce. The degree to which Irish-stock clerks and salespeople identified with the rest of the largely working-class Irish community remains unclear. Irish clerks and salespeople, if they participated in voluntary organizations, most likely became members of relatively conservative ethnic clubs that frowned on radical organized labor. These groups, such as the Ancient Order of Hibernians, were not neighborhood-based. Rather, they focused on the celebration of ethnicity and Catholicism.[21] Thus, in 1870 Irish clerical employees probably had a complicated group identity that in part emphasized the class differences separating them from blue-collar Irish. Yet some clung to their ethnic identity and saw themselves as leaders in their own ethnic group.

Whether they lived close enough to walk to their jobs or regularly commuted there, white-collar workers who lived in the Pine Street neighborhood enjoyed easy access to their workplaces. Indeed, the neighborhood's location offered office and sales employees who worked in the business district great flexibility in getting to work. They could either make the nearly half-mile walk, or they could catch a horsecar to their jobs. William Buchanan, for example, lived within the neighborhood at 329 Dean Street. A salesman for a liquor dealer, he worked at 1136 Market Street—exactly one-half mile away. Buchannan could choose to walk to work or not depending on how much spending money he had, the weather, his physical condition, and whim. Others surely toiled in offices and stores within or immediately nearby the neighborhood.

Nevertheless, this residential area was hardly dominated by office or sales employees. A section of the sampled neighborhood that stretched almost two full blocks north from Lombard Street and two blocks east of Thirteenth was the region most heavily populated by clerks. Skilled blue-collar workers, however, constituted the largest occupational category among the neighborhood's 628 gainfully employed individuals, totalling just over one-third of its residents. Semiskilled and unskilled blue-collar operatives combined for an additional 36 percent. Thus, even though nonmanual workers made up about 30 percent of the population there, the area had much more of a working-class complexion.[22] This indicates that the clerical workforce in early industrial Philadelphia did not have its own defined neighborhoods. Rather, these clerks were largely dependents who lived with parents in working-class enclaves. They most often came from families headed by widows, proprietors, or workers from the upper reaches of the blue-collar world.

By the 1920s the city had become an industrial metropolis, and its housing patterns more closely matched the Chicago school model.[23] Between 1870 and 1920 the distance between the city's white-collar residential areas and the CBD greatly increased. Just before the turn of the century Philadelphia had much more open land into which it could expand than did other East Coast cities. Philadelphia's residential structures thus spread out horizontally instead of climbing vertically.[24] In the 1910s North and West Philadelphians living far outside Center City relied on public transportation—electrified streetcars and subways—to get to work.[25] Map 3 illustrates this trend, for it indicates the much wider dispersion of residential addresses for the clerical workforce in 1920.[26] Large clusters existed in North Philadelphia, West Philadelphia, and the northern reaches of Kingsessing (southwest Philadelphia). The large tracts of newly constructed row houses and duplexes in these areas attracted white-collar Philadelphians and skilled blue-collar workers. An excellent

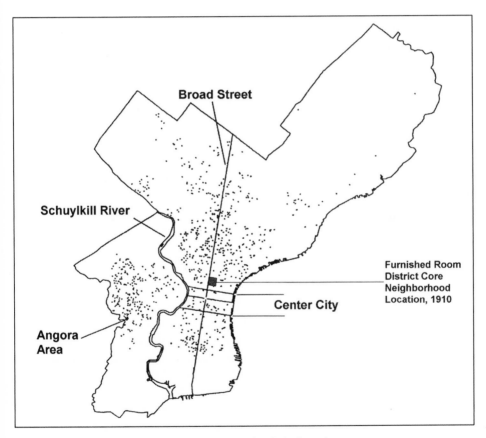

Map 3. Residential Patterns of Philadelphia's Clerical Workers, 1920

network of streetcars and subways rendered Center City work addresses only minutes away. To permit a more detailed analysis, I extracted a dense concentration of addresses from the 1920 federal manuscript census.[27] This sample comprised addresses on the border of two large regions in Philadelphia: West Philadelphia and Kingsessing. The addresses in the cluster came from the neighborhood of Angora, just inside Kingsessing, and was sandwiched between Cobb's Creek Park to the west and Fifty-eighth Street to the east. A short stretch of Baltimore Avenue formed the area's northern border, while Florence Avenue marked the southern edge. Founded in 1863 by two brothers, Robert and George Callaghan, Angora began as a small textile mill and villagelike enclave inside the city limits. They named it after Angora, Turkey, "the home of the long-haired goats."[28] Prior to the twentieth century, woodlands near Cobbs Creek gave the mill neighborhoods a bucolic feel.

Little housing development occurred in Angora prior to the early twentieth century,[29] but the area rapidly became a white-collar residential neighborhood between 1900 and 1920. Builders leveled wooded expanses and replaced them with streets lined by row houses and duplexes. Developers felled a stand of trees popularly known as Sherwood Forest on the eastern side of the neighborhood in 1912 to make way for residential expansion. The erection of row houses on the southern side of the 5800 block of Baltimore Avenue between 1918 and 1920 wrapped up home construction in the area. A yarn mill and glass works persisted in the northwest corner of the neighborhood (on the original site of the Callaghan brothers' mill), but this remained relatively isolated from the housing stock. Angora stood far removed from the city's CBD. It was also physically isolated from entertainment venues such as the big vaudeville theaters and movie houses in Center City. Of course, these amenities were only a short streetcar ride away and close to work for Angora's clerks and salespeople. One public recreational facility was near the neighborhood, however: Kingsessing Park, a little over one mile to the southeast. Dedicated in 1914, the park drew children and the elderly. On summer days old men playing checkers filled the park's recreation center (opened in 1918). Youthful clerks and salespeople likely did not want to spend their days off there, but the recreation center offered evening programs that might have caught their interest. In January 1919 it hosted the first of a series of "dancing academies" for youth, attracting eighty people. The instructor allowed students to dance only traditional waltzes. In the era of the Red Scare, the instructor frowned on more suggestive, radical dance steps deemed "Bolshevik Dancing."[30] It is unclear whether the "academy" drew younger, dependent clerks and salespeople living in the neighborhood, but this was one of the best nearby leisure venues.

Angora's social structure differed greatly from the Pine Street sample. For one thing, Philadelphia's neighborhoods had sorted out according to class by 1920. Unlike those in the 1870 Pine Street neighborhood, Angora's clerks and salespeople formed the major occupational group among the district's 893 workers. In fact, nonmanual workers constituted 73 percent of all workers in Angora, and clerical workers formed the largest group, almost 38 percent. Neither skilled nor semiskilled workers had the presence in Angora that they held in the Pine Street sample for 1870; they accounted for just under one-quarter of the workers in the neighborhood.[31] The ethnic mix, too, had changed. The native-born formed a larger percentage of the office and sales workers living in Angora than had those in the 1870 Pine Street area, providing 72 percent of the enclave's 337 clerks. At 12 percent, the Irish (both first- and second-generation) formed the largest ethnic group.[32]

From 1870 to 1920 the household status of clerical workers remained roughly the same. Dependents represented about 60 percent of the enclave; household heads, about 31 percent. The proportion of boarders and lodgers was smaller in 1920 than in 1870, which is a significant difference between the samples. Only 8 percent of Angora's clerks rented rooms. But this does not necessarily indicate that the number of clerks and salespeople who rented rooms declined in general. Rather, this development probably resulted from the differing class structures of the overall neighborhoods. Fewer Angora residents were blue-collar workers, who most often took in boarders or lodgers to help defray the costs of living. Regardless, throughout the late nineteenth and early twentieth centuries, a sizable segment of the clerical workforce remained dependent. At first this seems to contradict chapter 2's argument that between 1870 and 1920, male clerical workers increasingly stayed in the office or on the selling floor for their entire work lives. The feminization of the clerical workforce explains this discrepancy. The 1870 sample was only about 19 percent female, whereas women accounted for nearly 42 percent of the clerks in Angora. An astonishing 91 percent were dependents, but only about 40 percent of the men in Angora lived in their parents' households. As late as 1920 employers still expected women to quit their jobs once they married. They rarely had the chance to live independent of their families.

The 1870 and 1920 samples differ widely regarding the class backgrounds of dependent workers. This reflected the divergent class compositions of the neighborhoods. White-collar employees dominated Angora, and thus 61 percent of its dependent clerical workers came from white-collar families. The working class prevailed in the 1870 Pine Street sample, and thus the neighborhood's dependent clerks came from blue-collar families. More specifically, Angora had many more dependents from families headed by office or sales workers. About one-quarter of the young clerks living at home had parents who also toiled at clerical jobs.[33] This finding supports the argument that the early twentieth century saw increasing numbers of male clerks and salespeople who did not move into higher level managerial jobs or into small-business ownership as they aged. Rather, they remained in offices and on selling floors throughout their working lives, long enough to have their mature children follow them into the white-collar work world. The fact that only about 36 percent of the men in the 1870 sample headed households underscores this reality. In 1920, 51 percent had families. Overall, the differences between the two sampled neighborhoods resulted as much from changes in the clerical workforce as from citywide population shifts brought on by industrialization.

In the early twentieth century many single clerical workers chose to live outside typical residential neighborhoods such as Angora. They eschewed streets lined with row houses or duplexes where people like themselves lived with parents. Rather, they moved into the city's recently formed furnished-room district (FRD) and lived in the many lodging houses there. The FRD spread out around a core neighborhood north of Center City. The core's boundaries included Tenth Street to the east, Broad Street to the west, Poplar Street to the north, and Spring Garden Street to the south. The district's core neighborhood developed as a zone of lodging houses between 1900 and 1910 and was relatively near both the city's main commercial thoroughfares and its tenderloin. Our knowledge of furnished-room living in Philadelphia stems primarily from the work of Franklin Kline Fretz, whose Ph.D. dissertation, completed at the University of Pennsylvania around 1911, examined the FRD. Fretz focused on what he viewed as the district's social dysfunction, but he left us with a richly detailed glimpse into the lives of its lodgers.[34]

The clerks and salespeople living in this style of housing had direct antecedents in the mid-nineteenth-century city. Philadelphia's Center City witnessed a proliferation of residential hotels and boardinghouses, places such as the American Hotel, near Independence Hall. These structures provided shelter to many clerks, housing that was often close to their places of employment. Clerks frequently lived alongside other white-collar workers in such rental housing.[35] In the late nineteenth century, boardinghouses also dotted the area that became the furnished-room district. Furnished-room homes shared much in common with their predecessor, the boardinghouse. The proprietors of both types of establishments often specified the kinds of tenants they wanted—married or unmarried, male or female, black or white. Typically women ran both boarding- and lodging houses, and these institutions most often drew unmarried people. These houses differed in scope and purpose. At one extreme, families took in boarders or lodgers to make ends meet. At the other extreme, many boarding- and lodging houses were small businesses, some with as many as thirty residents that provided their proprietors their primary income. A boardinghouse on Green Street in the twentieth century's first decade housed sixteen male boarders, all native-born men except for one Russian (the female proprietor took in only men). Six held office or sales jobs.[36] The proprietor charged residents $5.50 per week. Boardinghouses offered regular meals at set times, and residents gathered at a table to eat, like a family. In addition, boardinghouses usually contained parlors where residents met guests, especially the opposite sex. Boarders also spent time together in the parlor entertaining one another, sharing daily news, and gossiping. To Fretz, the boardinghouse, with its parlor and common meals, formed an adequate, if inferior, substitute for family life.

The more modern furnished-room home was a different matter altogether.[37] Furnished-room houses rarely had parlors and did not offer communal meals. Thus, they did not offer lodgers as much opportunity to interact and develop close family-like ties, according to Fretz. In his view, furnished rooms isolated their occupants. After the early twentieth century, however, furnished-room houses quickly replaced boardinghouses in Philadelphia, and they attracted thousands of clerical workers. As I will show, Fretz refused to acknowledge that the anonymity he saw in furnished-room living might have actually attracted lodgers.

Furnished-room houses first appeared in the city in 1876 when thousands flocked to Philadelphia for the Centennial Exhibition. Many of these guests desired temporary lodging but did not want to pay for board. The first furnished-room houses emerged to meet this need.[38] Only after the turn of the century did they seriously compete with boarding establishments, most likely because up until that time, the web of services needed to support a lodging population did not exist. In the early twentieth century, however, cheap restaurants, cafés, laundries, and inexpensive entertainment could all be found in the area that became the FRD.

The district's core developed in what had been an affluent residential neighborhood during the 1870s and 1880s. A large number of the private homes were initially converted to boardinghouses in the 1890s as the area's wealthier denizens moved to peripheral urban areas and the suburbs. African Americans and immigrants moved to the side streets and alleyways of the district. Then, in the first decade of the twentieth century, enterprising souls converted most of the district's boardinghouses and almost all the remaining large private residences into furnished-room homes. The changeover occurred at a dizzying pace. In 1905, for instance, only two private homes remained on the 1100 block of Green Street. The rest were boardinghouses. By 1910 all the houses on this portion of Green had been transformed into furnished-room homes. That same year Fretz canvassed the core neighborhood of the FRD and found three hundred furnished-room houses and only twenty-seven boardinghouses. The furnished room houses clustered on the major thoroughfares in the area. The Lorraine, on the corner of Broad Street and Fairmount Avenue, was the area's only major hotel.[39]

Many of the lodging houses had once been well-appointed single-family dwellings; most had been built between 1850 and 1870. The typical house included a double parlor, dining room, and bump-out kitchen on the first floor, which featured stained-glass windows, marble mantles, ornate stucco work, and mahogany doors. The second floor usually contained two bedrooms and a bathroom. The third held two to four square rooms.[40] Turn-of-the-century clerks and salespeople thus lived in residences that a generation earlier had housed Philadelphia's business and professional elite. In their daily lives clerks touched the former dwellings of the class many of them aspired to join. In many cases the exteriors of these structures were well kept by lodging-house proprietors. The only way one could tell they were not private residences was by their window advertisements of rooms to let. Roomers paid either a weekly or a nightly rate; more reputable houses charged weekly.

Proprietors remade almost all the interior space in these once majestic homes, transforming them into shabbily furnished living areas with secondhand furniture. They subdivided parlors and turned them into lodgings. Owners partitioned larger bedrooms, forming two or three separate rooms to rent. It was much more difficult to add plumbing than to build a partition wall, however, so that many of the homes featured only one working bathroom for as many as thirty residents. If these homes resembled those in Boston's lodging-house district, dirt from heavy use clung to every corner and fixture in the bathrooms. Hot water was rare.[41] Fretz found that the furnaces installed in most homes failed to heat the residences adequately in winter.[42] Flimsy partition walls allowed much noise to pass through. Silence, like heat and hot water, was a luxury.

Fretz studied 100 furnished-room homes at the FRD's core and found that women ran 89. The houses accounted for a total of 962 roomers, 625 male and 337 female. The largest house contained twenty-nine rooms; some had only one. On Ridge Avenue, which ran diagonally through the district and was its hub, he found that many structures had storefronts on the first floor and rented rooms on upper levels.[43] Regarding the lodger population, Fretz reported that "the striking feature" was the "proportionately larger number of clerks than of skilled workers" in the core area. The investigator explained this by arguing that clerks and salespeople began their work lives with lower salaries than typical skilled workers. This encouraged clerical workers to rationalize remaining single for longer and living alone in furnished-room houses. To many it was an issue of status: "The average shopgirl [saleswoman] lives at home with her relatives . . . , but the ordinary clerk or salesman, earning less than the skilled mechanic, yet feeling himself on a higher plane than the latter, is for a long time unwilling to marry and assume the responsibility of home and family, and consequently remains in a furnished room house."[44] In a sample of 1,000 male denizens in the core area, 449 held jobs in offices or stores. Nearly 60 percent of the 200 women Fretz studied toiled as clerical or sales workers.[45] Most held jobs as saleswomen in smaller stores, which usually paid better than department stores did. Moreover, a "consciousness of kind" existed among lodgers. Clerks and salespeople tended to room with individuals of their own class status or even from the same workplace.[46] In fact, this finding contradicts Fretz's contention that the furnished-room home atomized its residents, for these lodgers did not need communal parlors and meals to socialize with others. Outside institutions had replaced these functions of the antiquated boardinghouse.

The dauntless researcher canvassed the district's streets looking for social dysfunction. He noticed that the area's thoroughfares largely emptied during the day. People thronged them only when lodgers went to or returned from work. He also noted that by 8:00 P.M. workers deserted the district in search of leisure: "All who could, have gone to see some play or 'movey' or have gone 'down-town' for a stroll."[47] Criticizing the modernization of society, Fretz saw this behavior as disrupting any semblance of home life lodgers could have created in their residences and viewed commercialized entertainment as prurient. He failed to realize that the city had become the parlor and dining room for lodging-house residents. Lodgers scrimped and saved to enjoy the fruits of the emerging leisure economy. They took their meals in cheap restaurants, cafés, dining rooms, lunch counters, or saloons. Interestingly, Fretz did not rail against saloons. In fact, he stressed that they provided lodgers a vital source of cheap food and socialization. The saloon was a place where men and occasionally women could meet friends, catch up on gossip, warm up or cool down (according to the weather), or get a hot and hearty meal—basically, leave their lodgings. In many nearby saloons a five-cent beer came with a free frankfurter, a roast-beef sandwich, soup, oysters, or fried clams. Women and men interacted in the back rooms of the district's saloons, which female patrons were allowed to enter.[48]

Indeed, the lodgers living in the core neighborhood of the FRD enjoyed easy access to many private businesses that met everyday needs. At least fifty-seven saloons slaked their collective thirst. More than two dozen eateries dotted the area, as did about three dozen barber shops and just above a score of laundries.[49] In the 1300 block of Ridge Avenue alone, just before Broad Street, seven drinking establishments, five restaurants, six barbershops, and two laundries beckoned to lodgers. Clearly, services had sprung up in the area to serve the needs of the lodging population. Furthermore, clerical workers utilized services close to their places of employment, too, and restaurants, theaters, and laundries abounded in and around Center City. For instance, after work they could grab dinner at Horn and Hardart's inexpensive, high-quality, no-frills Automat at 818 Chestnut Street. If a need for entertainment superseded hunger, they could take in a show at B. F. Keith's vaudeville house, three blocks west on Chestnut. Both establishments lay in the heart of Center City and within easy walking distance of department stores on Market Street or nearby bank and office buildings.

Eighth Street was the main entertainment strip near the district. Movie theaters, vaudeville houses, peep shows, and shooting galleries lined its blocks. Some of the bawdy shows scandalized Fretz, and the stockingless female vaudeville performers in Eighth Street's theaters horrified him. A woman who performed gymnastics while wearing a skintight bathing suit drew special ire. Four-fifths of the lodgers he interviewed did not admit to frequenting the Eighth Street theaters, but these responses probably should not be taken at face value. Who would openly admit to going to a peep show, especially if the interviewer posed the question in moralistic tones?[50] Be that as it may, Eighth Street and additional areas offered plenty of other leisure spots beyond these more risqué establishments. Lodgers habituated cheap movie houses, vaudeville, and variety theaters of the type described in chapter 4, and these were all available on Eighth Street as well as in Center City. Although clerks and salespeople had tight personal budgets, they had room for cheap entertainment. After paying for lodging and their meals, forty-five male clerks whom Fretz interviewed averaged $3.67 in spending money per week. Their female counterparts had about the same. Some of this went to carfare and to laundry, clothing, and sundries. If lodgers made it a priority, however, they could save enough for regular entertainment. Fretz noted that moving-picture shows abounded around the FRD, and they offered lodgers an hour of entertainment and pleasure for a mere nickel.[51]

Forgoing the temperance advice they received at work, lodgers occasionally indulged in "booze parties," generally quiet affairs held on Sunday nights within furnished-room homes. Both men and women came to these parties, and the partygoers most often came from the same occupational category or class. Lodgers created committees to organize these events, and some committees became permanent organizations that planned regular parties. They had names such as the Sunday Night club, the Bubble Organization, the Party-On Club, the Twice-A-Month Club, the Red Rose Social, the Not-Too-Often Club, and the Just One More Club. The organizations enjoyed the support of landladies, who often lent the clubs the use of their private dining rooms or kitchens for the parties. In return, clubs allowed the landladies to attend the festivities and turned over to them any alcohol remaining after the merriment. Bottled beer was the drink of choice. Wholesalers provided it at $1.00 per box. To cover beer costs, committees levied a fee on all club members. A typical party encompassed group singing and lively conversation. The mixed-gender revelry occasionally led to jealous fighting over dates; rarely, the parties disintegrated into outright fisticuffs and small-scale street rioting. These events were significant to the social lives of lodgers. Many women spent their Sundays preparing themselves for a party—mending dresses, applying makeup, and so on. Men likely devoted much time to preparation as well.[52]

One issue that troubled both Fretz and Albert Benedict Wolfe, an investigator of early twentieth-century Boston's lodging-house district, was what they saw as the lodgers' sexual promiscuity. For lodgers, the district offered vast opportunities for sexual experimentation. Joanne Meyerowitz suggests that "urban investigators identified the furnished room districts . . . as 'moral regions' of sorts, distinct neighborhoods where unconventional sexual behavior flourished." A variety of factors made this possible. Many furnished-room houses had both male and female lodgers living alone in close proximity. In addition, homes typically gathered people with similar occupational backgrounds, so that occupants identified with one another through work. Then, too, the neighborhood's various institutions provided men and women spaces in which to interact. They met in the back rooms of saloons, in movie theaters, and at booze parties. The populations of the districts were highly fluid, making temporary relationships typical. Family supervision was absent, and most landladies avoided personal involvement in their lodgers' lives. Furthermore, the denizens of the FRD (relatively) tolerated unconventional sexual practices, such as premarital heterosexual intercourse, prostitution, and homosexuality.[53] Finally, authorities usually looked the other way. Both Fretz and Wolfe lamented the many "temporary unions" forged between unmarried men and women.[54] Sexual interaction between men and women in the district ranged anywhere from casual dating to living together outside of marriage. Fretz attributed premarital sex and unmarried couples living together mostly to economic causes: lodgers were thrust into the sexually charged situation of shared rooms by their need to cut down on rent. And dating itself involved economic considerations. Even on the "most innocent" dates, men treated women. As Meyerowitz has noted, women responded by giving varying degrees of favors "ranging from charming companionship to sexual intercourse."[55] Such considerations, though valid, no doubt tell only part of the story. While economic factors greatly influenced sexual interaction, single men and women were sexually active in the FRD most likely because they had no immediate authority figures to oversee their behavior. In this environment men and women could more easily experiment sexually and rebel against traditional values. Wolfe speculated that experimentation prolonged the time clerks went unmarried, arguing that sexual promiscuity delayed marriage by providing intimate companionship without the burdens and costs of having a family. The fact that a clerk's wages could not support a family only exacerbated the situation.

The structuring of social space within the furnished-room home itself profoundly influenced the sexual atmosphere of the district. As Fretz worried, homes lacked parlors for intimate mixed-gender interaction. To find privacy, lodgers invited guests to their rooms. Most homes permitted such visitation by the opposite sex. In addition, the sexual atmosphere within homes containing both male and female lodgers was often much more relaxed than that of the outside world. Neighbors of both sexes visited one another's rooms unchaperoned. Residents treated their rooms and adjacent halls as semiprivate spaces in which they bent the rules of the outside world. For example, two female stenographers who roomed together in a furnished-room house became romantically involved with two men living in the adjoining room. The connecting door between the rooms was "generally open" as the couples shared their living space. Fretz believed this type of interaction would have scandalized the lodgers' families if they had witnessed it.[56] The nurturing of same-sex relationships was also quite possible under such circumstances. Intimate companions could pose as roommates with relative ease and attract little attention.

Fretz lumped casual sex and cohabitation together with prostitution, assuming that women who experimented sexually and challenged social convention made an easy transition from casual sex to prostitution. In 1912 the reformers who headed the Vice Commission of Philadelphia published a report noting that some clerical women engaged in what the commission dubbed "casual prostitution." Those who did usually worked as saleswomen in department stores during the day and involved themselves in prostitution to supplement their earnings. Critics of department stores often bemoaned the low salaries of saleswomen, which purportedly drove them into the sex trade to feed expensive consumer habits also learned in the store.[57] In 1894 a

Philadelphia saleswoman worried about the connection between prostitution and her coworkers:

> I must state that the majority of females who are employed in stores are not paid salaries sufficient for them to live upon. In some cases about enough is given them to pay their board. Then they are expected to present a respectable appearance; if they do not, they are not given employment, and in many cases a respectable and willing worker is turned away on that account. If better salaries were paid to working girls, fewer of them would have to resort to immorality to eke out a livelihood, and perhaps support an old father and mother as well.[58]

Of the 107 prostitutes the vice commission asked about their occupation, 23 said that they toiled in stores and supplemented their income as sex workers. Certainly most saleswomen did not dabble in prostitution, but it seems that lower-level white-collar workers did account for significant proportions of the city's prostitutes.[59]

Purchasing sex was an option widely available to male lodgers in and near the FRD. Fretz observed that one could easily find disreputable furnished-room houses there that sheltered prostitutes and openly catered to men interested in purchasing sex. Similarly, because they needed to maintain high levels of occupancy to turn a profit, some furnished-room house proprietors turned a blind eye to the sexual activities of resident prostitutes.[60] The Vice Commission of Philadelphia reported that within the tenderloin, several blocks south of the FRD's core, it was easy for men to find both female and male prostitutes.[61] Many male lodgers likely passed through the tenderloin on their way home from work. The commission discovered that men solicited prostitutes through a wide array of means. Parlor houses abounded in the tenderloin. These structures served as brothels, where a customer could ask for a prostitute and be ushered to her room. Houses charged anywhere from fifty cents to five dollars. Most common were "one-dollar houses." "Call houses" were much more expensive. The call-house proprietor telephoned a prostitute on behalf of a male customer and rented a room to her and her client. "Houses of assignation," akin to furnished-room homes renting a night's lodging for sex, offered another, cheaper, venue for prostitution.[62] Sex workers rented a room for a night and plied their trade at such places, but couples wishing to experiment in premarital intercourse could also lodge for an evening. Local saloonkeepers, bartenders, and waiters familiar with regularly visiting prostitutes knew where the women were staying in the nightly rate homes. More generally, prostitutes approached patrons in the area's many saloons, cafés, dance halls, and restaurants, and for their part, employees of these establishments often directed business toward them. Mas-

sage or manicure parlors, too, were commonly known as houses of prostitution. The vice commission singled out massage parlors as places where both
heterosexual and homosexual activity could be pursued. Finally, interested
men readily found streetwalking prostitutes, who clustered on thoroughfares
throughout the district. Overall, people involved in the sex trade had little
to fear regarding police. In exchange for kickbacks, officers often colluded
with people involved in the sex business.[63]

Whether or not lodgers wanted to be involved in prostitution, its existence
near the FRD's core transformed the district's gender-integrated spaces. Because of the nearby tenderloin's ubiquitous commerce in flesh, people such as
Fretz viewed the furnished-room district as a region of looser mores. Movie
theaters, saloons, restaurants, dance halls, beer gardens, cafés, and even the
streets themselves formed arenas in which sexual interaction (whether an
economic exchange or not) regularly occurred. Wide-open opportunities for
sexual contact, both paid and unpaid, existed in many establishments. Vice
commission investigators visited saloons in the district and noticed that an
interesting mix of unescorted women, single men, and prostitutes frequented
many locations.

One concert saloon less than half a block north of the FRD's core neighborhood allowed men and women to mingle near the bar. Single male and
female lodgers casually interacted at the tables. Prostitutes came and went
at will. If a man was interested in a prostitute, the bartender or a waiter
directed one his way. A male piano player and female singer entertained.
Beyond procuring sex for cash, the saloon provided an open environment
for male and female lodgers to flirt and woo. If courtship proved especially
successful for a couple and after dinner they decided to spend more of the
evening together, the two had the option of retiring to one of their own
furnished rooms. Alternatively, they could visit a cheap hotel. The saloon's
proprietor would unabashedly direct men and women to nearby inns where
they could register as married couples, no questions asked.[64] To sign in at a
hotel of this nature cost between one and two dollars, a substantial expense.
To avoid such costs, the couple could find a cheaper house of assignation. If
the two could not afford any of these options and did not want to return to
either of their rooms, they could take a trolley to Fairmount Park. The vice
commission noted that "the public parks are among the worst places [for
sexual activity]. The recesses of Fairmount Park are frequented throughout
the summer season by men and women who are seen to enter and depart
at all hours of the night."[65] Simply put, the FRD's environment of relatively
open sexuality surely encouraged many clerks and salespeople to challenge
larger society's mores.

* * *

Between 1870 and 1920 one constant in the residential patterns of clerks emerged. Their overall youth ensured that relatively few workers became household heads before leaving the clerical workforce. Rather, they lived either as dependents or lodgers. Beyond this, change rather than stability formed the overriding theme defining the housing patterns of Philadelphia's clerical workers. They were among the first residents to experience the separation of work and home brought on by industrialization. As early as 1870 the city's clerks and salespeople already lived on the peripheries of Center City. By 1920 almost all had moved further out, well beyond Center City, and commuted via rail to downtown businesses. The 1870 Pine Street sample shows that even in the most densely concentrated clerical residential areas in the early industrial city, clerks and salespeople did not form a plurality. In some of the outlying neighborhoods of the mature industrial city, they did. By 1920 neighborhoods where clerks resided were more homogeneous in terms of ethnicity and home to fewer boarders or lodgers than they had been in 1870. The fact that the 1870 sample neighborhood had a much higher proportion of boarders and lodgers among its clerks than the 1920 neighborhood did highlights the rise of the furnished-room district in the early twentieth century. The FRD siphoned potential lodgers from the newer peripheral urban neighborhoods to which the clerical workforce had moved. In the early twentieth century the boarding and lodging elements of the clerical workforce sifted out from dependents and household heads.

Numerous clerks residing in the FRD defied the sexual mores of larger society. For this group, the rather Victorian bromides about their work lives they received from their employers and social commentators—especially observations regarding temperance—presumably collided with their private lives. At the same time, they arguably lived as the first all-around consumers in American society. It is difficult to identify a facet of their lives untouched by the emerging consumer world. They rented their lodgings, ate at restaurants or saloons, washed their clothes at laundries, and entertained themselves in the institutions of the new leisure economy. They courted within movie theaters, restaurants, and vaudeville houses. Some even purchased sex while others sold themselves to make ends meet. Indeed, the lives of clerks who were lodgers in the early twentieth century approximated the lives of twenty-first-century Americans more closely than they did their industrial-era working-class counterparts: at work they managed information; at home they were consumers. In these regards, they were postmodern in the modern age.

Appendix: Occupational Rankings

This study trisects Philadelphia's white-collar workforce into professional, proprietary, and clerical (office and sales) segments. Any scholar relying on census material encounters some highly interpretable occupational designations. Workers counted as professional in this study had clear professional or managerial components to their work experiences. Foremen, forewomen, overseers, and floorwalkers all had heavy managerial responsibilities and thus are grouped with professionals. Bankers, commercial brokers, stockbrokers, and commission men do not fit under the clerical category, because they had higher status and pay than typical clerks and salespeople. The degree to which they were independent was also unclear, so they do not readily fit in the proprietary segment—hence their listing as professionals. People with occupations listed in the proprietary category basically ran independent businesses. Hucksters and peddlers are listed under the proprietary category because of their independence. Photographers are also grouped here, because, more often than not, they operated their own studios. Likewise, real estate agents often ran their own offices and are listed as proprietary for this study. Office or sales workers were those who held nonprofessional positions as "information workers" essential to the industrial-era office or selling floor. Accountants represent a special case. In the study they are considered clerical workers from 1870 to 1910, because their field was not fully professionalized in that period. For 1920 they are considered professional. Office and bundle boys are counted as office employees, because these positions were viewed by bosses and workers as the lowest rungs on the ladder into the clerical and indeed, white-collar realms. Insurance agents most often worked for large insurance firms in Philadelphia and thus are categorized as clerical workers. A handful of mail carriers appear in the 1920 census figures in this study. Their jobs dealt with information and were not simply blue-collar in nature. They also do not easily fit the proprietary or professional categories. All men, they made up less than 1 percent of the total clerical employees counted for that year.

Occupational Rankings

Professional	*Proprietary*	*Clerical*
Banker	Boardinghouse owner	Accountant
Buyer	Dealer	Agent
Chemist	Hosteler	Bookkeeper
Clergy	Hotelkeeper	Bundle boy
Commercial broker	Huckster	Canvasser
Commission man	Lodging-house owner	Cashier
Dentist	Manufacturer	Clerk
Designer	Merchant	Collector
Draftsman	Peddler	Copyist
Druggist	Photographer	Insurance agent
Engineer—	Real estate agent	Mail carrier
Civil	Restaurant owner	Messenger
Electrical	Retail dealer	Office boy
Mechanical	Saloonkeeper	Sales agent
Floorwalker	Small-business owner	Salesperson
Foreman	Trader	Stenographer
Forewoman	Undertaker	Telegrapher
Government official	Wholesale dealer	Telephone operator
Inspector	Traveler	Typewriter
Insurance co.		
official		
Intellectual		
Journalist		
Lawyer		
Manufacturing		
official		
Nurse		
Official		
Overseer		
Physician		
Stockbroker		
Superintendent		
Surgeon		
Teacher		
Veterinarian		

Notes

Introduction

1. "Biographical Sketch of Mr. T. James Fernley," *Peirce School Alumni Journal* 1 (Apr.–May 1896): 95, Peirce College Archives (hereinafter PCA), acc. 1, ser. 6, box 2, Peirce College, Philadelphia; "The Quarter Century Club, Fifteen New Members to Be Initiated This Year," *Strawbridge & Clothier Store Chat* 4 (Apr. 15, 1910): 111, Hagley Museum and Library, acc. 2117, ser. 7, box 60, Wilmington, Del.; "Biographical Sketches," *Peirce School Alumni Journal* 2 (Oct.–Nov. 1896): 40–41, PCA, acc. 1, ser. 6, box 2.

2. An immense amount of labor history on the industrial-era working class exists. The most prominent general studies include Herbert G. Gutman, *Work, Culture, and Society in Industrializing America: Essays in American Working-Class and Social History* (New York: Knopf, 1976); John T. Cumbler, *Working-Class Community in Industrial America: Work, Leisure, and Struggle in Two Industrial Cities, 1880–1930* (Westport, Conn.: Greenwood, 1979); Alice Kessler-Harris, *Out to Work: A History of Wage-Earning Women in the United States* (New York: Oxford University Press, 1982); and David Montgomery, *The Fall of the House of Labor: The Workplace, the State, and American Labor Activism, 1865–1925* (Cambridge: Cambridge University Press, 1987). On managers, see Alfred D. Chandler Jr., *The Visible Hand: The Managerial Revolution in American Business* (Cambridge, Mass.: Harvard University Press, 1977); Olivier Zunz, *Making America Corporate, 1870–1920* (Chicago: University of Chicago Press, 1990); and Clark Davis, *Company Men: White-Collar Life and Corporate Cultures in Los Angeles, 1892–1941* (Baltimore, Md.: Johns Hopkins University Press, 2000). Zunz examines primarily management, although he offers some discussion of office workers and traveling salesmen. Professionals have also been amply studied. For general studies, see Burton J. Bledstein, *The Culture of Professionalism: The Middle Class and the Development of Higher Education in America* (New York: Norton, 1978); Nathan O. Hatch, ed., *The Professions in American History* (Notre Dame, Ind.: Notre Dame University Press, 1988); Samuel Haber, *The Quest for Authority and Honor in the American Professions, 1750–1900* (Chicago: University of Chicago Press, 1991). For

information on professional women, see Barbara Harris, *Beyond Her Sphere: Women and the Professions in American History* (Westport, Conn.: Greenwood, 1978); Regina Markell Morantz-Sanchez, *Sympathy and Science: Women Physicians in American Medicine* (New York: Oxford University Press, 1985). Examples of studies on specific professions include Morton J. Horowitz, *The Transformation of American Law, 1870–1860* (Cambridge, Mass.: Harvard University Press, 1977); and Paul Starr, *The Social Transformation of American Medicine* (New York: BasicBooks, 1982). Three excellent general studies on proprietors are Mansell G. Blackford, *A History of Small Business in America* (New York: Twane, 1991); Stuart W. Bruchey, ed., *Small Business in American Life* (New York: Columbia University Press, 1980); and Ivan H. Light, *Ethnic Enterprise in America: Business and Welfare among Chinese, Japanese, and Blacks* (Berkeley: University of California Press, 1972).

3. Kenneth L. Kusmer, *Down and Out, On the Road: The Homeless in American History* (Oxford: Oxford University Press, 2002), 118–19.

4. These figures were derived from Secretary of the Interior, *The Statistics of the Population of the United States . . .* (Washington, D.C.: GPO, 1872), vol. 1, table 32, pp. 794–95; Department of Commerce and Labor, Bureau of the Census, *Occupations at the Twelfth Census,* special reports (Washington, D.C.: GPO, 1904), table 43, pp. 672–78; Department of Commerce, Bureau of the Census, *Population 1920, Occupations* (Washington, D.C.: GPO, 1923), vol. 4, table 2, pp. 1193–97.

5. See, for example, Susan Porter Benson, *Counter Cultures: Saleswomen, Managers, and Customers in the American Department Store, 1890–1940* (Urbana: University of Illinois Press, 1986); Stephen H. Norwood, *Labor's Flaming Youth: Telephone Operators and Worker Militancy, 1878–1923* (Urbana: University of Illinois Press, 1990); and Timothy B. Spears, *100 Years on the Road: The Traveling Salesman in American Culture* (New Haven, Conn.: Yale University Press, 1995); and Venus Green, *Race on the Line: Gender, Labor, and Technology in the Bell System, 1880–1980* (Durham, N.C.: Duke University Press, 2001).

6. Ileen A. DeVault, *Sons and Daughters of Labor: Class and Clerical Work in Turn-of-the-Century Pittsburgh* (Ithaca, N.Y.: Cornell University Press, 1990).

7. These include Margery W. Davies, *Woman's Place Is at the Typewriter: Office Work and Office Workers, 1870–1930* (Philadelphia: Temple University Press, 1982); and Lisa M. Fine, *The Souls of the Skyscraper: Female Clerical Work in Chicago, 1870–1930* (Philadelphia: Temple University Press, 1990); Miriam Cohen, *Workshop to Office: Two Generations of Italian Women in New York City, 1900–1950* (Ithaca, N.Y.: Cornell University Press, 1993). On the issue of gender in the white-collar workplace, see Sharon Hartman Strom, *Beyond the Typewriter: Gender, Class, and the Origins of Modern American Office Work, 1900–1930* (Urbana: University of Illinois Press, 1992); and Angel Kwolek-Folland, *Engendering Business: Men and Women in the Corporate Office, 1870–1930* (Baltimore, Md.: Johns Hopkins University Press, 1994). Clark Davis (*Company Men,* 143–70) discusses masculinity in the corporate setting from a business history perspective, focusing on management.

8. Venus Green, *Race on the Line,* provides an interesting discussion of race-related issues influencing workers in the Bell System, particularly after 1920.

9. C. Wright Mills, *White Collar: The American Middle Classes* (Oxford: Oxford University Press, 1951).

10. Ibid., xviii.

11. Although they do not focus on clerical workers, the best general studies of the types

of leisure activities that involved these workers are John F. Kasson, *Amusing the Million: Coney Island at the Turn of the Century* (New York: Hill and Wang. 1979); David Nasaw, *Going Out: The Rise and Fall of Public Amusements* (New York: BasicBooks, 1993); and Kathy Peiss, *Cheap Amusements: Working Women and Leisure in Turn-of-the-Century New York* (Philadelphia: Temple University Press, 1986). Excellent studies discussing advertising, which helped commercialize leisure pursuits, include Roland Marchand, *Advertising the American Dream: Making Way for Modernity, 1920–1940* (Berkeley: University of California Press, 1985); Susan Strasser, *Satisfaction Guaranteed: The Making of the American Mass Market* (New York: Pantheon Books, 1989); T. J. Jackson Lears, *Fables of Abundance: A Cultural History of Advertising in America* (New York: BasicBooks, 1994); and Richard M. Ohmann, *Selling Culture: Magazines, Markets, and Class at the Turn of the Century* (London: Verso, 1996).

Chapter 1: *Clerking and the Industrial-Era White-Collar Workforce*

1. Significant overviews of the industrial period include Samuel P. Hays, *The Response to Industrialization* (Chicago: University of Chicago Press, 1957); Robert H. Weibe, *The Search for Order, 1877–1920* (New York: Hill and Wang, 1967); Alan Trachtenberg, *The Incorporation of America: Culture and Society in the Gilded Age* (New York: Hill and Wang, 1982); Nell Irvin Painter, *Standing at Armageddon: The United States, 1877–1919* (New York: Norton, 1987); and Alan Dawley, *Struggles for Justice: Social Responsibility and the Liberal State* (Cambridge, Mass.: Harvard University Press, 1991).

2. Stuart M. Blumin observes that American historians have expended much effort studying both the upper crust of American society and blue-collar workers, "but only a beginning has been made toward fitting into this story of economic development and social transformation the experiences of large numbers of men and women who were neither elites nor manual workers" (Blumin, *The Emergence of the Middle Class: Social Experience in the American City, 1760–1900* [Cambridge: Cambridge University Press, 1989], 12). Blumin focuses most of his effort on the early republic and antebellum America. Jürgen Kocka, in *White-Collar Workers in America, 1890–1940: A Social-Political History in an International Perspective* (London: Sage, 1980), compares clerical workers in the United States to their European counterparts. The study centers on union organization among U.S. clerical workers. For an early and important study focused on professionals, see Burton J. Bledstein, *The Culture of Professionalism: The Middle Class and the Development of Higher Education in America* (New York: Norton, 1976).

3. Arno J. Mayer, "The Lower Middle Class as Historical Problem," *Journal of Modern History* 47 (Sept. 1975): 409–36, esp. 409.

4. Ibid., 409–36.

5. Walter Licht's *Industrializing America: The Nineteenth Century* (Baltimore, Md.: Johns Hopkins University Press, 1995) offers a concise and engaging overview of industrialization from a broad multiregional perspective.

6. Walter Licht, *Getting Work: Philadelphia, 1840–1950* (Cambridge, Mass.: Harvard University Press, 1992). Licht's first chapter (pp. 1–16) offers a wonderful, succinct description of Philadelphia's industrial structure from 1840 to 1950.

7. Lloyd M. Abernathy, "Progressivism, 1905–1919," in *Philadelphia: A 300–Year History,* ed. Russell F. Weigley, 524–65 (New York: Norton, 1982), 533.

8. Caroline Golab, in *Immigrant Destinations* (Philadelphia: Temple University Press, 1977), details this trend, especially for Polish immigrants.

9. Ibid., 11.

10. Blumin, *Emergence of the Middle Class,* 76. For more on the lives of clerks in antebellum America, see Thomas Augst, *The Clerk's Tale: Young Men and Moral Life in Nineteenth-Century America* (Chicago: University of Chicago Press, 2003).

11. Ellis Paxson Oberholtzer, *Jay Cooke: Financier of the Civil War,* 2 vols. (Philadelphia: George W. Jacobs, 1907), 1:27–42.

12. Harry Braverman has written that preindustrial clerical work "has been likened to a craft. The similarities are indeed apparent. Although the tools of the craft consisted only of a pen, ink, other desk appurtenances, and writing paper, envelopes, and ledgers, it represented a total occupation, the object of which was to keep current the records of the financial and operating condition of the enterprise, as well as its relationship to the external world" (Braverman, *Labor and Monopoly Capital: The Degradation of Work in the Twentieth Century* [New York: Monthly Review Press, 1974], 298–99).

13. Oberholtzer, *Jay Cooke,* 45–47.

14. Ibid., 47–48.

15. Ibid., 51–60.

16. George Rogers Taylor, "'Philadelphia in Slices,' by George G. Foster," *Pennsylvania Magazine of History and Biography,* January 1969, pp. 31–34.

17. For additional information on Cooke, Carnegie, and Rockefeller, as well as a lively read, see Matthew Josephson, *The Robber Barons: The Great American Capitalists, 1861–1901* (1934; repr., New York: Harcourt Brace Jovanovich, 1962).

18. Rosabeth Moss Kanter uses the term "Administrative Revolution"; see her *Men and Women of the Corporation* (New York: Basic Books, 1977), 18. For the best general study of the administrative or managerial revolution, see Alfred D. Chandler Jr., *The Visible Hand: The Managerial Revolution in American Business* (Cambridge, Mass.: Harvard University Press, 1977).

19. The rise of the department store and consumer culture in America has been interestingly discussed by William Leach in *Land of Desire: Merchants, Power, and the Rise of a New American Culture* (New York: Pantheon Books, 1993). Susan Porter Benson masterfully details the impact of all this on the work and consumer cultures of department stores; see Benson, *Counter Cultures: Saleswomen, Managers, and Customers in the American Department Store, 1890–1940* (Urbana: University of Illinois Press, 1986). Gunther Barth, too, examines department stores; see his *City People: The Rise of Modern City Culture in Nineteenth-Century America* (Oxford: Oxford University Press, 1980), 110–47. Bill Lancaster's book *The Department Store: A Social History* (London: Leicester University Press, 1995) discusses British department stores.

20. Ileen A. DeVault, *Sons and Daughters of Labor: Class and Clerical Work in Turn-of-the-Century Pittsburgh* (Ithaca, N.Y.: Cornell University Press, 1990), table 1, p. 12.

21. Sharon Hartman Strom, *Beyond the Typewriter: Gender, Class, and the Origins of Modern American Office Work, 1900–1930* (Urbana: University of Illinois Press, 1992), 2–5, 174. Also see Margery W. Davies, *Woman's Place Is at the Typewriter: Office Work and Office Workers, 1870–1930* (Philadelphia: Temple University Press, 1982).

22. DeVault, *Sons and Daughters,* 170–71.

23. See particularly Janice Harriet Weiss, "Educating for Clerical Work: A History of Commercial Education in the United States since 1850" (Ed.D. diss., Harvard University, 1987); and DeVault, *Sons and Daughters,* especially 24–47. For a discussion of women and schooling, consult John L. Rury, *Education and Women's Work: Female Schooling and the Division of Labor in Urban America, 1870–1930* (Albany: State University of New York Press, 1991).

24. Kendall Banning, "Six Brothers Build Success out of Failure," pt. 1, *System* 28 (Jan. 1916): 34–40; Banning, "Six Brothers Build Success out of Failure," pt. 2, *System* 29 (Feb. 1916): 160–65.

25. "On the Way up the Railroad Ladder," *Peirce School Alumni Journal* 20 (Apr. 1915): 3–4, Peirce College Archives (hereinafter PCA), acc. 1, ser. 6, box 2, Peirce College, Philadelphia.

26. Obituary, Edgar T. Wismer, *Strawbridge & Clothier Store Chat* 5 (Apr. 1907): 5, Hagley Museum and Library, acc. 2117, ser. 7, box 60, Wilmington, Del.

27. Arno J. Mayer uses a definition of lower middle class that includes small-business owners and professionals (Mayer, "The Lower Middle Class," 424). C. Wright Mills combines clerical workers with professionals and managers in his discussions of middle-class workers (Mills, *White Collar: The American Middle Classes* [Oxford: Oxford University Press, 1951]: 63–76).

28. Paul H. Douglas, *Real Wages in the United States: 1890–1920* (Boston: Houghton Mifflin, 1930), 367.

29. Louis E. Thayer, "Dig!" *Peirce School Alumni Journal* 18 (May 1913): 8, PCA, acc. 1, ser. 6, box 2.

30. On another level, the poem reminded young male clerical workers that hard work had eventual rewards.

31. Dale B. Light Jr., "Class, Ethnicity, and the Urban Ecology in a Nineteenth-Century City: Philadelphia's Irish, 1840–1890" (Ph.D. diss., University of Pennsylvania, 1979), 68.

32. Elyce J. Rotella, *From Home to Office: U.S. Women at Work, 1870–1920* (1977; repr., Ann Arbor, Mich.: University Microfilms, 1981), 197–99. The figure for male clerical workers is somewhat inflated, because Rotella's wage data, taken from the U.S. census, combined officials and managers with clerks and office workers.

33. Douglas, *Real Wages,* 367.

34. Stephan Thernstrom, *The Other Bostonians: Poverty and Progress in the American Metropolis, 1880–1970* (Cambridge: Cambridge University Press, 1973), 289–301. Thernstrom emphasizes the importance of the underemployment and cleanliness issues in differentiating office and sales workers from the labor aristocracy.

35. Alexander Keyssar, *Out of Work: The First Century of Unemployment in Massachusetts* (Cambridge: Cambridge University Press, 1986), 53–54. Clerical work provided more job security for Pittsburgh's workers, too, at the begining of the twentieth century (DeVault, *Sons and Daughters,* 52, 62).

36. They did slightly better at just under 4 percent.

37. The figures in this section were compiled from Department of Commerce and Labor, Bureau of the Census, *Occupations at the Twelfth Census,* special reports (Washington, D.C.: GPO, 1904), table 43, pp. 672–78.

38. Kocka, *White-Collar Workers*, 102.

39. Ibid., 87. Telegraphers founded their own international union in 1863. The Brotherhood of Telegraphers of the United States and Canada held major strikes in 1870 and 1883; both were unsuccessful. Most telegraphers were antiunion (see Edwin Gabler, *The American Telegrapher: A Social History, 1860–1900* [New Brunswick, N.J.: Rutgers University Press, 1988], 3–7, 145).

40. See especially David Montgomery, *The Fall of the House of Labor: The Workplace, the State, and Labor Activism, 1865–1925* (Cambridge: Cambridge University Press, 1987), for a broad overview.

41. Unless otherwise noted, figures used hereinafter in this chapter were drawn from Secretary of the Interior, *The Statistics of the Population of the United States . . . (Washington, D.C.: GPO, 1872)*, vol. 1, table 32, pp. 794–95; Department of Commerce and Labor, *Occupations at the Twelfth Census*, table 43, pp. 672–78; Department of Commerce, Bureau of the Census, *Population 1920, Occupations* (Washington, D.C.: GPO, 1923), vol. 4, table 2, pp. 1193–97.

42. The best discussion of these structural changes in corporate America is found in Chandler, *The Visible Hand*.

43. From 1870 to 1920 the clerical workforce grew from 14,970 to 157,313; the proprietary, from 16,460 to 56,032; and the professional, from 5,203 to 57,862.

44. DeVault, *Sons and Daughters*, 19.

45. In the late nineteenth century, Irish and German immigrants respectively ranked as the first- and second-largest foreign-born groups in Philadelphia's economy. After 1900 Russian (primarily Jewish) and Italian immigrants ranked first and third, respectively, with the Irish second and Germans fourth.

46. The 1880 federal census counted African Americans as native-born. It did not enumerate them in a separate category. Nonetheless, based on their low levels of participation in white-collar work as described in later censuses, it is likely that levels of African American participation in the white-collar world were small.

47. Between 1900 and 1920 second-generation immigrants held just under one-third of the city's white-collar jobs. Native-born individuals with native parents held about half of all white-collar jobs, while foreign-born workers held nearly one-fifth of Philadelphia's nonmanual jobs. Trisecting white-collar employment into professional, proprietary, and clerical categories yields a similar pattern from census to census. Native-born Philadelphians dominated the professional workforce. In the first two decades of the twentieth century, between about one-half to three-fifths of Philadelphia's native-born professionals had white, native-born parents. A bit over one-quarter were American-born children of immigrants (second-generation). The remaining 16 to 19 percent of professional positions were held by immigrants or nonwhites.

Business ownership also favored the native-born, but not as much as the professional sector did. Among the three segments of the white-collar workforce, the proprietary sector exhibited the most change in composition according to nativity. The percentage of small businesses owned by native-born Philadelphians declined from around 67 percent in 1870 to 50 percent in 1920. This decline was largely offset by gains among foreigners. Dividing the categories another way yields an additional inference. The 1900 and 1920 censuses show that second-generation men and women filled about a quarter of all proprietary occupations. Together immigrants and their children controlled 59 percent and 69 percent of all businesses in the city in 1900 and 1920, respectively. The segment of the proprietary sector held by immigrants was the largest group of foreign-born in the white-collar workforce during the period. Significantly, proprietors constituted only 38 percent of all native-born white-collar workers in 1870 and 13 percent in 1920. In contrast, this sector accounted for 68 percent of all foreign-born white-collar Philadelphians in 1870 and 51 percent in 1900. Between 1870 to 1900 one of every three proprietors in the city came from a foreign country. By 1920 this figure was almost one in every two. Thus, although the native-born held a majority of proprietary positions, small-business ownership defined the work experience for most foreign-born white-collar individuals. Chances were good that a consumer regularly encountered ethnic restauranteurs and merchants in the city, even though Philadelphia had relatively low proportions of immigrants in its population compared to cities in the industrial Midwest.

African Americans were underrepresented among proprietors. In the early 1900s the city's black businesses served a primarily African American clientele. Black barbers, restauranteurs, and insurance companies were fixtures in the African American community. Black business flowed to black entrepreneurs because their white counterparts usually refused to serve African Americans. Interestingly, although small-business ownership figured heavily in black nonmanual employment, it did not approach the levels among immigrants. For information on the city's black workforce, see R. R. Wright Jr., "A Study of the Industrial Conditions of the Negro Population in Pennsylvania and Especially the Cities of Philadelphia and Pittsburgh," in Pennsylvania Bureau of Industrial Statistics, *Annual Report of the Secretary of Internal Affairs, Part III, 1912* (Harrisburg, Pa.: William Stanley Ray, 1914), vol. 40, pp. 120–23.

48. Susan Porter Benson argues that department stores strove to "match their selling staffs to their desired clientele" (*Counter Cultures*, 209). In other words, African Americans and recent immigrants were not usually welcome as sales employees in department stores catering to white, middle-class women. Kenneth Lipartito also argues that telephone companies mainly hired native-born white operators to avoid any accents out of the mainstream. They wanted operators who "project[ed] a comfortable and genteel image to their customers." This was surely an oft-used excuse to keep blacks and immigrants from being operators (Lipartito, "When Women Were Switches: Technology, Work, and Gender in the Telephone Industry, 1890–1920," *American Historical Review* 99 [Oct. 1994]: 1084). Venus Green, in *Race on the Line: Gender, Labor, and Technology in the Bell System, 1880–1980* (Durham: Duke University Press, 2001), 62–67, details the selection standards used by the Bell system in hiring telephone operators prior to World War II. Kocka (*White-Collar Workers*, 136–37) stresses that the nature of their occupations differentiated second-generation clerical workers from blue-collar immigrants.

49. W. E. B. Du Bois, *The Philadelphia Negro*, ed. Elijah Anderson, centennial edition (Philadelphia: University of Pennsylvania Press, 1996), 132, 342.

50. Ibid., 327–28, 32.

51. Ibid., 332, 344, 346.

52. Ibid., 131–33, 324, 336, 342, 344.

53. Wright, "A Study," 21–195; Du Bois, *The Philadelphia Negro*, 131–33.

54. Wright, "A Study," 123–29.

55. DuBois, *The Philadelphia Negro,* 328.

56. For other cities, see Allan H. Spear, *Black Chicago: The Making of a Negro Ghetto, 1890–1920* (Chicago: University of Chicago Press, 1967), 29, 30–34, 152–55; Kenneth L. Kusmer, *A Ghetto Takes Shape: Black Cleveland, 1870–1930* (Urbana: University of Illinois Press, 1976), 78–80; and Joe William Trotter Jr., *Black Milwaukee: The Making of an Industrial Proletariat* (Urbana: University of Illinois Press, 1985), 81–82.

57. White-collar men constituted roughly 19 percent of male workers in 1870 Philadelphia. This percentage jumped to about 31 in 1920. White-collar women constituted 10 percent of all women employed in 1870. This figure almost reached 19 percent in 1900 and then leapt to nearly 40 percent over the next twenty years.

58. Not only did male workers abound in the professions, but native-stock men predominated from 1900 to 1920. Native-born men of native parents and second-generation men combined to hold around 60 percent of all professional positions between 1900 and 1920. The native-born provided over 80 percent of the male professional workforce. In the first two decades of the twentieth century, foreign-born men and the progeny of immigrants made slight inroads into the dominance of natives in the male professional workforce. Native-born and second-generation women formed the backbone of female participation in the professions from 1900 to 1920. Native-born women with native parents constituted just over one-half of the female professional workforce in the period. Second-generation workers constituted about one-third of female professionals in the city during the first two decades of the twentieth century.

59. The clerical labor pool grew by 15,786 women between 1870 and 1900. In the two following decades it grew by 47,173 women.

60. Strom, *Beyond the Typewriter,* 20. On Taylor, see especially Robert Kanigel, *The One Best Way: Frederick Winslow Taylor and the Enigma of Efficiency* (New York: Viking, 1997).

61. Strom, *Beyond the Typewriter,* 174.

62. Rather than argue for the blurring I suggest, Strom (in *Beyond the Typewriter*) and Angel Kwolek-Folland (in *Engendering Business: Men and Women in the Corporate Office, 1870–1930* [Baltimore, Md.: Johns Hopkins University Press, 1994]) depict gender relationships in the office and on selling floors along management (male) and general workforce (female) lines.

63. "Women at the Bar," *Philadelphia Evening Bulletin,* June 20, 1883.

64. DeVault, *Sons and Daughters,* 73–104.

65. Roughly between 60 and 66 percent did so.

66. In 1900 the figure was just over 15 percent.

Chapter 2: In the Office and the Store

1. Walter Licht, *Getting Work: Philadelphia, 1840–1950* (Cambridge, Mass.: Harvard University Press, 1992), 256–63.

2. *The Union Business College of Philadelphia* (Philadelphia: Henry B. Ashmead, 1865), 13, Peirce College Archives (hereinafter PCA), acc. 1, ser. 7G, box 1, Peirce College, Philadelphia.

3. Throughout the 1890s and after the turn of the century, Peirce published lists of graduates and their occupational placements in promotional pamphlets. The school

also published letters from employers requesting qualified applicants. Testimonials from successfully placed students appear in this literature.

4. Pamphlet (Philadelphia: Peirce, 1900), PCA, acc. 1, ser. 6G, box 1.

5. "Chances for Success," *Peirce School Alumni Journal* 8 (Mar. 1903): 8, PCA, acc. 1, ser. 6, box 2.

6. "Back to the Great Days," *Peirce School Alumni Journal* 15 (Oct. 1909): 12–13, PCA, acc. 1, ser. 6, box 2.

7. *There Is Room in the Business World for YOU* (Philadelphia: Peirce, 1906), 11, PCA, acc. 1, ser. 7G, box 1.

8. Ibid., 18–19.

9. *Secretarial Positions for Women* (Philadelphia: Peirce, 1913), 4, PCA, acc. 1, ser. 6G, box 1.

10. *Tom Brown at Peirce School* (Philadelphia: Peirce, 1919), 10, PCA, acc. 1, ser. 6G, box 1.

11. *Are You Acquainted with These Facts concerning Peirce School* (Philadelphia: Peirce, 1912), 6, PCA, acc. 1, ser. 7G, box 1; *Peirce School of Business Administration: Circular of Condensed Information* (Philadelphia: Peirce, 1921), 12, PCA, acc. 1, ser. 6G, box 1.

12. "School Notes," *Peirce School Alumni Journal* 11 (Dec. 1905): 8, PCA, acc. 1, ser. 6, box 2; "A Glimpse into the Work of the Employment Department," *Peirce School Alumni Journal* 15 (Sept. 1909): 10, PCA, acc. 1, ser. 6, box 2.

13. "A Glimpse," 10.

14. "The Year 1914–1915 at Peirce School," *Peirce School Alumni Journal* 20 (June 1915): 10, PCA, acc. 1, ser. 6, box 2.

15. "Plenty of Room in the Business World for Peirce Graduates," *Peirce School Alumni Journal* 16 (Oct. 1910): 9, PCA, acc. 1, ser. 6, box 2.

16. "School Notes," *Peirce School Alumni Journal* 11 (Jan. 1906): 10–11, PCA, acc. 1, ser. 6, box 2.

17. "The Advantage of Being a Peirce Graduate," *Peirce School Alumni Journal* 20 (Nov. 1914): 8, PCA, acc. 1, ser. 6, box 2.

18. "When It Comes to Employment," *Peirce School Alumni Journal* 10 (Apr. 1905): 6, PCA, acc. 1, ser. 6, box 2.

19. "How Peirce School Is of Service," *Peirce School Alumni Journal* 11 (May 1906): 7, PCA, acc. 1, ser. 6, box 2.

20. "School Notes," *Peirce School Alumni Journal* 11 (Dec. 1905): 8, PCA, acc. 1, ser. 6, box 2.

21. "Positions Recently Filled," *Peirce School Alumni Journal* 11 (Nov. 1905): 10, PCA, acc. 1, ser. 6, box 2.

22. "School Notes," *Peirce School Alumni Journal* 11 (Dec. 1905): 8.

23. "A Glimpse," 11.

24. *Report for 1915* (Philadelphia: Bureau of Occupations for Trained Women, 1916), Urban Archives, Temple University (hereinafter UATU), Free Library Pamphlet Collection, box 4, "Bureau of Occupations for Trained Women 1914–1916" file, Temple University, Philadelphia; *Report for 1914* (Philadelphia: Bureau of Occupations for Trained Women, 1915), UATU, Free Library Pamphlet Collection, box 4, "Bureau of Occupations for Trained Women 1914–1916" file.

25. Pamphlet (Philadelphia: Bureau of Occupations for Trained Women, 1915), UATU,

Free Library Pamphlet Collection, box 4, "Bureau of Occupations for Trained Women 1914–1916" file.

26. The evidence seems to suggest that "college training" meant four-year college experience. The bureau probably lumped business-college experience under its "special training" statistical category.

27. These included bookkeepers, statisticians, treasurers, clerks, typists, general office assistants, executive secretaries, and stenographers. Stenographers accounted for 65 percent of filled clerical positions; see *Report for 1914*.

28. Lisa Fine, *The Souls of the Skyscraper: Female Clerical Workers in Chicago, 1870–1930* (Philadelphia: Temple University Press, 1990): 127–33.

29. "Our Carpet Chief," *Strawbridge & Clothier Store Chat* 3 (Oct. 15, 1909): 258–59, Hagley Museum and Library (hereinafter HML), acc. 2117, ser. 7, box 60, Wilmington, Del.

30. "The Quarter Century Club," *Strawbridge & Clothier Store Chat* 4 (Apr. 15, 1910): 111–12, HML, acc. 2117, ser. 7, box 60.

31. "Biographical Sketches," *Peirce School Alumni Journal* 3 (Oct.–Nov. 1896): 40–41, PCA, acc. 1, ser. 6, box 2; "Banker and Merchant," *Peirce School Alumni Journal* 15 (May 1910): 3–4, PCA, acc. 1, ser. 6, box 2.

32. "Hall of Fame," *Strawbridge & Clothier Store Chat* 8 (June 10, 1914): 168–69, HML, acc. 2117, ser. 7, box 60.

33. For a discussion of ethnicity and race as factors in the hiring process, see Suzanne Model, "The Ethnic Niche and the Structure of Opportunity: Immigrants and Minorities in New York City," in *The "Underclass" Debate: Views from History,* ed. Michael B. Katz (Princeton, N.J.: Princeton University Press, 1993), 161–93.

34. Ellis Paxson Oberholtzer, *Jay Cooke: Financier of the Civil War,* 2 vols. (Philadelphia: George W. Jacobs, 1907), 1:48–53.

35. "Applying for a Position," *Peirce School Alumni Journal* 3 (Dec. 1897): 78, PCA, acc. 1, ser. 6, box 2.

36. James Glentworth to president and directors of the Fourth Street National Bank, July 30, 1886, HML, acc. 1658, FSNB Corporate, box 10, "Personnel" file.

37. William K. Houpt to W. W. Kurtz, July 27 and August 10, 1886, HML, acc. 1658, FSNB Corporate, box 10, "Personnel" file.

38. David Faust to S. F. Tyler and members of the board of directors of Fourth Street National Bank, August 6, 1886, HML, acc. 1658, FSNB Corporate, box 10, "Personnel" file.

39. "'Don'ts' When Applying for a Position," *Peirce School Alumni Journal* 10 (June 1905): 7, PCA, acc. 1, ser. 6, box 2.

40. "Dress That Commands Respect," *Peirce School Alumni Journal* 11 (Feb. 15, 1906): 10–11 (repr. from *Success*), PCA, acc. 1, ser. 6, box 2.

41. "To Get and Hold Employment," *Strawbridge & Clothier Store Chat* 5 (Jan. 15, 1911): 30, HML, acc. 2117, ser. 7, box 60.

42. E.g., ibid.

43. "Be Clean," *Peirce School Alumni Journal* 9 (June 1901): 6, PCA, acc. 1, ser. 6, box 2.

44. "'Don'ts' When Applying," 7; "A Stenographer's Story," *Strawbridge & Clothier Store Chat* 3 (Apr. 15, 1909): 92, HML, acc. 2117, ser. 7, box 60.

45. C. R. Evans, "Vocational Training for Women in Its Relation to Secretarial Courses," *Peirce School Alumni Journal* 24 (June 1919): 6, PCA, acc. 1, ser. 6, box 2.

46. *Peirce School Alumni Journal* 8 (Apr. 1903): 6, PCA, acc. 1, ser. 6, box 2.

47. Margery W. Davies, *Woman's Place Is at the Typewriter: Office Work and Office Workers, 1870–1930* (Philadelphia: Temple University Press, 1982), 120.

48. Stuart M. Blumin found that during every decade from 1820 to 1860, between 25 and 38 percent of Philadelphia's clerical workers experienced upward occupational mobility. Only 5 to 10 percent of craftsmen did so (Blumin, *The Emergence of the Middle Class: Social Experience in the American City, 1760–1900* [Cambridge: Cambridge University Press, 1989], 121).

49. Earlier published federal censuses break down workers' ages too broadly to be useful in this study. Figures for this section and for the corresponding section on women workers were drawn from Secretary of the Interior, *The Statistics of the Population of the United States . . .* (Washington, D.C.: GPO, 1872), vol. 1, table 32, pp. 794–95; Department of Commerce, Bureau of the Census, *Population 1920, Occupations* (Washington, D.C.: GPO, 1923), vol. 4, table 2, pp. 1193–97.

50. Alyson Marie Blant, "Avenues of Advancement or Clerk Factories?: A History of Private Business Schools, 1865–1900" (master's thesis, University of Virginia, 1988), 53–54. Blumin (*Emergence of the Middle Class*, 77) uses age to discuss mobility among lower-level nonmanual workers in 1860.

51. *Peirce School Alumni Journal* 1 (Feb.–Mar. 1896): 75–76, PCA, acc. 1, ser. 6, box 2.

52. "Some Modest Stories of Success," *Peirce School Alumni Journal* 11 (Dec. 1905): 10, PCA, acc. 1, ser. 6, box 2.

53. "Biographical Sketches," *Peirce School Alumni Journal* 3 (Oct.–Nov. 1896): 40–41, PCA, acc. 1, ser. 6, box 2.

54. "New Members of the Quarter Century Club," *Strawbridge & Clothier Store Chat* 3 (Apr. 15, 1909): 108, HML, acc. 2117, ser. 7, box 60.

55. Most American women in the industrial era who worked for wages outside the home did so only until marriage. Numerous African American women, however, whether married or not, worked outside their homes throughout their lives.

56. Philadelphia and Reading R. R. Athletic Association, *Official Program, Grand Benefit Held at Chestnut Street Theater* (Philadelphia, 1894), 73; Charles Darrach Gobrecht, *The Design, Installation, and Maintenance of the Modern Office Building* (Philadelphia: Franklin Institute, 1906); George Morgan, *The City of Firsts* (Philadelphia: Historical Publication Society of Pennsylvania, 1926), 593.

57. Robert H. Weibe, *The Search for Order, 1877–1920* (New York: Hill and Wang, 1967), 111–32. Oddly enough, Weibe omits the office and sales workforce from his description of American industrialization.

58. Alfred D. Chandler Jr., *The Visible Hand: The Managerial Revolution in American Business* (Cambridge, Mass.: Harvard University Press, 1977).

59. Elyce J. Rotella, "The Transformation of the American Office: Changes in Employment and Technology," *Journal of Economic History* 41 (Mar. 1981): 53.

60. Davies, *Woman's Place*, 37.

61. "A Matter of Classification," *Peirce School Alumni Journal* 3 (Nov. 1897): 57 (repr. from *The Phonographic Magazine*), PCA, acc. 1, ser. 6, box 2.

62. "The Frantic Typist," *Peirce School Alumni Journal* 24 (Dec. 1918): 13, PCA, acc. 1, ser. 6, box 3.

63. M. S. Tennent, "The Typewriter's First Day Back," *Peirce School Alumni Journal* 4 (Oct. 1898): 221 (repr. from *The Stenographer*), PCA, acc. 1, ser. 6, box 2.

64. "How to Cure a Headache," *Peirce School Alumni Journal* 2 (Oct.–Nov. 1896): 43 (repr. from *Ladies' Home Journal*), PCA, acc. 1, ser. 6, box 2.

65. "'She,'" *Peirce School Alumni Journal* 3 (Oct. 1897): 41, PCA, acc. 1, ser. 6, box 2.

66. John H. Sinberg, "A Stenographer's Opportunities," *Peirce School Alumni Journal* 7 (Jan. 1902): 10–11, PCA, acc. 1, ser. 6, box 2.

67. "Don'ts for Stenographers," *Peirce School Alumni Journal* 1 (Dec. 1895–Jan. 1896): 65, PCA, acc. 1, ser. 6, box 2.

68. Ibid.

69. "The New Stenographer," *Peirce School Alumni Journal* 3 (Oct. 1897): 41–42, PCA, acc. 1, ser. 6, box 2.

70. Fine, *The Souls of the Skyscraper,* 93.

71. "From Stenographer to Traction Official," *Peirce School Alumni Journal* 15 (Nov. 1909): 3–4, PCA, acc. 1, ser. 6, box 2.

72. Kenneth Lipartito, "When Women Were Switches: Technology, Work, and Gender in the Telephone Industry, 1890–1920," *American Historical Review* 99 (Oct. 1994): 1085. Telephone companies tried to hire men as operators but often found them too gruff with callers.

73. Davies, *Woman's Place,* 130–46.

74. Rosabeth Moss Kanter, *Men and Women of the Corporation* (New York: BasicBooks, 1977), 27.

75. "Secretarial Positions," *Peirce School Alumni Journal* 8 (Sept. 1912): 12, PCA, acc. 1, ser. 6, box 2.

76. Edwin Gabler, *The American Telegrapher: A Social History, 1860–1900* (New Brunswick, N.J.: Rutgers University Press, 1988), 58.

77. "Hall of Fame," *Strawbridge & Clothier Store Chat* 8 (Feb. 15, 1914): 52, HML, acc. 2117, ser. 7, box 60.

78. "The Proper Care of the Records and Correspondence of a City," *Peirce School Alumni Journal* 18 (June 1913): 3–7, PCA, acc. 1, ser. 6, box 2.

79. The best source on traveling salesmen is Timothy B. Spears, *100 Years on the Road: The Traveling Salesman in American Culture* (New Haven, Conn.: Yale University Press, 1995).

80. "The Common Cause," *Strawbridge & Clothier Store Chat* 3 (Dec. 15, 1908): 8–9, HML, acc. 2117, box 60.

81. This definition comes from Susan Porter Benson, *Counter Cultures: Saleswomen, Managers, and Customers in American Department Stores, 1890–1940* (Urbana: University of Illinois Press, 1986), 14–17. Also interesting is William Leach, *Land of Desire: Merchants, Power, and the Rise of a New American Culture* (New York: Pantheon, 1993).

82. Benson, *Counter Cultures,* 23.

83. Ibid., 180.

84. "The Quarter Century Club," *Strawbridge & Clothier Store Chat* 4 (Apr. 15, 1910): 110–12, HML, acc. 2117, ser. 7, box 60; "New Members of the Quarter Century Club,"

Strawbridge & Clothier Store Chat 3 (Apr. 15, 1909): 106–8, HML, acc. 2117, ser. 7, box 60; "New Members of the Quarter Century Club," *Strawbridge & Clothier Store Chat* 3 (Mar. 15, 1909): 73, HML, acc. 2117, ser. 7, box 60.

85. "Do You Want to Sell Goods?" *Strawbridge & Clothier Store Chat* 1 (Nov. 1907): 1, HML, acc. 2117, ser. 7, box 60.

86. Emma Johnson, "The 'I Will' Girl," *Strawbridge & Clothier Store Chat* 3 (Sept. 15, 1909): 218 (repr. from the *Chicago Tribune*), HML, acc. 2117, ser. 7, box 60.

87. Benson, *Counter Cultures,* 232–35.

88. Pennsylvania Bureau of Industrial Statistics, "Women in Industry," *Annual Report of the Secretary of Internal Affairs of the Commonwealth of Pennsylvania, Part III, Industrial Statistics, 1894* (Harrisburg, Pa.: Clarence M. Busch, 1895), vol. 22, pp. 4.A–A.5 (quotation on 36.A).

89. Ibid., A.64–115.A.

90. Ibid., A.5.

91. "The Employees' Dining Room," *Strawbridge & Clothier Store Chat* 1 (Jan. 1907): 4, HML, acc. 2117, ser. 7, box 60.

92. "The New Roof Garden," *Strawbridge & Clothier Store Chat* 4 (Aug. 15, 1910): 224–25, HML, acc. 2117, ser. 7, box 60.

93. "Our New Hospital," *Strawbridge & Clothier Store Chat* 3 (Oct. 15, 1909): 260–61, HML, acc. 2117, ser. 7, box 60.

94. "The Relief Association," *Strawbridge & Clothier Store Chat* 1 (Oct. 1906): 12, HML, acc. 2117, ser. 7, box 60.

95. "About That Vacation," *Strawbridge & Clothier Store Chat* 3 (June 15, 1909): 147, HML, acc. 2117, ser. 7, box 60.

96. Leach, *Land of Desire,* 34.

97. "A Business Palace," *Philadelphia Press,* Apr. 12, 1887; "Strawbridge & Clothier: Twentieth Anniversary of Their First Extension in 1868," *Philadelphia Ledger and Transcript,* October 11, 1888, HML, acc. 2117, ser. 7, box 75, "Clippings Scrapbook January 1887–January 1894."

98. Ample interior lighting was always an issue in nineteenth-century department stores, and many favored a rotunda design allowing for skylights; see Benson, *Counter Cultures,* 39.

99. Ibid., 231–40.

100. The following draws on Deborah C. Andrews, "Bank Buildings in Nineteenth-Century Philadelphia," in *The Divided Metropolis: Social and Spatial Dimensions of Philadelphia, 1800–1975,* ed. William W. Cutler and Howard Gillette Jr. (Westport, Conn.: Greenwood, 1980), 57–83.

101. Angel Kwolek-Folland notes that after World War I, some banks began to hire women because they wanted to please female clients, who were a growing part of their business. Banks began to create women's departments staffed by women and serving women. See Kwolek-Folland, *Engendering Business: Men and Women in the Corporate Office, 1870–1930* (Baltimore, Md.: Johns Hopkins University Press, 1994), 171.

102. Olivier Zunz, *Making America Corporate, 1870–1920* (Chicago: University of Chicago Press, 1990), 103–25.

103. "An Every-Day Stenographer," pt. 1, *Peirce School Alumni Journal* 4 (Jan. 1899): 260,

PCA, acc. 1, ser. 6, box 2. Lisa M. Fine (*Souls of the Skyscraper,* 65–75) offers a discussion of stories in *The Phonographic World* that incorporated female clerical workers.

104. Sharon Hartman Strom, *Beyond the Typewriter: Gender, Class, and the Origins of Modern American Office Work, 1900–1930* (Urbana: University of Illinois Press, 1992), 369–70.

105. Kwolek-Folland, *Engendering Business,* 63. Fine (*Souls of the Skyscraper,* 108–9) discusses fictionalized women office workers who married their bosses and reproduces two postcards depicting office women on the laps of supervisors.

106. "A Good Woman's Good Influence in a Business Establishment," *Strawbridge & Clothier Store Chat* 4 (Jan. 15, 1910): 23, HML, acc. 2117, ser. 7, box 60; "A Stenographer's Story," 92.

107. Mary Clay Whiteley, "Women's Sphere," *Peirce School Alumni Journal* 2 (Dec. 1896–Jan. 1897): 59, PCA, acc. 1, ser. 6, box 2.

108. Mary Clay Whiteley, "Women and Their Ways," *Peirce School Alumni Journal* 3 (Oct. 1897): 40, PCA, acc. 1, ser. 6, box 2.

109. Kwolek-Folland, *Engendering Business,* 113.

110. Millicent S. Renshaw, "Women in the Stenographic Field" *Peirce School Alumni Journal* 5 (Nov. 1899): 6, PCA, acc. 1, ser. 6, box 2.

111. "The Graduating Exercises of the 37th class of Peirce School," *Peirce School Alumni Journal* 8 (Dec. 1902): 6–8, PCA, acc. 1, ser. 6, box 2. Merriam had been a banker (among other things), and at the time of the commencement he was the director of the U.S. Census.

112. Fine, *Souls of the Skyscraper,* 93–96.

113. Gabler, *The American Telegrapher,* 58.

114. Albert W. Niemi Jr., "The Male-Female Earnings Differential: A Historical Overview of the Clerical Occupations from the 1880s to the 1970s," *Social Science History* 7 (Winter 1983): 97–107.

115. Pennsylvania Bureau of Industrial Statistics, "Women in Industry," 40.A.

116. Blue-collar women workers also felt this way. For a discussion of the issue of equal pay versus equal work, see Alice Kessler-Harris, *In Pursuit of Equity: Women, Men, and the Quest for Economic Citizenship in 20th-Century America* (Oxford: Oxford University Press, 2001), 53–56; Kessler-Harris, "The Double Meaning of Equal Pay," *A Woman's Wage: Historical Meanings and Social Consequences* (Lexington: University of Kentucky Press, 1990), 81–112.

117. Renshaw, "Women," 6–7.

Chapter 3: Pursuing "Noble Endeavor"

1. *Tom Brown at Peirce School* (Philadelphia: Peirce, 1915), Peirce College Archives (hereinafter PCA), acc. 1, ser. 7G, box 1, Peirce College, Philadelphia.

2. Ibid., 2.

3. Obituary, Thomas May Peirce, *Peirce School Alumni Journal* 2 (June–July 1896): 3, PCA, acc. 1, ser. 6, box 2.

4. *To Our Graduates* (Philadelphia: Peirce, 1904), PCA, acc. 1, ser. 7G, box 1; William Wirt Mills, "The Peirce School in Philadelphia," in *Peirce School in Philadelphia: The Most*

Eminent School of Business in America, King's Booklets (New York: Moses King, 1907), 2, PCA, acc. 1, ser. 7G, box 1.

5. *Peirce School* (Philadelphia: Peirce, ca. 1915), PCA, acc. 1, ser. 7G, box 1.

6. Isaac Costa, *Gopsill's Philadelphia City Directory for 1881* (Philadelphia: James Gopsill, 1881).

7. *The Philadelphia* Record *Educational Guide* (Philadelphia: *Philadelphia Record,* 1920), 22–27, PCA, acc. 1, ser. 7G, box 1. The Wanamaker Institute was not a business college in the strictest sense. Rather, it offered courses in a variety of subjects ranging from dressmaking to stenography and bookkeeping.

8. Janet Harriet Weiss, "Educating for Clerical Work: A History of Commercial Education in the United States since 1850" (Ph.D. diss., Harvard University, 1978). Weiss offers the only national study of business education. She outlines the growth of public and private business schools and focuses on the way educators, who saw the potential to serve a larger clientele, encouraged the development of business education in public high schools. Specifically, public educators wanted to broaden the socioeconomic community that these institutions served. Weiss suggests that, as part of the vocational education movement, business education helped to democratize public and private schooling.

9. Earl P. Strong, *The Organization, Administration, and Supervision of Business Education* (New York: Gregg, 1944), 50–51.

10. *The Union Business College of Philadelphia* (Philadelphia: Henry B. Ashmead, 1865), 13, PCA, acc. 1, ser. 7G, box 1.

11. Ibid., 30.

12. *Peirce School Catalog, 1900–1901* (Philadelphia: Peirce, 1900), 22, PCA, acc. 1, ser. 7G, box 1.

13. *Announcement to College Students and Those About to Enter College* (Philadelphia: Peirce, 1910), PCA, acc. 1, ser. 7G, box 1.

14. *Are You Acquainted with These Facts concerning Peirce* (Philadelphia: Peirce, 1912), PCA, acc. 1, ser. 7G, box 1.

15. *There Is Room in the Business World for YOU* (Philadelphia: Peirce, 1906), 3, PCA, acc. 1, ser. 7G, box 1.

16. "The Jennie W. Rogers Loan Fund," *Peirce School Alumni Journal* 19 (Oct. 1914): 8, PCA, acc. 1, ser. 6, box 2; "The Jennie W. Rogers Loan Fund," *Peirce School Alumni Journal* 26 (Jan.–Feb. 1920): 7, PCA, acc. 1, ser. 6, box 2.

17. *The Union Business College and Writing Institute* (Philadelphia: Henry B. Ashmead, 1866), 30, PCA, acc. 1, ser. 7G, box 1.

18. *Announcement to College Students and Those About to Enter College* (Philadelphia: Peirce, 1906), 3, PCA, acc. 1, ser. 7G, box 1.

19. *Relation of Peirce School to the Public Schools* (Philadelphia: Peirce, 1910), 2–3, PCA, acc. 1, ser. 7G, box 1.

20. *This May Give You a New View-point* (Philadelphia: Peirce, ca. 1915), PCA, acc. 1, ser. 7G, box 1.

21. *To Our Graduates* (Philadelphia: Peirce, 1904), 2, PCA, acc. 1, ser. 7G, box 1.

22. *Are You Acquainted.*

23. *There Is Room.*

24. For a discussion of the definition of success in industrial-era America, see John

G. Cawelti, *Apostles of the Self-Made Man* (Chicago: University of Chicago Press, 1965), 167–95.

25. *In Reference to Its Courses of Study* (Philadelphia: Peirce, 1912), 12, PCA, acc. 1, ser. 7G, box 1.

26. Department of Commerce and Labor, Bureau of the Census, *Occupations at the Twelfth Census,* special reports (Washington, D.C.: GPO, 1904), table 43, pp. 672–78; Department of Commerce, Bureau of the Census, *Population 1920, Occupations* (Washington, D.C.: GPO, 1923), vol. 4, table 2, pp. 1193–97; Angel Kwolek-Folland, *Engendering Business: Men and Women in the Corporate Office, 1870–1930* (Baltimore, Md.: Johns Hopkins University Press, 1994), 30.

27. *There Is Room.*

28. *Announcement to College Students and Those About to Enter College* (Philadelphia: Peirce, 1910), 7.

29. The preceding section is based on the following sources: *The Circular of Peirce's Union Business College* (Philadelphia: Thomas May Peirce, 1880); *The Circular of Peirce's Union Business College* (Philadelphia: Thomas May Peirce, 1890); *Peirce School Year Book, Winter, Spring '96, '97* (N.p.: n.p., n.d.); Peirce catalog for 1900–1901 (N.p.: n.p., n.d.); *Announcement to College Students; Are You Acquainted;* Carl Fassl, *Peirce Means Business: A History of Peirce Junior College, 1865–1989* (Philadelphia: Peirce Junior College, 1990). The first three items can be found at PCA, acc. 1, ser. 7G, box 1.

30. *Union Business College,* 27.

31. Ibid. This catalog lists the names and addresses of enrolled students for the 1865–1866 schoolyear.

32. Janet F. Davidson, "'Now That We Have Girls in the Office': Clerical Work, Masculinity, and the Refashioning of Gender for a Bureaucratic Age," in *Boys and Their Toys? Masculinity, Class, and Technology in America,* ed. Roger Horowitz (London: Routledge, 2001), 59.

33. "Peirce School under War Conditions," *Peirce School Alumni Journal* 23 (Sept. 1917): 8, PCA, acc. 1, ser. 6, box 2.

34. "Discarded Gloves Wanted to Provide Leather Waistcoats for Soldiers," *Peirce School Alumni Journal* 23 (Nov. 1917): 12, PCA, acc. 1, ser. 6, box 2; "Our Boys," *Peirce School Alumni Journal* 23 (Feb. 1918): 8, PCA, acc. 1, ser. 6, box 2; "Peirce School in the Third Liberty Loan," *Peirce School Alumni Journal* 23 (June 1918): 4, PCA, acc. 1, ser. 6, box 2; "Captured Hun Helmet Presented to the School by a Student of 1916–1917," *Peirce School Alumni Journal* 24 (Nov.–Oct. 1918): 12, PCA, acc. 1, ser. 6, box 2; "Peirce School in the Victory Loan," *Peirce School Alumni Journal* 24 (May 1919): 6, PCA, acc. 1, ser. 6, box 2.

35. "The Secretarial Course," *Peirce School Alumni Journal* 15 (June 1910): 9, PCA, acc. 1, ser, 6, box 2.

36. "Biographical Sketch of Mr. T. James Fernley," *Peirce School Alumni Journal* 1 (Apr.–May 1896): 95, PCA, acc. 1, ser. 6, box 2.

37. The 1880, 1900, and 1910 enrollments were selected because of the following considerations: (1) The first complete existing class roster that matches a census year is 1880. (2) Fire destroyed the 1890 manuscript census. (3) Enrollment rosters do not exist for 1920. The existing enrollment ledgers for the 1880 calendar year do not differentiate between the 1879–1880 and 1880–1881 classes. Taking a stratified, proportionate 10 percent sample

of the male enrollments listed in these ledgers produced a group of 56; the female sample included 49 women. Because there were significantly fewer women listed in the 1879–81 ledgers, the female sample was the average of the total number of women listed in each ledger. I drew 10 percent samples from both the male and the female enrollments shown in the 1899–1900 registration ledgers. The male sample numbered 96; the female, 41. The same procedure was used for the 1909–1910 class, which produced samples of 69 women and 130 men.

38. Entries in the ledgers followed the order of student registration. They were not alphabetized. Also, the registrars did not sort them in any other way. Sampling was done to compensate for potential factors that could have slanted results. For example, because some students likely registered in friendship groups, student records were sampled to avoid possibly acquainted individuals.

39. This supports what Margery W. Davies asserts: "The endemic financial insecurity of many small business men often meant not only that their children were reluctant to follow them in an unstable occupation, but also, in many cases, that the children were forced to support themselves" (*Woman's Place Is at the Typewriter: Office Work and Office Workers, 1870–1930* [Philadelphia: Temple University Press, 1982], 61).

40. DeVault, *Sons and Daughters,* 43.

41. I have not found explicit statements of policy suggesting that immigrants, African Americans, or any other socioeconomic group was barred from enrollment at Peirce between 1865 and 1920. This of course does not preclude the existence of bias or discrimination on the part of the administration.

42. Since the 1870 and 1880 federal censuses do not enumerate nativity beyond the rather crude categories of "foreign-born" and "native-born," the numbers of second-generation individuals in the clerical workforce cannot be discerned from them.

43. I followed two basic rules when sorting the Peirce samples for ethnicity. First, I considered anyone ethnic if he or she was an immigrant or second-generation with parents sharing an ethnicity. If parents were of mixed nativity (one American-born and the other foreign), the native-born parent had to be second-generation of the same ethnicity as the foreign-born parent for the student to be deemed of a specific ethnic category. This is a relatively stringent set of strictures. For a comparison of methodologies, see Theodore Hershberg, Alan N. Burstein, Eugene P. Ericksen, Stephanie W. Greenberg, and William Yancey, "A Tale of Three Cities: Blacks, Immigrants, and Opportunity in Philadelphia, 1850–1880, 1930, 1970," in *Philadelphia: Work, Space, Family, and Group Experience in the 19th Century,* ed. Hershberg (London, 1981), 471.

44. The statistics regarding Philadelphia's immigrant population in this section are drawn from Hershberg et al., "Tale of Three Cities," 471.

45. Joel Perlmann, *Ethnic Differences: Schooling and Social Structure among the Irish, Italians, Jews, and Blacks in an American City, 1880–1915* (Cambridge: Cambridge University Press, 1988), 122–62. Perlmann examines Russian Jews in Providence, Rhode Island. Twelve of the fifteen Jewish students in the 1910 Peirce sample had Russian backgrounds. Philadelphia's census enumerators utilized the term *Yiddish* to designate Jews.

46. For examples of scholars stressing the transformative, intergenerational impacts of industrial society on ethnic identity, see Lizabeth Cohen, *Making a New Deal: Industrial Workers in Chicago, 1919–1939* (Cambridge: Cambridge University Press, 1990); Richard

D. Alba, *Ethnic Identity: The Transformation of White America* (New Haven, Conn.: Yale University Press, 1990); Miriam Cohen, *Workshop to Office: Two Generations of Italian Women in New York City, 1900–1950* (Ithaca, N.Y.: Cornell University Press, 1993); Ewa Morawska, "In Defense of the Assimilation Model," *Journal of American Ethnic History,* (Winter 1994): 76–87; David A. Hollinger, *Postethnic America: Beyond Multiculturalism* (New York: BasicBooks, 1995); Gary Gerstle, "Liberty, Coercion, and the Making of Americans," *Journal of American History* (Sept. 1997): 524–58; and Jonathan Zimmerman, "Ethnics against Ethnicity: European Immigrants and Foreign-Language Instruction, 1890–1940," *Journal of American History* (Mar. 2002): 1383–1404.

Chapter 4: After Hours

1. This concept of a commercialized leisure economy comes from John F. Kasson, *Amusing the Million: Coney Island at the Turn of the Century* (New York: Hill and Wang, 1979), 36. Kasson describes vaudeville theaters, movie houses, and theme parks as major components in the new urban leisure economy. See also Kathy Peiss, *Cheap Amusements: Working Women and Leisure in Turn-of-the-Century New York* (Philadelphia: Temple University Press, 1986); and David Nasaw, *Going Out: The Rise and Fall of Public Amusements* (New York: BasicBooks, 1993). Nasaw and Peiss focus on the highly commercialized leisure activities of urban Americans. For studies of fraternalism, which involved many office and sales employees, see Mark Carnes, *Secret Ritual and Manhood in Victorian America* (New Haven, Conn.: Yale University Press, 1989); and Mary Ann Clawson, *Constructing Brotherhood: Class, Gender, and Fraternalism* (Princeton, N.J.: Princeton University Press, 1989).

2. Nasaw, *Going Out,* 2–9. Another general source on nightlife is Lewis A. Erenberg, *Steppin' Out: New York Nightlife and the Transformation of American Culture, 1890–1930* (Westport, Conn.: Greenwood, 1981).

3. See especially Peiss, *Cheap Amusements.*

4. Nasaw, *Going Out,* 36–37.

5. Michael Kimmel, *Manhood in America: A Cultural History* (New York: Free Press, 1996), 173; Carnes, *Secret Ritual,* 3; *Fifth Annual Report of the Bank Clerks' Beneficial Association of Philadelphia* (Philadelphia: Ledger Job Printing Office, 1874), Urban Archives, Temple University (hereinafter UATU), Free Library Pamphlet Collection, box 3, "Bank Clerks' Beneficial Association" file, Temple University, Philadelphia; *Fifteenth Annual Report of the Bank Clerks' Beneficial Association of Philadelphia* (Philadelphia: Burk and McKetridge, 1884), UATU, Free Library Pamphlet Collection, box 3, "Bank Clerks' Beneficial Association" file; *Peirce School Alumni Journal* 6 (Oct. 1900): 4, Peirce College Archives (hereinafter PCA), acc. 1, ser. 6, box 2, Peirce College, Philadelphia; "Bookkeepers' Beneficial Association of Phila.," *Peirce School Alumni Journal* 3 (Dec. 1897): 70, PCA, acc. 1, ser. 6, box 2; "The Bookkeepers' Beneficial Association of Philadelphia," *Peirce School Alumni Journal* 3 (Apr. 1898): 148, PCA, acc. 1, ser. 6, box 2; "Of Interest to Bookkeepers," *Peirce School Alumni Journal* 5 (Sept. 1899): 3, PCA, acc. 1, ser. 6, box 2.

6. "A Good Example: A Great Business Establishment and How It Entertains Its Employees," *Philadelphia North American,* April 19, 1882, Hagley Museum and Library (hereinafter HML), acc. 2117, ser. 7, box 75, clippings scrapbook 1882–84, Wilmington, Del.

7. Ibid.

8. "Caring for Their Employees: Strawbridge & Clothier Inaugurate an Admirable Idea," *Philadelphia Evening Bulletin,* April 19, 1882, HML, acc. 2117, ser. 7, box 75, clippings scrapbook 1882–84.

9. See ibid. and "Entertaining Their Employees: An Enterprising Firm Setting Merchants a Good Example," *Philadelphia Chronicle Herald,* October 19, 1882, HML, acc. 2117, ser. 7, box 75, clippings scrapbook 1882–84; "Entertaining Their Employes [sic]: How Messrs. Strawbridge & Clothier Furnish Rest and Amusement to Their Clerks," *Philadelphia Evening News,* December 13, 1882, HML, acc. 2117, ser. 7, box 75, clippings scrapbook 1882–84; "Egypt, Old and New: The Subject upon Which Mr. Wilson Lectured to Strawbridge & Clothier's Employes [sic]," *Philadelphia Evening Bulletin,* February 10, 1883, HML, acc. 2117, ser. 7, box 75, clippings scrapbook 1882–84; "A Liberal Firm: Strawbridge & Clothier Again Entertain Their Employees at the Academy," *Philadelphia Inquirer,* November 22, 1883, HML, acc. 2117, ser. 7, box 75, clippings scrapbook 1882–84; "Strawbridge & Clothier's Entertainment to Their Employes [sic]," *Philadelphia Public Ledger and Daily Transcript,* January 13, 1887, HML, acc. 2117, ser. 7, box 75, clippings scrapbook January 1887–January 1894; "The Boston Symphony Orchestra: Entertained Messrs. Strawbridge & Clothier's Employees at the Academy Last Night," *Philadelphia Inquirer,* March 15, 1889, HML, acc. 2117, ser. 7, box 75, clippings scrapbook January 1887–January 1894. Clark Davis discusses corporate-sponsored leisure in *Company Men: White-Collar Life and Corporate Cultures in Los Angeles, 1890–1941* (Baltimore, Md.: Johns Hopkins University Press, 2000), 171–96.

10. "Twenty-One Years of Steady Progress: A Brief History of the Alumni Association," *Peirce School Alumni Journal* 18 (Apr. 1913): 3–6, PCA, acc. 1, ser. 6, box 2.

11. "Exercise and Business," *Peirce School Alumni Journal* 10 (Feb. 1905): 8, PCA, acc. 1, ser. 6, box 2.

12. "Exercise Important," *Peirce School Alumni Journal* 21 (Dec. 1914): 8, PCA, acc. 1, ser. 6, box 2; "Gymnasium Classes," *Peirce School Alumni Journal* 22 (Oct. 1916): 12, PCA, acc. 1, ser. 6, box 2.

13. Advertisement on playbill for B. F. Keith's Theater, weeks of September 21, 1914, and January 1, 1917, the Free Library of Philadelphia Theatre Collection (hereinafter FLPTC), "Keith's 11th & Chestnut," Free Library of Philadelphia, Philadelphia, Pa.

14. "From Carpenter to Corporation President," *Peirce School Alumni Journal* 15 (Oct. 1909): 4, PCA, acc. 1, ser. 6, box 2.

15. Harvey Green, *Fit for America: Health, Fitness, Sport, and American Society* (New York: Pantheon Books, 1986), 184–95.

16. "Thomas Martindale Dies in Wilderness," *Philadelphia Evening Bulletin,* September 16, 1916, UATU, *Philadelphia Evening Bulletin* clippings collection, "Thomas-Merchant-Dead, Phila." file.

17. Thomas Martindale, "Why Women Should Walk," *Strawbridge & Clothier Store Chat* 6 (Apr. 15, 1912): 104–6, HML, acc. 2117, ser. 7, box 60.

18. Kimmel, *Manhood in America,* 182–88.

19. "An Entertainment," *Peirce School Alumni Journal* 1 (Apr.–May 1896): 93, PCA, acc. 1, ser. 6, box 2.

20. "Alaska and Its Big Game: A Lecture by Thomas Martindale," *Peirce School Alumni*

Notes to Pages 87–91

Journal 21 (Jan. 1916): 3–7, PCA, acc. 1, ser. 6, box 3. This article includes introductory remarks by the Peirce Alumni Association's president John H. Sinberg.

21. Steven A. Reiss, *City Games: The Evolution of American Urban Society and the Rise of Sports* (Urbana: University of Illinois Press, 1989), 61–67.

22. For works that broadly discuss the development of the sport creed, see Green, *Fit for America,* 181–208; Reiss, *City Games,* 29–31; and Steven Hardy, *How Boston Played: Sport, Recreation, and Community, 1865–1915* (Boston: Northeastern University Press, 1982), 53–67.

23. Hardy, *How Boston Played,* 53; Kimmel, *Manhood In America,* 177–81; Green, *Fit for America,* 181–215; Reiss, *City Games,* 29–30, 156–58; Clifford Putney, *Muscular Christianity: Manhood and Sports in Protestant America, 1880–1920* (Cambridge, Mass.: Harvard University Press, 2001).

24. Steven M. Gelber, "'Their Hands Are All Out Playing': Business and Amateur Baseball, 1845–1917," *Journal of Sport History* 11 (Spring 1984): 17. For information on Philadelphia's cricket clubs in the nineteenth century, see J. Thomas Jable, "Social Class and the Sport of Cricket in Philadelphia, 1850–1880," *Journal of Sport History* 18 (Summer 1991): 205–23.

25. J. Thomas Jable, "Sports: Philadelphia's Sporting and Athletic Clubs in the Nineteenth Century," in *Invisible Philadelphia: Community through Voluntary Organizations,* ed. Jean Barth Toll and Mildred S. Gilliam, 1138–41 (Philadelphia: Atwater Kent Museum, 1995), 1140.

26. Philadelphia and Reading Railroad Athletic Association, *Official Program, Grand Benefit Held at Chestnut Street Theater* (Philadelphia, 1894), 7. The rest of this section relies on this booklet.

27. "Strawbridge & Clothier's Picnic to Three Hundred of Their Employes [*sic*]," *Philadelphia Public Ledger & Daily Telegraph,* July 5, 1884, HML, acc. 2117, ser. 7, box 75, clippings scrapbook 1881–84. The store also held entertainments for cash boys at other times during the year; see "Cash Boys, Strawbridge & Clothier Entertain Theirs at Wesley Hall," *Philadelphia Inquirer,* April 19, 1884, HML, acc. 2117, ser. 7, box 75, clippings scrapbook 1881–84.

28. "New Athletic Grounds," *Strawbridge & Clothier Store Chat* 7 (June 15, 1910): 172–73, HML, acc. 2117, ser. 7, box 60.

29. Photograph, *Strawbridge & Clothier Store Chat* 5 (Oct. 15, 1911): 245, HML, acc. 2117, ser. 7, box 60.

30. "Our Gymnasium Opening," *Strawbridge & Clothier Store Chat* 6 (Mar. 15, 1912): 84, HML, acc. 2117, ser. 7, box 60.

31. "Memorial Day Meet," *Strawbridge & Clothier Store Chat* 5 (June 15, 1911): 160–61, HML, acc. 2117, ser. 7, box 60.

32. "Our Gymnasium Opening," 84.

33. "Our New Athletic Grounds," *Strawbridge & Clothier Store Chat* 4 (Aug. 15, 1910): 224, HML, acc. 2117, ser. 7, box 60.

34. Gelber, "'Their Hands Are All Out,'" 6.

35. Ibid., 23. Occasionally, interfirm rivalries grew heated, and company owners hired professional players to fill skilled positions and ensure victory.

36. "More Baseball," *Strawbridge & Clothier Store Chat* 3 (May 15, 1909): 128, HML, acc. 2117, ser. 7, box 60.

37. Peirce students also formed a baseball team in the late 1890s. In 1898 the school's team played Philadelphia's Manual Training School and Central High School's second team, winning both games ("School Notes," *Peirce School Alumni Journal* 3 [May 1898]: 178, PCA, acc. 1, ser. 6, box 2; "Baseball Notes," *Peirce School Alumni Journal* 4 [June 1898]: 195, PCA, acc. 1, ser. 6, box 2).

38. "Theatrical," *Strawbridge & Clothier Store Chat* 2 (Oct. 1908): 6–7, HML, acc. 2117, ser. 7, box 60; "Baseball," *Strawbridge & Clothier Store Chat* 1 (Oct. 1906): 7, HML, acc. 2117, ser. 7, box 60; "Baseball," *Strawbridge & Clothier Store Chat* 1 (Sept. 1907): 5, HML, acc. 2117, ser. 7, box 60; "Executive Win Third Game of Series," *Strawbridge & Clothier Store Chat* 2 (May 1908): 4, HML, acc. 2117, ser. 7, box 60.

39. The proceeds of the game, donated to the store's pension fund, amounted to one hundred dollars.

40. Reiss, *City Games,* 76–77.

41. "Bowling Records," *Strawbridge & Clothier Store Chat* 3 (May 15, 1909): 178, HML, acc. 2117, ser. 7, box 60; "With the Bowlers," *Philadelphia Evening Bulletin,* 9 May 1905.

42. "The Strawbridge & Clothier Bowling Team," *Strawbridge & Clothier Store Chat* 3 (May 15, 1909): 129, HML, acc. 2117, ser. 7, box 60; "The S. & C. Retail Bowling Team," *Strawbridge & Clothier Store Chat* 4 (Apr. 15, 1910): 117, HML, acc. 2117, ser. 7, box 60.

43. "Store People at Play," *Strawbridge & Clothier Store Chat* 4 (Sept. 15, 1909): 268, HML, acc. 2117, ser. 7, box 60; "Store People at Play," *Strawbridge & Clothier Store Chat* 4 (Dec. 15, 1909): 15, HML, acc. 2117, ser. 7, box 60.

44. "Women Form Gym Class," *Strawbridge & Clothier Store Chat* 6 (Nov. 15, 1912): 291, HML, acc. 2117, ser. 7, box 60.

45. The huge front wheel was designed for speed, because the ordinary did not have a chain drive; instead, its pedals were attached directly to the front wheel. The tiny back wheel minimized weight.

46. Material on the ordinary is drawn from Hardy, *How Boston Played,* 147–67. This is the best general but brief source on bicycling in late nineteenth- and early twentieth-century America. Other important sources include Richard Harmond, "Progress and Flight: An Interpretation of the American Cycle Craze of the 1890s," *Journal of Social History* 5 (Winter 1971–72): 235–57; Robert A. Smith, *A Social History of the Bicycle: Its Early Life and Times in America* (New York: American Heritage, 1972); Gary Allen Tobin, "The Bicycle Boom of the 1890s: The Development of Private Transportation and the Birth of the Modern Tourist," *Journal of Popular Culture* 7 (Spring 1974): 838–49; and George D. Bushnell, "When Chicago Was Wheel Crazy," *Chicago History* 4 (Fall 1975): 167–75.

47. "Proposed Bicycle Club," *Peirce School Alumni Journal* 3 (June–July 1897): 4, PCA, acc. 1, ser. 6, box 2.

48. "The Cyclers," *Peirce School Alumni Journal* 3 (Sept. 1897): 29–30, PCA, acc. 1, ser. 6, box 2; "Our Club," *Peirce School Alumni Journal* 3 (Jan. 1898): 105–7, PCA, acc. 1, ser. 6, box 2.

49. John H. Sinberg, "New Club House Secured," *Peirce School Alumni Journal* 3 (Oct. 1897): 44, PCA, acc. 1, ser. 6, box 2.

50. "Echoes of the Watermelon Run," *Peirce School Alumni Journal* 3 (Oct. 1897): 44, PCA, acc. 1, ser. 6, box 2.

51. "Peirce Alumni Cyclers," *Peirce School Alumni Journal* 3 (Nov. 1897): 59–61, PCA, acc. 1, ser. 6, box 2.

52. "A Few Don't's to the Ladies," *Peirce School Alumni Journal* 4 (June 1898): 193, PCA, acc. 1, ser. 6, box 2.

53. Ellen Gruber Garvey, "Reframing the Bicycle: Advertising-Supported Magazines and Scorching Women," *American Quarterly* 47 (Mar. 1995): 72–78, 85–89. Garvey notes that the mixed-gender nature of cycling formed a theme in cycling-related short stories in popular magazines of the late nineteenth century. She also points out that some Americans found the image of cycling women and their mobility to be particularly threatening.

54. Cindy S. Aron, *Working at Play: A History of Vacations in the United States* (New York: Oxford University Press, 1999), 25, 69–100. Aron shows that in some nineteenth-century vacation resorts, middle-class men and women occasionally mingled while engaged in athletic pursuits such as bowling or swimming. However, many beachfront resorts segregated swim times.

55. Smith, *Social History*, 109–11.

56. Ibid., 113–15.

57. "Peirce Alumni Cyclers," *Peirce School Alumni Journal* 3 (Nov. 1897): 59–61, PCA, acc. 1, ser. 6, box 2.

58. "Our Club," 105–7.

59. "The Package Party," *Peirce School Alumni Journal* 3 (Feb. 1898): 120–21, PCA, acc. 1, ser. 6, box 2.

60. "Peirce Alumni Cyclers: Weekly Entertainments," *Peirce Alumni Journal* 3 (Apr. 1898): 155–56, PCA, acc. 1, ser. 6, box 2.

61. Jable, "Sports," 1139; Associated Cycling Clubs of Philadelphia, *Official Catalog and Souvenir of the A.C.C. Cycle Show* (Philadelphia: n.p., 1892), 9, 19, UATU, Free Library Pamphlet Collection, box 15, "Cycling 1892" file. In 1892, while the bicycle was still a fairly elite vehicle, the A.C.C. estimated that there were 28,000 cyclists in Philadelphia.

62. Smith, *Social History*, 51–53.

63. Ibid., 75.

64. Hart Cycle Company, *Cyclegraphs* (Philadelphia, 1892), 4–17, UATU, Free Library Pamphlet Collection, box 15, "Cycling 1892" file.

65. Harmond, "Progress and Flight," 239.

66. Smith, *Social History*, 35–37.

67. Hardy (*How Boston Played*, 162) notes that even the low prices of used bikes did not draw many blue-collar workers into cycling.

68. Associated Cycling Clubs of Philadelphia, *Official Catalog and Souvenir*.

69. "Wheeling Notes," *Peirce School Alumni Journal* 3 (Apr. 1898): 157, PCA, acc. 1, ser. 6, box 2.

70. Ibid.

71. "Peirce Alumni Cyclers," *Peirce School Alumni Journal* 3 (Mar. 1898): 137–39, PCA, acc. 1, ser. 6, box 2.

72. Tobin, "Bicycle Boom," 841.

73. Ibid., 842.

74. "Our Club," 107.

75. Associated Cycling Clubs, *Official Catalog and Souvenir,* 4.

76. "Bryn Mawr Run," *Peirce School Alumni Journal* 3 (Nov. 1897): 59–60, PCA, acc. 1, ser. 6, box 2.

77. "Peirce Alumni Cyclers," *Peirce School Alumni Journal* 4 (Sept. 1898): 209, PCA, acc. 1, ser. 6, box 2.

78. Hardy, *How Boston Played,* 164–66.

79. "The Fourteenth Annual Meeting of the Alumni Association," *Peirce School Alumni Journal* 11 (May 1906): 5–6, PCA, acc. 1, ser. 6, box 2.

80. "The Lecture and Organ Recital," *Peirce School Alumni Journal* 18 (Mar. 1913): 5–7, PCA, acc. 1, ser. 6, box 2.

81. "The Dance," *Peirce School Alumni Journal* 5 (May 1900): 8, PCA, acc. 1, ser. 6, box 2.

82. "Opening Dance a Success," *Strawbridge & Clothier Store Chat* 11 (July 15, 1915): 119, HML, acc. 2117, ser. 7, box 60.

83. "The Strawbridge & Clothier Chorus," *Strawbridge & Clothier Store Chat* 3 (Apr. 15, 1909): 104–5, HML, acc. 2117, ser. 7, box 60.

84. "The S&C Chorus at Willow Grove," *Strawbridge & Clothier Store Chat* 3 (July 15, 1909): 179, HML, acc. 2117, ser. 7, box 60.

85. "Christmas Echoes," *Strawbridge & Clothier Store Chat* 3 (Jan. 15, 1909): 29, HML, acc. 2117, ser. 7, box 60.

86. "Mandolin Club," *Strawbridge & Clothier Store Chat* 1 (Sept. 1907): 7, HML, acc. 2117, ser. 7, box 60.

87. Irvin R. Glazer, *Philadelphia Theaters A–Z: A Comprehensive Record of 813 Theaters Constructed Since 1724* (New York: Greenwood, 1986), 18.

88. Geraldine Duclow, "Philadelphia," in *Cambridge Guide to American Theatre,* ed. Don B. Wilment and Tice L. Miller, 373–75 (Cambridge: Cambridge University Press, 1993). Duclow counts one German-language, nine legitimate, five variety, and two minstrel theaters.

89. Glazer, *Philadelphia Theatres,* 23.

90. Dance-hall culture and professional sports have been discussed by others.

91. Glazer, *Philadelphia Theatres,* 15. Glazer notes that the Academy of Music (1857) was named an "academy" because the city's elite frowned on terms such as *opera house* or *theater.*

92. Nasaw, *Going Out,* 14–18.

93. Ibid., 16; Robert C. Allen, *Horrible Prettiness: Burlesque and American Culture* (Chapel Hill: University of North Carolina Press, 1991), 180–85; Frank Brookhouser, "A Girl Was Safe at Keith's," *Philadelphia Evening Bulletin,* January 10, 1971, Sunday edition, FLPTC, "Keith's 11th & Chestnut." Prior to opening the museum, Keith and his partner, E. F. Albee, sold electric shocks for a nickel on Boston streets. After they jolted customers, the duo sold them popcorn and scientific literature. Keith went on to own theaters in New York, Philadelphia, Boston, Pawtucket, and Providence. Keith's Philadelphia Bijou was named after his first theater, in Boston.

94. Glazer, *Philadelphia Theatres,* 18.

95. Nasaw, *Going Out,* 31; Allen, *Horrible Prettiness,* 182.

96. Glazer, *Philadelphia Theatres,* 22–23; Irvin R. Glazer, *Philadelphia Theaters: A Pictorial Architectural History* (New York and Philadelphia: Athenaeum of Philadelphia/Dover, 1994), xx.

97. Frank Brookhouser, "Dust over the Old Bijou Covers Lusty Chapter of Song-and-Dance History," *Philadelphia Evening Bulletin,* July 16, 1967, Sunday edition, FLPTC, "Bijou."

98. Charles Bell, untitled promotional booklet, 1912, FLPTC, "Keith's 11th & Chestnut"; flyer for week of September 21, 1914, B. F. Keith's Theater, FLPTC, "B. F. Keith's 11th & Chestnut" file.

99. Harry Harris, "Keith's Days of Glory End . . . but Memories Linger On," clipping from unknown newspaper, June 6, 1949, FLPTC, "Keith's 11th & Chestnut." (A tidbit in *Store Chat* suggested the familiarity Strawbridge & Clothier's workers had with Keith's. In the spring of 1911, after a banquet held in honor of a store bowling team, the participants "all went in a body to Keith's Theatre, which made a nice closing to the evening's exercise" ["The Bowlers," *Strawbridge & Clothier Store Chat* 5 (May 15, 1911): 136, HML, acc. 2117, ser. 7, box 60].)

100. Ibid.

101. Bell, untitled promotional booklet.

102. Program, B. F. Keith's Theater, week of January 1, 1912, FLPTC, "B. F. Keith's 11th & Chestnut" file; Glazer, *Philadelphia Theaters,* 142–45.

103. "Hammerstein Sells Out to Metropolitan," *Philadelphia Evening Bulletin,* April 28, 1910, UATU, mounted clippings collection, box 119, "Metropolitan Opera House—Operation and Sale of by Hammerstein" file; "Movie Houses Springing Up on All Sides," *Philadelphia Evening Bulletin,* September 1, 1928, UATA, mounted clippings collection, box 119, "Metropolitan Opera House—Sale to Lu Lu Temple and Operation since 1920" file; "Opera Night at the Academy, Ghost Night at the 'Met,'" *Philadelphia Evening Bulletin,* November 25, 1941, UATU, mounted clippings collection, box 119, "Metropolitan Opera House—Operation and Sale of by Hammerstein" file.

104. "Grand Opera Party," *Peirce School Alumni Journal* 15 (Dec. 1909): 9–10, PCA, acc. 1, ser. 6, box 2.

105. "Mr. E. T. Stotesbury," *Peirce School Alumni Journal* 11 (Mar. 1906): 5, PCA, acc. 1, ser. 6, box 2.

106. "Alumni Association to See John Drew," *Peirce School Alumni Journal* 21 (Feb. 1917): 14, PCA, acc. 1, ser. 6, box 3.

107. Glazer, *Philadelphia Theatres,* 72–3.

108. "About That Vacation," *Strawbridge & Clothier Store Chat* 3 (June 15, 1909): 147, HML, acc. 2117, ser. 7, box 60. For an excellent discussion of vacationing, see Aron, *Working at Play.*

109. "From Carpenter to Corporation President," 4.

110. "About That Vacation," 147.

111. Ibid.; "Vacation and Its Lessons," *Peirce School Alumni Journal* 7 (Sept. 1901): 3, PCA, acc. 1, ser. 6, box 2.

112. "A Trip to Chinatown, (San Francisco)," *Peirce School Alumni Journal* 1 (Aug. 1895): 22, PCA, acc. 1, ser. 6, box 2; "A Trip to Chinatown, (San Francisco)," *Peirce School Alumni Journal* 1 (Oct.–Nov. 1895): 41–42, PCA, acc. 1, ser. 6, box 2.

113. Carroll B. Grace and George Hoffman, "A Flying Trip to the Golden Gate," *Peirce School Alumni Journal* 3 (Feb. 1898): 119, PCA, acc. 1, ser. 6, box 2.

114. Lawrence M. Friedman, *Crime and Punishment in American History* (New York: BasicBooks, 1993), 137; David T. Courtwright, *Dark Paradise: A History of Opiate Addiction in America,* 2d ed. (Cambridge, Mass.: Harvard University Press, 2001), 62–81.

115. Jennie W. Rogers, "A Trip across the Continent," *Peirce School Alumni Journal* 4 (Dec. 1895–Jan. 1896): 53, PCA, acc. 1, ser. 6, box 2.

116. "Vacation Personals," *Peirce School Alumni Journal* 4 (Sept. 1898): 211, PCA, acc. 1, ser. 6, box 2, lists vacations taken by members during the summer of 1898. Destinations along the Jersey Shore predominate, with Atlantic City being the alumni's favorite vacation spot. Workers stayed in rented cottages or inexpensive hotels.

117. "A Company That Cares," *Strawbridge & Clothier Store Chat* (Apr. 1968): 12, HML, acc. 2117, ser. 7, box 60; "Ho for the Seashore," *Strawbridge & Clothier Store Chat* 3 (June 15, 1909): 154, HML, acc. 2117, ser. 7, box 60.

118. "Your Invitation to Wildwood," *Strawbridge & Clothier Store Chat* 4 (June 15, 1910): 168, HML, acc. 2117, ser. 7, box 60.

119. "Two Happy Days by the Sea at Wildwood," *Strawbridge & Clothier Store Chat* 4 (July 15, 1910): 207–8, HML, acc. 2117, ser. 7, box 60.

120. "Ho for the Seashore," 154.

121. Pennsylvania Bureau of Industrial Statistics, "Women in Industry," *Annual Report of the Secretary of Internal Affairs of the Commonwealth of Pennsylvania, Part III, Industrial Statistics, 1894* (Harrisburg, Pa.: Clarence M. Bush, 1895), vol. 22, p. A.23.

122. Charles E. Funnell, *By the Beautiful Sea: The Rise and High Times of That Great American Resort, Atlantic City* (New York: Knopf, 1975), 12.

123. Ibid., 33.

124. Kasson, *Amusing the Million,* 38. Kasson notes that "Coney Island drew upon all social classes and especially upon the rising middle class and more prosperous working-class visitors, salesmen, clerks, tradesmen, secretaries, shop attendants, laborers, and the like." The opportunities for play available at Willow Grove mirrored those at Coney Island, and the two parks doubtlessly attracted the same type of clientele.

125. Nasaw, *Going Out,* 80–95.

126. Jean Barret, "Willow Grove Music Pavilion Is No More; Hey Day of Sousa and Herbert Is Recalled," *Philadelphia Evening Bulletin,* date unknown, UATU, *Philadelphia Evening Bulletin* clippings collection, "Willow Grove Park–History and Description" file; Frank Brookhouser, "Amusement Center Observes 60th Year," *Philadelphia Evening Bulletin,* July 10, 1955, UATU, *Philadelphia Evening Bulletin* clippings collection, "Willow Grove Park–History and Description" file; Robert Fowler, "Age Hasn't Dimmed Fun Parks," *Philadelphia Inquirer,* June 24, 1973, UATU, *Philadelphia Evening Bulletin* clippings collection, "Willow Grove Park–History and Description" file.

127. "Happy Happenings around the Store," *Strawbridge & Clothier Store Chat* 1 (Oct. 1906): 11, HML, acc. 2117, ser. 7, box 60.

128. Esther M. Klein, *Fairmount Park: History and Guidebook, World's Largest Landscaped Municipal Park* (Bryn Mawr, Pa.: Harcum Junior College Press, 1974), 21–23.

129. T. A. Daly, ed. *The Wissahickon* (Philadelphia: Garden Club of Philadelphia, 1922), 39; Richard R. Nicolai and John McIlhenny, "The Fairmount Park Commission," in *Invis-*

ible Philadelphia: Community Through Voluntary Organization, ed. Jean Barth Toll and
Mildred S. Gillian, 848–51 (Philadelphia: Atwater Kent Museum, 1995), 848.

130. Daly, *The Wissahickon,* 39.

131. Ibid., 39–40.

132. Klein, *Fairmount Park,* 23.

Chapter 5: Workplace Virtues, Rebellion, and Race

1. Judy Hilkey, *Character Is Capital: Success Manuals and Manhood in Gilded Age America*
(Chapel Hill: University of North Carolina Press, 1997), 22. The manuals were most often
read by small-town or rural Americans, however. For discussions of loyalty in the white-
collar workplace, see Olivier Zunz, *Making America Corporate, 1870–1920* (Chicago: University of Chicago Press, 1990), 187–89; Clark Davis, *Company Men: White-Collar Life and
Corporate Cultures in Los Angeles, 1892–1941* (Baltimore, Md.: Johns Hopkins University
Press, 2000), 42–49, 95–100. For an overview of success as a theme in American culture,
see John G. Cawelti, *Apostles of the Self-Made Man* (Chicago: University of Chicago Press,
1965).

2. "A Good Example," *The North American,* April 19, 1882, Hagley Museum and Library
(hereinafter HML), acc. 2117, ser. 7, box 75, clippings scrapbook 1882–84, Wilmington,
Del.

3. "Ideals," *Strawbridge & Clothier Store Chat* 1 (Oct. 1906): 5, HML, acc. 2117, ser. 7,
box 60.

4. "Following Ideals," *Peirce School Alumni Journal* 11 (Dec. 1905): 3–4, Peirce College
Archives (hereinafter PCA), acc. 1, ser. 6, box 2, Peirce College, Philadelphia.

5. "A Few Helpful Hints," *Peirce School Alumni Journal* 9 (Nov. 1903): 8, PCA, acc. 1,
ser. 6, box 2.

6. "Work, Work, Work," *Peirce School Alumni Journal* 7 (Sept. 1901): 12, PCA, acc. 1, ser.
6, box 2; "Easy Positions," *Peirce School Alumni Journal* 8 (Mar. 1903): 7, PCA, acc. 1, ser.
6, box 2.

7. Manly M. Gillam, "Doing No More Than You Are Paid For," *Strawbridge & Clothier
Store Chat* 3 (July 15, 1909): 168, HML, acc. 2117, ser. 7, box 60.

8. David Starr Jordan, "The Habit of Self-Denial," *Strawbridge & Clothier Store Chat*
1 (May 1907): 8 (repr. from *Macy Monthly*), HML, acc. 2117, ser. 7, box 60.

9. G. W. Flemming, "Acorns and Dimes," *Strawbridge & Clothier Store Chat* 3 (Aug. 15,
1909): 193–94, HML, acc. 2117, ser. 7, box 60.

10. "The Relief Association," *Strawbridge & Clothier Store Chat* 1 (Oct. 1906): 12, HML,
acc. 2117, ser. 7, box 60; "The Twenty-Fifth Birthday of the Strawbridge & Clothier Saving
Fund," *Strawbridge & Clothier Store Chat* 3 (June 15, 1909): 145–46, HML, acc. 2117, ser. 7,
box 60; "Strawbridge & Clothier Pension and Aid Fund Principal Sum of $50,000 to Be
Completed by the Generosity of Our Firm," *Strawbridge & Clothier Store Chat* 6 (Apr.
15, 1912): supplemental insert, HML, acc. 2117, ser. 7, box 60; "A Company That Cares,"
Strawbridge & Clothier Store Chat (Apr. 1968): 9–12, HML, acc. 2117, ser. 7, box 60.

11. "An S. & C. Girl's Prize," *Strawbridge & Clothier Store Chat* 3 (Nov. 1909): 303, HML,
acc. 2117, ser. 7, box 60.

12. Fr. Joseph L. J. Kirlin, "Strong Drink from a Business Point of View," *Strawbridge & Clothier Store Chat* 3 (Aug. 15, 1909): 191–92, HML, acc. 2117, ser. 7, box 60.

13. "The Alphabet of Success," *Peirce School Alumni Journal* 8 (May 1903): 8 (repr. from *Ladies' Home Journal*), PCA, acc. 1, ser. 7G, box 1.

14. "Temperance Question," *Peirce School Alumni Journal* 3 (Nov. 1897): 51–52, PCA, acc. 1, ser. 7G, box 1.

15. "How Success Is Achieved," *Peirce School Alumni Journal* 4 (May 1899): 339 (repr. from *The Archive*), PCA, acc. 1, ser. 7G, box 1.

16. Jordan, "Habit of Self Denial," 8.

17. "Success," *Strawbridge & Clothier Store Chat* 3 (Feb. 15, 1909): 52 (repr. from *Filene's Echo*), HML, acc. 2117, ser. 7, box 60.

18. A good example is Russell H. Conwell, "'Be Not Slothful in Business'—Romans 12," *Strawbridge & Clothier Store Chat* 3 (Sept. 15, 1909): 217–18, HML, acc. 2117, ser. 7, box 60. Conwell was also the minister of Grace Baptist Church in North Philadelphia and a well-traveled speaker who preached to anyone who would listen about the value of hard work and generating wealth.

19. Hilkey, *Character Is Capital*, 46–47, 157–58; Angel Kwolek-Folland, *Engendering Business: Men and Women in the Corporate Office, 1870–1930* (Baltimore, Md.: Johns Hopkins University Press, 1994), 44–52. Kwolek-Folland argues persuasively that management valued aggressiveness among male workers in the industrial-era office, but this attitude was tempered with an increasing focus on service.

20. "Aim High," *Peirce School Alumni Journal* 10 (Oct. 1904): 8, PCA, acc. 1, ser. 6, box 2.

21. "Merit, Not Favor," *Peirce School Alumni Journal* 10 (Oct. 1904): 8, PCA, acc. 1, ser. 6, box 2.

22. "Opportunities to Win Success," *Peirce School Alumni Journal* 6 (May 1901): 4, PCA, acc. 1, ser. 6, box 2; "Are You a Success?" *Strawbridge & Clothier Store Chat* 1 (June 1906): 11, HML, acc. 2117, ser. 7, box 60; "Where Success Is Found," *Strawbridge & Clothier Store Chat* 3 (May 15, 1909): 119–20, HML, acc. 2117, ser. 7, box 60.

23. "A Leader in One of Philadelphia's Greatest Industries," *Peirce School Alumni Journal* 15 (Mar. 1910): 9–10, PCA, acc. 1, ser. 6, box 2.

24. Mary Clay Whiteley, "Contentment," *Peirce School Alumni Journal* 3 (Dec. 1897): 72–73, PCA, acc. 1, ser. 6, box 2; "The Results of 'Going to Peirce's,'" *Peirce School Alumni Journal* 10 (June 1905): 4–5, PCA, acc. 1, ser. 6, box 2.

25. "Business Girls as Wives," *Strawbridge & Clothier Store Chat* 4 (May 15, 1910): 155, HML, acc. 2117, ser. 7, box 60.

26. "The Girl Who Goes into Business," *Peirce School Alumni Journal* 6 (Sept. 1901): 11 (repr. from the *Philadelphia Evening Telegraph*), PCA, acc. 2117, ser. 6, box 2.

27. "A Stenographer's Story," *Strawbrigde & Clothier Store Chat* 3 (Apr. 15, 1909): 92–93, HML, acc. 2117, ser. 7, box 60.

28. "Results of 'Going to Peirce's,'" 4–5.

29. C. Wright Mills suggested that status was especially important to mid-twentieth-century professionals, managers, and clerical workers who wanted to differentiate themselves from blue-collar operatives. This "status psychology," as Mills dubbed it, kept many

white-collar workers from joining unions (Mills, *White Collar: The American Middle Classes* [Oxford: Oxford University Press, 1951]: 312).

30. Pennsylvania Bureau of Industrial Statistics, "Women in Industry," *Annual Report of the Secretary of Internal Affairs of the Commonwealth of Pennsylvania, Part III, Industrial Statistics, 1894* (Harrisburg, Pa.: Clarence M. Busch, 1895), vol. 22, p. A.31.

31. The authors of the following works discuss unionization among clerks from 1870 to 1920: Jürgen Kocka, *White Collar Workers in America, 1890–1940: A Social-Political History in International Perspective* (London: Sage, 1980)—Kocka offers the most on unionization, which he discusses throughout his book; Edwin Gabler, *The American Telegrapher: A Social History, 1860–1900* (New Brunswick, N.J.: Rutgers University Press, 1988), 3–29; Susan Porter Benson, *Counter Cultures: Saleswomen, Managers, and Customers in American Department Stores, 1890–1940* (Urbana: University of Illinois Press, 1986), 269–70; Stephen H. Norwood, *Labor's Flaming Youth: Telephone Operators and Worker Militancy, 1878–1923* (Urbana: University of Illinois Press, 1990); Lisa Fine, *The Souls of the Skyscraper: Female Clerical Workers in Chicago, 1870–1930* (Philadelphia: Temple University Press, 1990), 133–36; Sharon Hartman Strom, *Beyond the Typewriter: Gender, Class, and the Origins of Modern American Office Work, 1900–1930* (Urbana: University of Illinois Press, 1992), 203–4; Kenneth Lipartito, "When Women Were Switches: Technology, Work, and Gender in the Telephone Industry, 1890–1920," *American Historical Review* 99 (Oct. 1994): 1108; and Janet F. Davidson, "'Now That We Have Girls in the Office': Clerical Work, Masculinity, and the Refashioning of Gender for a Bureaucratic Age," in *Boys and Their Toys? Masculinity, Class, and Technology in America*, ed. Roger Horowitz, 55–90 (London: Routledge, 2001).

32. Benson, *Counter Cultures*, 269.

33. Pennsylvania Bureau of Industrial Statistics, "Women in Industry," table, 64–115.

34. Elbert Hubbard, "The Two Kinds," *Strawbridge & Clothier Store Chat* 2 (May 1908): 3, HML, acc. 2117, ser. 7, box 60.

35. Benson, *Counter Cultures*, 25–26.

36. "A Message from the Firm," *Strawbridge & Clothier Store Chat* 3 (Nov. 15, 1909): 281–82, HML, acc. 2117, ser. 7, box 60.

37. "Obedience," *Strawbridge & Clothier Store Chat* 3 (July 15, 1909): 172–73, HML, acc. 2117, ser. 7, box 60.

38. See Susan Porter Benson's definitive comments in "'The Clerking Sisterhood': Saleswomen's Work Culture," chap. 6 of *Counter Cultures* (227–82).

39. "Who Is This?" *Strawbridge & Clothier Store Chat* 3 (Jan. 15, 1909): 32, HML, acc. 2117, ser. 7, box 60; "A Chewing Gum Story," *Strawbridge & Clothier Store Chat* 3 (Feb. 15, 1909): 56, HML, acc. 2117, ser. 7, box 60; "A Thoughtless Action," *Strawbridge & Clothier Store Chat* 4 (Dec. 15, 1909): 12, HML, acc. 2117, ser. 7, box 60.

40. "Some Elevator 'Don't's," *Strawbridge & Clothier Store Chat* 3 (Aug. 15, 1909): 209, HML, acc. 2117, ser. 7, box 60; "Elevator Entrances and Exits," *Strawbridge & Clothier Store Chat* 3 (Nov. 15, 1909): 294, HML, acc. 2117, ser. 7, box 60; "Elevator Courtesy," *Strawbridge & Clothier Store Chat* 4 (Jan. 15, 1910): 27, HML, acc. 2117, ser. 7, box 60.

41. Internal memorandum, undated, Fourth Street National Bank, HML, acc. 1658, FSNB Corporate, box 10, "Embezzlement" file; R. H. Rushton to the American Surety Company, December 8, 1897, HML, acc. 1658, FSNB Corporate, box 10, "Embezzlement" file.

42. Application for bond of the American Surety Company of New York, Gustave A. Meyer, February 1, 1899, HML, acc. 1658, FSNB Corporate, box 10, "Theft, Gustave Meyer" file; Fisher A. Baker to R. H. Rushton, November 24, 1899, HML, acc. 1658, FSNB Corporate, box 10, "Theft, Gustave Meyer" file; E. F. Shanbacker to Fisher A. Baker, November 25, 1899, HML, acc. 1658, FSNB Corporate, box 10, "Theft, Gustave Meyer" file; manager of the Chartered Bank of India, Australia, and China to FSNB, December 12, 1899, HML, acc. 1658, FSNB Corporate, box 10, "Theft, Gustave Meyer" file; memorandum, "Extracts from Bombay Letters of 1899," undated, HML, acc. 1658, FSNB Corporate, box 10, "Theft, Gustave Meyer" file.

43. "A Clerk Accused of Embezzlement," *New York Times,* July 11, 1879; "Fall of a Confidential Clerk," *New York Times,* July 12, 1879; "A Confidential Clerk Absconds," *New York Times,* July 24, 1884. On the rationalization of embezzlement, see "Defalcations and How to Stop Them," *Merchants' Magazine and Commercial Review* (Nov. 1870): 339; George E. Pond, "Drift-Wood," *The Galaxy* 16 (July 1873): 128; A. R. Barrett, "Era of Fraud and Embezzlement; Its Causes and Remedies," *The Arena* 14 (Oct. 1895): 197; and Alfred A. Thomas, *The Temptations of Employes [sic] Who Handle Money* (Dayton, Ohio: National Cash Register, 1905), 7. James William Coleman ("Toward an Integrated Theory of White-Collar Crime," *American Journal of Sociology* 93 [Sept. 1987]: 410–11) notes that the rationalization of "temporarily borrowing money" is still popular among modern embezzlers.

44. "'As a Crushing Blow,'" *Philadelphia Evening Bulletin,* July 28, 1886; untitled editorial, *Philadelphia Evening Bulletin,* July 28, 1886; "Two More Defaulters," *New York Times,* July 28, 1886; "A Mania for Speculation," *Philadelphia Evening Bulletin,* July 29, 1886; "The American Baptists," *New York Times,* July 29, 1886; "The Supreme Folly of It All," *Philadelphia Evening Bulletin,* July 29, 1886; "Guilty of Embezzlement," *New York Times,* December 28, 1886.

45. Thomas, *Temptations of Employes,* 3–4; James W. Coleman, "Toward an Integrated Theory," 410–34. Coleman emphasizes that the quest for the "fast buck" lies at the heart of most contemporary white-collar crime. For more on modern-day white-collar crime, see Donald R. Cressey, *Other People's Money* (Glencoe, Ill.: Free Press, 1953); Susan B. Shapiro, "Collaring the Crime, Not the Criminal: Reconsidering the Concept of White-Collar Crime," *American Sociological Review* 55 (June 1990): 347–52; Gary S. Green, "White-Collar Crime and the Study of Embezzlement," *The Annals* 525 (Jan. 1993): 96–105; James W. Coleman, *The Criminal Elite: Understanding White-Collar Crime,* 4th ed. (New York: St. Martin's, 1998), 2–7, 15–93, 178–99. Green and Shapiro focus on embezzlement as a crime that, at its root, involves the violation of trust.

46. *Philadelphia Evening Bulletin,* July 28, 1886.

47. Jerome P. Bjelopera, "'Mr. Smith's Prolonged Vacation': White-Collar Criminals in the Late-Nineteenth-Century American Office Setting," paper delivered at the 2002 meeting of the Social Science History Association, St. Louis, Mo.

48. Certainly Philadelphia's clerks (and business owners) were aware of high-profile thefts involving clerks on the city's payroll. Two such late nineteenth-century cases made frontpage headlines in the *New York Times.* Philadelphia's water department charged Isaac R. Mulock with embezzling undisclosed amounts on several occasions in 1879. The water department's accounts bore a discrepancy of around $1,000 for that year, but the

shortage could not be directly connected to Mulock. The clerk allegedly returned $210, blaming his clerical "mistakes" on the "pressure of business." Regardless, Mulock was found guilty of thieving by a Philadelphia court. In a similar case, during September 1890 Lewis T. Young, the chief clerk of the Philadelphia Health Office, fled the city after having illicitly pocketed about $12,000 from his place of work. Young had been stealing from the city's coffers since 1888. His family repaid the money the chief clerk had peculated. Young intended to use the money to finance a run for a political office in the city and had begun to lavish his windfall on women friends—especially an opera singer. Locals had noticed the chief clerk spending huge amounts at restaurants with his paramours. He had also dropped $700 on a ring at Tiffany's in New York. See "Quarter Sessions—Judge Biddle," *Philadelphia Inquirer,* January 1, 1879; *New York Times,* January 2, 1879; "Young's Peculation," *Philadelphia Inquirer,* September 15, 1890; "Short in His Accounts," *New York Times,* September 15, 1890. For other Philadelphia cases of employee theft that made headlines, see "Embezzlement in Philadelphia," *New York Times,* April 8, 1877; "Brothers All, Says Accused," *Philadelphia Press,* March 9, 1905 (repr. in Thomas, *Temptations of Employes,* 26); "Clerk Missing and His Accounts Short," *Philadelphia Evening Bulletin,* March 11, 1905 (repr. in Thomas, *Temptations of Employes,* 39); "Insane When He Forged, They Say," *Philadelphia Press,* March 12, 1905 (repr. in Thomas, *The Temptations of Employes,* 36). Some regional cases of theft made national headlines. In January 1883 Camden's chief clerk of the municipal water department fled town with over $600 he had lifted from his office's coffers ("Camden's Water Clerk," *New York Times,* February 9, 1883). See also "Defalcation in the Wilmington (Del.) Post Office," *New York Times,* October 30, 1873; "The Wilmington Postmastership," *New York Times,* December 8, 1873.

49. C. R. Evans, "An Every-Day Stenographer," *Peirce School Alumni Journal* 4 (Feb. 1899): 273, PCA, acc. 1, ser. 6, box 2.

50. For a significant exception, see Venus Green, *Race on the Line: Gender, Labor, and Technology in the Bell System, 1880–1980* (Durham, N.C.: Duke University Press, 2001).

51. U.S. Census, 1900, Special Reports, table 43, pp. 672–78; U.S. Census, 1920, vol. 4, table 2, pp. 1193–97. Foreign-born employees accounted for just over 11 percent of the clerical workforce between 1900 and 1920.

52. Matthew Frye Jacobson, *Whiteness of a Different Color: European Immigrants and the Alchemy of Race* (Cambridge, Mass.: Harvard University Pres, 1998), 9.

53. On minstrelsy, see especially Robert C. Toll, *Blacking Up: The Minstrel Show in Nineteenth-Century America* (New York: Oxford University Press, 1974); David R. Roediger, *The Wages of Whiteness: Race and the Making of the American Working Class* (London: Verso, 1991); Eric Lott, *Love and Theft: Blackface Minstrelsy and the American Working Class* (New York: Oxford University Press, 1993); Michael Rogin, *Blackface, White Noise: Jewish Immigrants in the Hollywood Melting Pot* (Berkeley: University of California Press, 1996); and William J. Mahar, *Behind the Burnt Cork Mask: Early Blackface Minstrelsy and Antebellum American Popular Culture* (Urbana: University of Illinois Press, 1999). Venus Green discusses the involvement of Bell telephone operators in blackface minstrelsy (*Race on the Line,* 135, 206).

54. Roediger, *Wages of Whiteness,* 116, 127.

55. Ibid., 116–17. The quotation drawn from Roediger's excellent study refers to Lewis A. Erenberg, *Steppin' Out: New York Nightlife and the Transformation of American Culture, 1890–1930* (Westport, Conn.: Greenwood, 1981), 73.

56. Roediger, *Wages of Whiteness,* 123.

57. Frank Dumont, *The Witmark Amateur Minstrel Guide and Burnt Cork Encyclopedia* (Chicago: M. Witmark and Sons, 1899), 1.

58. James H. Dormon, "Shaping the Popular Image of Post-Reconstruction American Blacks: The 'Coon Song' Phenomenon of the Gilded Age," *American Quarterly* 40 (Dec. 1988): 450.

59. "A 'Telephony,'" *Strawbridge & Clothier Store Chat* 5 (Oct. 15, 1911): 248 (excerpted from *Lippincott's Magazine*), HML, acc. 2117, ser. 7, box 60.

60. "By Aid of Scissors," *Peirce School Alumni Journal* 9 (Mar. 1904): 6, PCA, acc. 2117, ser. 6, box 2.

61. "Unlooked for Examples," *Strawbridge & Clothier Store Chat* 3 (Oct. 15, 1909): 112, HML, acc. 2117, ser. 7, box 60.

62. "Mandolin Club," *Strawbridge & Clothier Store Chat* 1 (Sept. 1907): 7, HML, acc. 2117, ser. 7, box 60. The club's central activities are discussed in more detail in chapter 4.

63. "Mandolin Club's Minstrel Show," *Strawbridge & Clothier Store Chat* 4 (May 15, 1910): 138, HML, acc. 2117, ser. 7, box 60.

64. "The Mandolin Club," *Strawbridge & Clothier Store Chat* 6 (May 15, 1912): 137, HML, acc. 2117, ser. 7, box 60; "The Mandolin Club and Orchestra Entertainment," *Strawbridge & Clothier Store Chat* 6 (June 15, 1912): 153, HML, acc. 2117, ser. 7, box 60.

65. Frank Dumont, *Burnt Cork or the Amateur Minstrel* (New York: Wehman Bros., 1881), 43–44.

66. Toll, *Blacking Up,* 162–63, 183–84; Roediger, *Wages of Whiteness,* 125.

67. "Mandolin Club's Minstrel Show," 138.

68. Benson, *Counter Cultures,* 235–36.

69. Roediger, *Wages of Whiteness,* 117.

70. "The Argyle Minstrels," *Strawbridge & Clothier Store Chat* 6 (May 15, 1912): 134–35, HML, acc. 2117, ser. 7, box 60.

71. "Heed Club's Minstrels," *Strawbridge & Clothier Store Chat* 7 (June 15, 1910): 182, HML, acc. 2117, ser. 7, box 60.

72. "The Ham and Egg Club," *Peirce School Alumni Journal* 16 (June 1911): 6–7, PCA, acc. 1, ser. 6, box 2.

73. Jacobson, *Whiteness of a Different Color,* 7; see also 1–14, 39–90.

74. Rogin, *Blackface, White Noise,* is an excellent study of blackface minstrelsy's role in the Americanization of Jewish immigrants.

75. Ibid., 1–2.

76. Undated note in Free Library of Philadelphia Theater Collection, "Dumont's Arch Street at Ninth" file, Free Library of Philadelphia.

77. "Sixth Annual Outing," *Strawbridge & Clothier Store Chat* 4 (Sept. 15, 1910): 255–57, HML, acc. 2117, ser. 7, box 60.

78. Dumont, *Witmark Amateur Minstrel Guide,* 7.

79. "Minstrels' Home Is Closed Forever," *Philadelphia Evening Bulletin,* April 20, 1909, Urban Archives, Temple University, mounted clippings collection, box 32, "Dumont's Theater" file, Temple University, Philadelphia. The Eleventh Street Opera House closed in 1911. Perhaps the closing described in this article was temporary or the article is misdated.

80. Ibid. In addition, satires of Gilbert and Sullivan operettas, such as *H.M.S. Pinafore,* were extremely popular in the 1870s and 1880s. At the turn of the twentieth century send-ups of local political infighting and scandals pleased crowds. The Eleventh Street Opera's stage productions also sallied into national politics. The theater attracted large audiences by using Theodore Roosevelt and his family as blackface subjects. In the fall of 1901, early in his presidency, Roosevelt asked the African American educator and national figure Booker T. Washington to confer with him in the nation's capital regarding Republican political appointments to be made throughout the South. Washington made two trips, and Roosevelt invited him to dinner at the White House during the second visit. The renowned educator dined with the first family and afterward discussed political matters with the president. Within days many southern newspapers seized on the dinner as an example of Roosevelt's trying to undermine Jim Crow. Southerners quickly popularized a vicious coon song castigating both Washington and Roosevelt:

> Coon, coon, coon,
> Booker Washington is his name;
> Coon, coon, coon,
> Ain't that a measly shame?
> Coon, coon, coon,
> Morning, night, and noon,
> I think I'd class Mr. Roosevelt
> With a coon, coon, coon.

This animosity filtered north to Philadelphia. A nasty skit based on the 1906 wedding of Alice Roosevelt (the president's daughter) ran for ten consecutive weeks at the Eleventh Street Opera House. The previously quoted song is reproduced in Samuel R. Spencer Jr., *Booker T. Washington and the Negro's Place in American Life* (Boston: Little, Brown, 1955), 135.

81. Dumont's short theatrical pieces were initially performed by professional minstrels and later published for widespread amateur consumption. Among the many one-act plays Dumont penned were *An Awful Plot* (Chicago, 1880), *The Black Brigands* (New York, 1884), *Jack Sheppard and Joe Blueskin; or Amateur Road Agents* (Chicago, 1897), *How to Get a Divorce* (Chicago, 1897), and *Society Acting* (Chicago, 1898).

82. Frank Dumont, *Scenes in Front of a Clothing Store* (New York, 1889).

83. Dumont, *Burnt Cork;* Dumont, *Witmark Amateur Minstrel Guide.*

84. Dumont, *Witmark Amateur Minstrel Guide,* 14–16.

85. "Harry L. Sampson," *Strawbridge & Clothier Store Chat* 8 (Mar. 15, 1914): 6, HML, acc. 1, ser. 7, box 60.

Chapter 6: Home and Neighborhood

1. Sam Bass Warner Jr. dubs the city during the 1920s the "industrial metropolis" (see *The Private City: Philadelphia in Three Periods of Its Growth* [Philadelphia: University of Pennsylvania Press, 1968], 161–224).

2. Theodore Hershberg et al., "A Tale of Three Cities: Blacks, Immigrants, and Opportunity in Philadelphia, 1850–1880, 1930, 1970," in *Philadelphia: Work, Space, Family, and*

Group Experience in the Nineteenth Century: Essays Towards an Interdisciplinary History of the City, ed. Hershberg (New York: Oxford University Press, 1981), 470–73.

3. These are all factors emphasized in Hershberg et al., "Tale of Three Cities," 472. For an excellent study on housing construction in the antebellum city, see Donna J. Rilling, *Making Houses, Crafting Capitalism: Builders in Philadelphia, 1790–1850* (Philadelphia: University of Pennsylvania Press, 2001).

4. See Warner, *The Private City;* Hershberg et al., "Tale of Three Cities"; and Howard Gillette Jr., "The Emergence of the Modern Metropolis: Philadelphia in the Age of Its Consolidation," in *The Divided Metropolis: Social and Spatial Dimensions of Philadelphia, 1800–1975,* ed. William W. Cutler III and Howard Gillette Jr., 3–25 (Westport, Conn.: Greenwood, 1980).

5. Gillette, "Emergence of the Modern Metropolis," 14–16.

6. The data for maps 1 and 2 were culled from *Gopsill's Philadelphia City Directory* (Philadelphia: James Gopsill, 1870). A representative sample of office and sales workers was drawn from the city directory. Each name had a home address, and many had business addresses listed as well. The initial sample included 884 names and residential addresses. About 70 percent of these (620) could be accurately mapped. Of the 884 names drawn, 621 also included work addresses. About 76 percent (471) of these could be accurately mapped.

7. Warner, *The Private City,* table 7, p. 55.

8. The sample included 442 clerical workers who worked in Center City. Of these, 297 (67 percent) lived beyond the boundaries of Center City. The 442 sampled were chosen from *Gopsill's Philadelphia City Directory* (1870). Their listings in the directory included traceable home and work addresses.

9. Gillette, "Emergence of the Modern Metropolis," 15.

10. Theodore Hershberg, Harold E. Cox, Dale B. Light Jr., and Richard Greenfield, "'The Journey-to-Work': An Empirical Investigation of Work, Residence, and Transportation, Philadelphia, 1850 and 1880," in *Philadelphia: Work, Space, Family, and Group Experience in the Nineteenth Century,* ed. Hershberg (Oxford: Oxford University Press, 1981), 129–43. Hershberg et al. indicate that by 1880, clerical workers in banks probably commuted to their jobs in the central business district from homes well beyond its outskirts. Kenneth T. Jackson provides an interesting discussion of the improved transportation technology's effects on city geography; see Jackson, *Crabgrass Frontier: The Suburbanization of the United States* (New York: Oxford University Press, 1985), 20–44.

11. Gillette, "Emergence of the Modern Metropolis," 16–17. Kenneth T. Jackson notes that the neighborhoods in the Penn region of North Philadelphia in 1860 were becoming increasingly populated by the middle class and office and sales workers moving out from Center City (*Crabgrass Frontier,* table 2-2, p. 24).

12. The 1870 federal manuscript census contains no address listings. To work around this dilemma, I accessed raw data from the Philadelphia Social History Project (PSHP) holdings at the University of Pennsylvania. The PSHP divided the city into seven thousand gridsquares, each containing about 1¼ city blocks. The PSHP also used the manuscript census and identified residential addresses within each of the blocks. This study examines blocks 051-596, 052-596, and 053-596. I chose these blocks because they reflect a particularly dense cluster of address hits derived from data used in map 1. I examined several address

clusters in the federal manuscript census, and this area yielded the greatest concentration. In addition, the census manuscripts for this area were in the best condition among those for the areas sampled. Finally, the neighborhood was particularly interesting geographically. It lay within walking distance of the business district but far enough away to justify occasional commuting.

13. Men accounted for 81.5 percent of the sample; women, 18.5 percent.

14. Pennsylvania Bureau of Industrial Statistics, "Women in Industry," *Annual Report of the Secretary of Internal Affairs of the Commonwealth of Pennsylvania, Part III, Industrial Statistics, 1894* (Harrisburg, Pa.: Clarence M. Busch, 1895), vol. 22, pp. A.1–237.A, and table, pp. A.64–115.A.

15. Franklin Kline Fretz, "The Furnished Room Problem in Philadelphia" (Ph.D. diss. University of Pennsylvania, 1911), 70.

16. I used Stephan Thernstrom, *The Other Bostonians: Poverty and Progress in the American Metropolis, 1880–1970* (Cambridge, Mass.: Harvard University Press, 1973), 289–301, as a guide in discerning the occupational breakdown of both the 1870 and 1920 samples.

17. Claudia Goldin notes that a "family without a father was more likely to have both its sons and daughters in the labor force, although the impact was stronger for the sons" (Goldin, "Family Strategies and the Family Economy in the Late Nineteenth Century: The Role of Secondary Workers," in *Philadelphia: Work, Space, Family, and Group Experience in the Nineteenth Century,* ed. Theodore Hershberg, 277–310 [Oxford: Oxford University Press, 1981], 289–90).

18. The other categories accounted for the following percentages: professional, 11.8; clerical, 4.7; semiskilled, 2.4; unskilled 9.4.

19. All other ethnic groups contributed 8.5 percent of the sample, while African Americans made up 3.0 percent.

20. Dale B. Light, "Class, Ethnicity, and the Urban Ecology in a Nineteenth Century City: Philadelphia's Irish, 1840–1890" (Ph.D. diss., University of Pennsylvania, 1979), 29.

21. Ibid., 111–12. Light notes that many of the men involved in such groups were drawn from low-level white-collar and proprietary occupations.

22. Among white-collar workers the percentages ranked as follows: professionals, 6.1; business owners, 8.9; clerical workers, 14.3.

23. Warner, *The Private City,* 162–233. Warner also writes that by 1930 Philadelphia's core was an area of "poverty, low skills, and low status surrounded by a ring of working-class and middle-class homes" (171). Hershberg et al. argue that the industrial city followed the concentric zones of the Chicago school ("Tale of Three Cities," 474).

24. John F. Sutherland, "Housing the Poor in the City of Homes: Philadelphia at the Turn of the Century," in *The Peoples of Philadelphia: A History of Ethnic Groups and Lower-Class Life, 1790–1940,* ed. Allen F. Davis and Mark H. Haller, repr. with new preface, 175–201 (Philadelphia: University of Pennsylvania Press, 1998), 176. Sutherland notes that in 1898 Philadelphia "had 83,000 acres upon which to build, while New York had only 25,000."

25. Warner, *The Private City,* table 20, p. 192.

26. These addresses were drawn from *Boyd's Philadelphia Combined City and Business Directory* (Philadelphia, 1921). Map 3 contains 847 addresses.

27. I chose these blocks because they reflected a particularly dense cluster of address

hits derived from data used in map 3. Several address clusters were examined in the federal manuscript census, and this area proved to have by far the greatest concentration of clerical workers. The sample was enumeration district 1497 in the census. It was bounded by Baltimore Avenue, Fifty-eighth Street, Florence Avenue, and Cobbs Creek Park.

28. The information about the neighborhood is drawn from William Bucke Campbell, "Old Towns and Districts of Philadelphia," *Philadelphia History* 4, no. 5 (1942): 116–17; and *Jackson's Philadelphia Year Book for 1919* (Philadelphia: Joseph Jackson, 1919), 10.

29. As late as 1900 much of the land in the neighborhood was empty. Only the area between Fifty-ninth and Sixtieth streets and the block between Ashland and Thomas streets had extensive residential development (George W. Bromley and Walter S. Bromley, *Atlas of the City of Philadelphia: Complete in One Volume* [Philadelphia: G. W. Bromley, 1901], pls. 24 and 25).

30. "Park Dedicated as Recreation Center," *Philadelphia Evening Bulletin*, May 17, 1914, Urban Archives, Temple University (hereinafter UATU), *Philadelphia Evening Bulletin* clippings collection, "Kingsessing Recreation Center" file, Temple University, Philadelphia; "'Crazy' Steps Banished at City Dancing Schools," *Philadelphia Evening Bulletin*, January 23, 1919, UATU, *Philadelphia Evening Bulletin* clippings collection, "Kingsessing Recreation Center" file; "Human 'Sun Dial' in City Playground," *Philadelphia Evening Bulletin*, March 29, 1919, UATU, *Philadelphia Evening Bulletin* clippings collection, "Kingsessing Recreation Center" file.

31. Outside of office and sales workers, the occupational categories broke down thus: professionals, 24.1 percent; business owners, 11.3; skilled workers, 11.5; semiskilled workers, 11.6; unskilled laborers, 2.5; unknown, 1.2.

32. A smattering of other ethnic groups (first- and second-generation) provided 16.2 percent of the populace.

33. Professionals were the breadwinners in 21.3 percent of the households with dependent clerks; business owners, in 15.4 percent; blue-collar workers, in 18.4 percent. Parents who held no jobs, including widows, contributed another 18.4 percent, while the status of 2.2 percent of the household heads remains unknown.

34. For primary glimpses into lodging-house life, see Franklin Kline Fretz, "Furnished Room Problem"; Albert Benedict Wolfe, *The Lodging House Problem in Boston* (Boston: Houghton Mifflin; Cambridge, Mass.: Riverside, 1916); and Harvey Warren Zorbaugh, *The Gold Coast and the Slum: A Sociological Study of Chicago's Near North Side* (Chicago: University of Chicago Press, 1929). Excellent secondary sources include Howard P. Chudacoff, *The Age of the Bachelor: Creating an American Subculture* (Princeton, N.J.: Princeton University Press, 1999); Paul Groth, *Living Downtown: The History of Residential Hotels in the United States* (Berkeley: University of California Press, 1994); George Chauncey, *Gay New York: Gender, Urban Culture, and the Making of the Gay Male World, 1890–1940* (New York: BasicBooks, 1994); Joanne Meyerowitz, "Sexual Geography and Gender Economy: The Furnished Room Districts of Chicago, 1890–1930," in *Gender and American History Since 1890*, ed. Barbara Melosh (London: Routledge, 1993), 43–71; and Mark Peel, "On the Margins: Lodgers and Boarders in Boston, 1860–1900," *Journal of American History* 72 (Mar. 1986): 813–34.

35. Stuart M. Blumin, *The Emergence of the Middle Class: Social Experience in the American City, 1760–1900* (Cambridge: Cambridge University Press, 1989), 167–69.

36. The rest included one carpenter, one electrician, one machinist, one tailor, two dental students, and two druggists (Fretz, "Furnished Room Problem," 35).

37. Ibid., 35–40.

38. Ibid., 30–33.

39. Ibid., 19–30, 43.

40. Ibid., 10, 43.

41. Albert Benedict Wolfe, *The Lodging House Problem*, 35.

42. Fretz, "Furnished Room Problem," 10–11.

43. Ibid., 50.

44. Ibid., 69.

45. Ibid., 68–68. Fretz found that 119 (59.5 percent) of the 200 women in his sample were clerical workers.

46. Ibid., 70.

47. Ibid., 47.

48. Ibid., 112–15. Excellent studies of the working-class saloon experience include Madelon Powers, *Faces along the Bar: Lore and Order in the Workingman's Saloon, 1870–1920* (Chicago: University of Chicago Press, 1998); Roy Rosenzweig, *Eight Hours for What We Will: Workers and Leisure in an Industrial City, 1870–1920* (New York: Cambridge University Press, 1983); Perry R. Duis, *The Saloon: Public Drinking in Chicago and Boston 1880–1920* (Urbana: University of Illinois Press, 1983).

49. Ernest Hexamer and Son, *Insurance Maps of the City of Philadelphia* (Philadelphia: Ernest Hexamer and Son, 1907), vol. 5, pls. 62, 64, 67, 68, 69, 70, 72; C. E. Howe Company, compilers, *1911 Boyd's Co-Partnership and Residence Business Directory of Philadelphia City* (Philadelphia: C. E. Howe, 1911). These sources list only relatively prominent business establishments, so the figures likely undercount the many saloons, eateries, laundries, and barbershops that lodgers had at their disposal.

50. Fretz, "Furnished Room Problem," 95–108.

51. Ibid., 71–74.

52. Ibid., 116–18.

53. Meyerowitz, "Sexual Geography," 45, 47–48.

54. Fretz, "Furnished Room Problem," 164–65; Wolfe, *Lodging House Problem*, 153–63.

55. Meyerowitz, "Sexual Geography," 51.

56. Fretz, "Furnished Room Problem," 48.

57. Susan Porter Benson, *Counter Cultures: Saleswomen, Managers, and Customers in American Department Stores, 1890–1940* (Urbana: University of Illinois Press, 1986), 135–36.

58. Pennsylvania Bureau of Industrial Statistics, "Women in Industry," 36.A.

59. Vice Commission of Philadelphia, *A Report on Existing Conditions with Recommendations to the Honorable Rudolph Blankenburg, Mayor of Philadelphia* (Philadelphia: n.p., 1913), 101. Timothy J. Gilfoyle notes that a 1912 survey of almost 500 New York City prostitutes found that 30 percent of them worked as sales clerks. Together, office workers, stenographers, telephone operators, and teachers contributed an additional 15 percent. See Gilfoyle's masterful *City of Eros: New York City, Prostitution, and the Commercialization of Sex, 1790–1920* (New York: Norton, 1992), 290.

60. Fretz, "Furnished Room Problem," 130.

61. Vice Commission of Philadelphia, *Report*, 1–5. The commission comprised private citizens appointed by the Progressive reform mayor Rudolph Blankenburg. The commission hired trained investigators from the American Vigilance Association to study the city.

62. Gilfoyle, *City of Eros*, 172–73.

63. Vice Commission of Philadelphia, *Report*, 6–21. The commission described massage parlors as locations where "perversion" occurred. This likely meant sodomy involving either heterosexual partners or males.

64. Vice Commission of Philadelphia, *Report*, 62–63.

65. Ibid., 21.

Index

74–75; differences between clerical workers and, 2
Blumenthal, Joseph, 14–15
Blumin, Stuart, 11, 167n2, 175n48
boardinghouse keepers, 29
boardinghouses: description of, 152–53
Bookkeepers' Beneficial Association (BBA), 82
bookkeeping, 28, 43
Braverman, Harry, 168n12
Breerwood, Charles H., 41
Broad Street Station, 43, 89
Brotherhood of Telegraphers, 170n39
Brown, Tom (character in Peirce School promotional literature), 33–34, 59
Brush Electric Company, 104
Bryn Mawr, 101
Bryson, Harold, 36
Bureau of Occupations for Trained Women, 37
business colleges, 14; job placement by, 33; in Philadelphia, 61; training clerical workers, 21
Business Educators' Association, 61

Carnegie, Andrew, 13, 118
Carver, George Washington, 135
cash boys, 49, 89–90
Cattell, Henry S., 42
C. B. Porter and Company, 41
Centennial Exhibition, 93, 153
central business district, Philadelphia (CBD), 43, 143, 145, 149
Cheltenham Electric Light, Heat, and Power Company, 41
Chicago school of sociology, 143
Chinatown (San Francisco), 108–9
clerical revolution, 20, 26
clerical work: conditions of, 2, 43; de-skilling of, 18; experiences, female, 13–14; experiences, male, 13–14; feminine views of, 4; feminization of, 28; gender issues in, 31; gender segregation in, 54–55; job security, 17; masculine views of, 4; mechanization of, 13–14; promotion and pay in, 57; qualities of, 16–18; upward mobility in, 19, 44; upward mobility in, of African Americans, 24; upward mobility in of men, 14, 15–16, 18, 21, 120; upward mobility in, of women, 42, 120–22; women in, 3, 10, 13; workers views of, 4, 5. *See also* hiring process; workplace virtues
clerical workers: job experiences of, 49–50;

as part of white-collar workforce, 2; pre-industrial, 11–13; residential patterns for, in 1870, 144–46; residential patterns for, in 1920, 149; salaries for, 2, 17; unionization of, 18, 122–23, 128; and whiteness, 116, 132; widowhood of, 42; women in preindustrial workplace, 12. *See also* workplace virtues
clerical workforce: African Americans in, 22–25; gender composition of, 25–31; growth of, 19–20; immigrants in, 22; industrial-era changes in, 9, 13; job diversity in, 43; nativity of, 21–22, 29; position of, in white-collar workforce, 17; position of, in urban society, 18; racial composition of, 22–25; relationship of, to blue-collar workforce, 17, 18; structure, 4, 16; youthfulness of, 40, 79–80
Clothier, Clarkson, 83–84, 116
Clothier, Isaac H., 89
Clover Mandolin Club, 103, 114. *See also* blackface minstrelsy: and Clover Mandolin Club
Cohen, Miriam, 77
Comfort Kit Club. *See* Peirce School: and World War I
Commercial Department, Pittsburgh School District, 75
commercial leisure economy (entertainment economy), 6, 79, 80, 81, 87, 104, 110, 113. *See also* blackface minstrelsy: and commercial leisure economy; furnished-room district (FRD): and commercial leisure economy
Coney Island, 80
Conwell, Rev. Russell H., 102, 118, 191n18
Cooke, Jay: early career of, 11–12, 15; and E. W. Clarke and Company; and Washington Packet Line, 11; and William G. Moorehead, 11, 12
Cowan, Henry, 147
Cutter Electric Manufacturing Company, 36
cycling. *See* amateur athletics: Peirce Alumni Cyclers

DaCosta, George, 125
Davidson, Janet F., 69
Davies, Margery W., 48, 181n39
Dawson's Grotto, 133
DeLong Hook and Eye Company, 36
department stores: architecture of, 53; general description of, 50; hiring of women

From 2000 to 2003 JEROME P. BJELOPERA was an assistant professor at Bradley University, in Peoria, Illinois, where he earned the 2000–2001 First-Year Faculty Award for outstanding teaching. From 2003 to 2004 he taught at Bowie State University in Bowie, Maryland. He currently lives and works in the Washington, D.C., area.

The Working Class in American History

Worker City, Company Town: Iron and Cotton-Worker Protest in Troy and Cohoes, New York, 1855–84   *Daniel J. Walkowitz*

Life, Work, and Rebellion in the Coal Fields: The Southern West Virginia Miners, 1880–1922   *David Alan Corbin*

Women and American Socialism, 1870–1920   *Mari Jo Buhle*

Lives of Their Own: Blacks, Italians, and Poles in Pittsburgh, 1900–1960   *John Bodnar, Roger Simon, and Michael P. Weber*

Working-Class America: Essays on Labor, Community, and American Society   *Edited by Michael H. Frisch and Daniel J. Walkowitz*

Eugene V. Debs: Citizen and Socialist   *Nick Salvatore*

American Labor and Immigration History, 1877–1920s: Recent European Research   *Edited by Dirk Hoerder*

Workingmen's Democracy: The Knights of Labor and American Politics   *Leon Fink*

The Electrical Workers: A History of Labor at General Electric and Westinghouse, 1923–60   *Ronald W. Schatz*

The Mechanics of Baltimore: Workers and Politics in the Age of Revolution, 1763–1812   *Charles G. Steffen*

The Practice of Solidarity: American Hat Finishers in the Nineteenth Century   *David Bensman*

The Labor History Reader   *Edited by Daniel J. Leab*

Solidarity and Fragmentation: Working People and Class Consciousness in Detroit, 1875–1900   *Richard Oestreicher*

Counter Cultures: Saleswomen, Managers, and Customers in American Department Stores, 1890–1940   *Susan Porter Benson*

The New England Working Class and the New Labor History   *Edited by Herbert G. Gutman and Donald H. Bell*

Labor Leaders in America   *Edited by Melvyn Dubofsky and Warren Van Tine*

Barons of Labor: The San Francisco Building Trades and Union Power in the Progressive Era   *Michael Kazin*

Gender at Work: The Dynamics of Job Segregation by Sex during World War II   *Ruth Milkman*

Once a Cigar Maker: Men, Women, and Work Culture in American Cigar Factories, 1900–1919   *Patricia A. Cooper*

A Generation of Boomers: The Pattern of Railroad Labor Conflict in Nineteenth-Century America   *Shelton Stromquist*

Work and Community in the Jungle: Chicago's Packinghouse Workers, 1894–1922   *James R. Barrett*

Workers, Managers, and Welfare Capitalism: The Shoeworkers and Tanners of Endicott Johnson, 1890–1950   *Gerald Zahavi*

Men, Women, and Work: Class, Gender, and Protest in the New England Shoe Industry, 1780–1910   *Mary Blewett*

Workers on the Waterfront: Seamen, Longshoremen, and Unionism in the 1930s   *Bruce Nelson*

The University of Illinois Press
is a founding member of the
Association of American University Presses.

———————————————————

Composed in 10.5/13 Minion
by Jim Proefrock
at the University of Illinois Press
Manufactured by Sheridan Books, Inc.

University of Illinois Press
1325 South Oak Street
Champaign, IL 61820-6903
www.press.uillinois.edu